T0319827

Comparative Capitalism and the Transitional Periphery

NEW HORIZONS IN INTERNATIONAL BUSINESS

Series Editor: Peter J. Buckley, *Centre for International Business, University of Leeds (CIBUL), UK*

The New Horizons in International Business series has established itself as the world's leading forum for the presentation of new ideas in international business research. It offers pre-eminent contributions in the areas of multinational enterprise – including foreign direct investment, business strategy and corporate alliances, global competitive strategies, and entrepreneurship. In short, this series constitutes essential reading for academics, business strategists and policy makers alike.

Titles in the series include:

Comparative Capitalism and the Transitional Periphery

Firm Centred Perspectives

Edited by

Mehmet Demirbag

Professor of International Business and Deputy Dean, Essex Business School, University of Essex, UK

Geoffrey Wood

Dean and Professor of International Business, Essex Business School, University of Essex, UK

NEW HORIZONS IN INTERNATIONAL BUSINESS

Edward **Elgar**
PUBLISHING

Cheltenham, UK • Northampton, MA, USA

Published by
Edward Elgar Publishing Limited
The Lypiatts
15 Lansdown Road
Cheltenham
Glos GL50 2JA
UK

Edward Elgar Publishing, Inc.
William Pratt House
9 Dewey Court
Northampton
Massachusetts 01060
USA

A catalogue record for this book
is available from the British Library

Library of Congress Control Number: 2018944729

This book is available electronically in the **Elgar**online
Business subject collection
DOI 10.4337/9781786430892

ISBN 978 1 78643 088 5 (cased)
ISBN 978 1 78643 089 2 (eBook)

Typeset by Servis Filmsetting Ltd, Stockport, Cheshire
Printed and bound in Great Britain by TJ International Ltd, Padstow

Contents

PART III   OTHER TRANSITIONAL PERIPHERY

Contributors

Yusaf H. Akbar is Associate Professor in Management at Central European University (CEU), Hungary. Yusaf's current research interests are focused on three topics: the internationalization capabilities of small and medium-sized enterprises into emerging markets; non-market strategies of multinational firms; and strategic impacts of the sharing economy. He was awarded a Research Fellowship at CEU's Institute for Advanced Studies, 2016. He completed Visiting Researcher positions at University of Trieste, Italy and the Wirtschaftsuniversiteit in Vienna, Austria in 2013. He has published in peer-reviewed journals including the *Journal of World Business, Journal of International Management, Business and Politics, Cross-Cultural Management, Global Governance, Global Business and Organizational Excellence, Harvard Business Review, International Business Review, Thunderbird International Business Review, Journal of Air Transport Management* and *World Competition.* He has published two books, the first entitled *EU Enlargement and Central Europe: Regulatory Convergence and the Multinational Enterprise,* and another volume, *Global Antitrust: Trade and Competition Linkages.* He is co-editor (with Rustam Jamilov) of a book entitled *Neo-Transition Economics* published in 2015. He has a forthcoming book on *Strategic Management in Emerging Markets* in 2018 (co-authored with Krassimir Todorov). He has served as an Editorial Advisory Board member on the following journals: *Thunderbird International Business Review, Journal of Asia-Pacific Business* and the *European Journal of International Management.* He has authored or co-authored numerous business case studies of both large and smaller entrepreneurial firms including BMB Group, ING Insurance, Datwyler, Philips, Smollan Group, Vendedy, Vienna International Airport, Zwack Unicum and Hummus Bar. His current roles in the academy and beyond include Founding Editor of the *International Journal of Emerging Markets* and as an advisor to governmental authorities. His consulting and professional references include Citibank, Deutsche Telekom, Siemens and Toyota. He has extensive teaching and executive education experience in more than ten countries, including MIB School of Management, Italy; Hult International Business School, USA; Shanghai Jiaotong University, China; Stockholm School of Economics, Sweden; and the University of Michigan, USA.

Dr Ahmad Arslan is currently working as a Senior Research Fellow (International Business) at the Department of Marketing, Management & International Business, Oulu Business School, University of Oulu, Finland. Previously, he has worked in academia in the UK and Finland as a Senior Lecturer, Assistant Professor and Researcher. His core areas of research interests include Cross-Border Mergers & Acquisitions, Entrepreneurship, Emerging Economies, Foreign Market Entry Strategies, Internationalization of Small Firms, and Multinational Enterprises' (MNEs) Strategies. His earlier research has been published in prestigious academic journals such as *British Journal of Management, International Business Review, International Marketing Review, Scandinavian Journal of Management, Journal of Strategic Marketing, Journal for East European Management Studies, and Journal of Global Marketing,* among others. Moreover, he has also contributed book chapters to edited handbooks addressing different international business and strategy topics. Finally, he is an editorial board member of two academic journals (*Journal of East-West Business* and *International Journal of Export Marketing*).

Professor Richard Croucher is Professor of Comparative Employment Relations at Middlesex University Business School, London, UK. Previously Senior Research Fellow at Cranfield School of Management, UK, he earned his PhD from the University of Warwick, UK in 1976. He worked with five global union federations on projects to restructure trade unions in the former Soviet Union from the late 1990s to 2010. His main interests are in comparative employment and labour issues at the international level. He is a member of the editorial committee of the *British Journal of Management.* He has conducted numerous research projects funded by, amongst others, the UK's Department of Trade and Industry, the Low Pay Commission, the International Labour Organization and the Leverhulme Trust. He has published more than 120 articles in journals including *Journal of Management, Human Relations, Industrial Relations: A Journal of Economy and Society, British Journal of Management, Work, Employment and Society* and *British Journal of Industrial Relations.*

Dr Hanna Danilovich is a Research Fellow in Business, Labour and Society in Transition, Middlesex University Business School, UK. After obtaining her PhD in 2013, her main research interests are focused on labour relations, organizational change and industrial relation in the economies of the former Soviet Union. Another area of interest is in workplace analytics and developing methodologies that compensate for the lack of secondary data on companies in post-Soviet economies. Her work has been published in academic journals including *Work, Employment and Society, Economic and Industrial Democracy* and *International Business Review*.

Professor Mehmet Demirbag is Professor of International Business and Deputy Dean of Essex Business School at the University of Essex, UK. Previously he was Head of Department of Strategy and Organisation at Strathclyde Business School, UK. His current research interest focuses around multinational enterprises in and from emerging markets, offshore research and development activities of multinational enterprises, and the impact of institutional factors on multinational enterprises' operations, high-performance work systems and talent management practices in emerging markets. He has authored or co-authored more than 70 papers on these topics, published in journals such as the *Journal of Management Studies, Human Resource Management, Journal of World Business, British Journal of Management, Human Resource Management Journal, Management International Review, International Journal of Human Resource Management* and *International Business Review*. He has co-guest edited eight journal Special Issues, including *Human Resource Management, British Journal of Management, Journal of World Business, International Business Review, Journal of Business Research* and *International Marketing Review*, on emerging markets and emerging market multinational enterprises (MNEs). He is a co-author of a book (Palgrave Macmillan), and co-editor of three books (Edward Elgar Publishing) and author of numerous book chapters. Mehmet serves on the editorial boards of the *Journal of World Business, British Journal of Management, Management International Review* and *Journal of Asia Business Studies*, among others.

Dr Aleksandr V. Gevorkyan is Assistant Professor of Economics at the Department of Economics and Finance of the Peter J. Tobin College of Business at St John's University in New York City, USA. He is a Senior Research Fellow at the Vincentian Center for Church and Society and a Research Fellow at the Center for Global Business Stewardship, New York, USA. Dr Gevorkyan is also Economics Subject Matter Expert for the Permanent Observer Mission of the Holy See to the United Nations. Dr Gevorkyan's teaching and research experience covers themes in open economy macroeconomics, economic development, international financial economics and post-socialist transition economics. He is the author of *Transition Economies: Transformation, Development, and Society in Eastern Europe and the Former Soviet Union* (Routledge, 2018); co-editor (with Otaviano Canuto) of *Financial Deepening and Post-Crisis Development in Emerging Markets* (Palgrave Macmillan, 2016); and the author of *Innovative Fiscal Policy and Economic Development in Transition Economies* (Routledge, 2013 in paperback, 2011 in hardback).

Maciej Kisilowski is Associate Professor of Law and Public Management at Central European University (CEU), Budapest, Hungary. He received his doctorate and master's in law degrees from Yale Law School, USA; MPA in economics and public policy from Princeton University's Woodrow Wilson School of Public and International Affairs, USA; and MBA with distinction from INSEAD. He also holds another PhD and MA in law from Warsaw University, Poland. In 2016, he was awarded the CEU Distinguished Teaching Award and the Warsaw University of Technology Instructor of 2014–16 award for his teaching at the Katalyst Executive MBA (KEMBA) Program offered in partnership with CEU. His research interests include the theory of regulation and public management. He has consulted for numerous public and nonprofit organizations. His research appears in leading academic journals, including *Law and Social Inquiry* and *International Business Review.* His latest co-authored book, *Administrategy: Achieving Personal Success when Managing Public Administration*, has been published in Hungary, Poland, and Romania. His earlier, edited book, *Free Market in Its Twenties: Modern Business Decision-Making in Central and Eastern Europe*, was published in 2014 with a Foreword by George Soros. In 2011, a case study he authored won an award at the Annual Congress of the Academy of Management in Boston, MA, USA. His recent academic work has appeared in *Law and Social Inquiry* and the *International Business Review*. His popular commentary has appeared, among others, in *Politico*, *Foreign Policy*, *Euronews*, *Project Syndicate*, *EU Observer* and *EURactiv.*

Dr Jorma Larimo is a Professor of International Marketing at the University of Vaasa, Finland. He is currently Vice Dean of the School of Marketing and Communications and Head of the doctoral programme of Business Studies at the University of Vaasa. His areas of interest include small and medium-sized enterprise internationalization and foreign entry strategies of multinational enterprises, especially foreign direct investment, mergers and acquisitions, and international joint venture strategies and performance. He has edited six books addressing various aspects of international business. His research has been published in well-ranked academic journals including the *International Business Review*, *Journal of International Business Studies*, *Journal of International Marketing*, *Management International Review*, *Journal of World Business*, *Journal of Global Marketing*, *Journal of East–West Business* and *Journal for East European Management Studies*. He has also contributed book chapters to several edited books.

Dr Dilshod Makhmadshoev is a Lecturer at Strathclyde Business School, UK. He completed his PhD in the same institution and holds an MSc from Queen's University Belfast, UK. His research is interdisciplinary, spanning the fields of international business, entrepreneurship and small and medium-sized enterprises (SMEs), and development studies. He focuses on the development and international expansion of transition-economy SMEs and emerging-market multinational enterprises, and has particular interest in ongoing interactions between actors and their institutional contexts. Theoretically, his work is influenced by institutionalist perspectives (for example, new institutional economics, comparative institutionalism, institutional change), internationalization approaches and the global value chain lens. His work has been published in journals such as the *International Business Review* and *International Marketing Review*, edited book volumes, and presented at national and international academic conferences.

Dr Saranzaya Manalsuren is a Researcher and Lecturer at London South Bank University, UK. She is passionate about exploring the intertwining relationships between cultures and their influence on our thinking. Her research focuses on management and institutional changes in emerging countries including Mongolia, Kazakhstan and Russia. She writes on the topics of managerial roles, symbols in an organizational context and the relationship between culture and institutions in the case of Mongolia and other transitional economies. She also works as an independent consultant for cultural awareness in business negotiations and managing human resources for companies which operate in Mongolia, or are considering doing so in the future. She is a frequent speaker at both academic and non-academic international conferences and business events.

Dr Marina Michalski is a lecturer at the Organisation Studies and Human Resource Management Group at Essex Business School, University of Essex, UK, where she teaches Organisational Behaviour and International Employment Relations. Her recent research has focused on skills development in rest-of-the-world countries, having, for instance, cooperated with the BBC College of Journalism on a project with the Arabic Group. Her current research project investigates interactions of organizational, institutional and cultural contexts with respect to sustainable labour markets and human resources management practice in Brazil.

Dr Giovanni O. Serafini is a Lecturer in International Business and Management at the Essex Business School, University of Essex, UK. His research interests focus on host country institutional effects on human resources management policies and practices application by multinational enterprises in transitional periphery economies.

Professor Martyna Śliwa is Professor of Management and Organisation Studies and Dean of Postgraduate Research and Education at the

University of Essex, UK. Her research interests focus on language(s) and power in organizations in the global context, professional identities, professional mobility and migration, gender, intersectionality and higher education. Her work has been published in a range of international journals including the *British Journal of Management, Gender, Work and Organization, Journal of International Business Studies, Management Learning* and *Organization*. She is an Associate Editor of *Management Learning*.

Dr Leslie T. Szamosi is a Senior Lecturer and the Academic Director of the MBA programme at CITY College, International Faculty of the University of Sheffield, and a Founder and Co-Director of the Laboratory for Strategic People Management at CITY College. He is a member of the International Faculty of the Association of MBAs (AMBA) and has worked both in the private and public sectors in Canada. He is a highly sought-after presenter and has undertaken seminars and workshops for a variety of international organizations and institutions. He has published in a wide variety of academic and practitioner-oriented journals.

Professor Shlomo Y. Tarba is a Professor in Business Strategy, Head of Department of Strategy and International Business, and a member of Senior Management Team of the Birmingham Business School, University of Birmingham, UK, and a Visiting Professor in Recanati Business School, Tel-Aviv University, Israel. Previously he has been an Assistant Professor (Lecturer) at the University of Sheffield, UK. In addition, Dr Tarba has vast teaching experience in the leading research-intensive institutions in Israel such as the Hebrew University of Jerusalem, Tel-Aviv University, Ben-Gurion University, and others. He received his PhD in Strategic Management from Ben-Gurion University and Master's in Biotechnology and BSc in Agriculture at the Hebrew University of Jerusalem, Israel. His research interests include ambidexterity, resilience, strategic agility, and mergers and acquisitions. Dr Tarba is a member of the editorial boards of *Journal of Management Studies, Human Resource Management* (US, Wiley), *British Journal of Management, Journal of World Business, Long Range Planning* and *Management International Review.* His research papers are published or forthcoming in journals such as the *Journal of Management (SAGE), Journal of Organizational Behavior, Human Relations, Human Resource Management* (US), *British Journal of Management, Journal of World Business, Academy of Management Perspectives, California Management Review, Long Range Planning, Management International Review, International Business Review, Group and Organization Management, International Journal of Production and Economics, Technological Forecasting and Social Change, International Journal of Human Resource Management, Human Resource Management*

Review, *International Studies of Management and Organization* and *Thunderbird International Business Review*. One of his papers was selected and published in *Best Paper Proceedings of the Academy of Management* (USA) in 2006. His consulting experience includes biotechnological and telecom companies, as well as industry associations such as the Israeli Rubber and Plastic Industry Association, and the US–Israel Chamber of Commerce.

Professor Ali Resul Usul is a Professor at the Department of Political Science and International Relations at Istanbul Medipol University, Turkey, and also serves as Dean of the School of Humanities and Social Science there. He completed his PhD at the Department of Government, University of Essex, UK. He has published extensively on Turkey–European Union (EU) relations, the issues and problems of democratization, politics in the Middle East and North Africa (MENA) countries, Central Asian politics and various theoretical issues in the international relations discipline. One of his books, *Democracy in Turkey: The Impact of EU Political Conditionality*, was published by Routledge in 2011. He also served as Chair of the Center for Strategic Studies at the Turkish Ministry of Foreign Affairs between 2014 and 2016.

Professor Geoffrey Wood is Dean and Professor of International Business at Essex Business School, University of Essex, UK. Previously he was Professor of International Business at Warwick Business School, UK. He has authored, co-authored or edited 16 books, and more than 160 articles in peer-reviewed journals. He holds honorary positions at Griffith and Monash University in Australia, and Witwatersrand and Nelson Mandela Universities in South Africa. His research interests centre on the relationship between institutional setting, corporate governance, firm finance, and firm-level work and employment relations. He is Editor in Chief of the *British Journal of Management*, the official journal of the British Academy of Management (BAM). He also serves on the BAM Council. He is also Co-Editor of the *Annals of Corporate Governance* and Associate Editor of *Academy of Management Perspectives*. He is also Editor of the Chartered ABS Journal Ranking list. He has received numerous research grants, including funding councils (for example, the Economic and Social Research Council, ESRC), government departments (for example, the US Department of Labor, and the UK Department of Works and Pensions), charities (for example, the Nuffield Foundation), the labour movement (for example, the International Transport Workers' Federation, ITF) and the European Union.

Professor Sayım Yorgun is a Professor at the Faculty of Economics, Department of Labour Economics and Industrial Relations, Istanbul University, Turkey. Previously he was an Associate Professor at the

Department of Labor Economics and Industrial Relations at Kocaeli University, Turkey. He served as a Visiting Research Fellow for two years between 2001 and 2003 at New York State School of Industrial and Labor Relations, Cornell University, USA. He was also a Visiting Researcher for three months at the Department of Management, Birkbeck, University of London, UK, in 2011. He has published eight books and a large number of articles. He is the Editor of the *Journal of Social Policy Conferences* (academic journal) and the *Journal of Tourism and Research* (academic journal).

Introduction

Geoffrey Wood and Mehmet Demirbag

This book seeks to shed further light on the type of capitalism that has emerged in Central Asia, the Caucasus and other peripheral areas of the post-state socialist world, drawing out the implications for both domestic and overseas firms from a broad perspective that is founded in the literature on comparative institutional analysis. We call this cluster of countries the 'transitional periphery economies', to set them apart from other emerging and more mature types of capitalism; this reflects the more complex mix of political and market mediation, and informal personal ties, than is encountered in the more developed states of the post-state socialist world. This collection is a wide-ranging one, and incorporates both detailed country studies and chapters dealing with broad thematic issues. What these accounts have in common is that liberalization is not a one-way street, and that there is little connection between liberalization and growth. At the same time, international firms are pragmatic and creative in finding ways of coping with quite different yet durable forms of institutional mediation and coverage.

COMPARATIVE CAPITALISM AND THE TRANSITIONAL PERIPHERY

Although the early literature on comparative capitalism focused on the case of the developed world, there has been a growing interest in the types of institutional arrangements prevalent in key emerging markets (Lane and Wood, 2012; Wood and Demirbag, 2012; Demirbag and Yaprak, 2015). The early literature on comparative capitalism held that only in the developed world were there the institutional foundations for stable and sustained growth and high levels of overall prosperity, and in other economies there would be strong pressures to converge with either the liberal or coordinated market ideal (Hall and Soskice, 2003). However, since the early 2000s, it has become clear that many emerging markets have proved capable of generating significant growth despite a failure to evolve towards one or other of the mature institutional archetypes, and others have become locked on suboptimal trajectories, with little prospect of meaningful institutional redesign (Lane and Wood, 2012). This has led to efforts to identify new capitalist archetypes that might best describe such persistently different economies. Again, much of the early comparative literature on institutions has tended to focus on the firm as a transmission belt, whereby specific sets of institutional pressures resulted in some outcome or other; what went on inside the firm was, at best, described in terms of stylistic ideal-types (Wood et al., 2014). This, in turn, has led to a subsequent interest in exploring variations in intra-organizational practice, and the effects of the entrants of new players from abroad.

The project of identifying persistently distinct types of capitalism beyond the coordinated and liberal market economies (CMEs and LMEs) encountered in the advanced societies led to the development of a number of alternative capitalist archetypes. These included the 'hierarchical market economies' of Latin America (characterized by particular patterns of stratification and elite composition) and the 'segmented business systems' of tropical Africa (characterized by large pre-modern peasant and informal sectors, and persistently durable uneven institutional coverage) (Wood and Frynas, 2006). Hancke et al. (2007) argued that the Mediterranean economies had similarly distinct features of their own, including a tightly regulated large firms sector, a weakly regulated small business sector, and a prominent role for family ownership. There was a similar recognition that in the case of post-state socialist Central and Eastern Europe, initial expectations of a swift transition to the LME or CME models were misplaced, with the exception of Slovenia, and possibly Estonia and Slovakia (Lane and Myant, 2016). The title of 'emerging market economy' has been used to describe the bulk of economies in the region (Nölke and Vliegenthart, 2009). Key features would include the revival of pre-Soviet traditions of corporate law but also, at least in some instances, the persistence of specific modes of Soviet-era practice in large organizations, despite market reforms (ibid.). Again, such economies are characterized by limited institutional alignment and coupling (Lane and Wood, 2012).

A feature of this model was the neglect of a large swathe of post-state socialist countries, most notably those of the Caucasus and Central Asia. This stimulated the development of a new archetype, the 'transitional peripheral economy' (TPE) to describe such states (Wood and Demirbag, 2012). TPEs were characterized by the persistence of informal networks that pre-date, but persisted through the Soviet era, with extended ties and networks which, in many instances, correspond with clans (Wood and Demirbag, 2012; Northrop, 2000; Collins, 2006). Of course, extended networks of support are a feature of many emerging markets. However, in the case of Central Asia, what sets them apart are the extent to which core features have survived all manner of internal and external shocks. If one considers *guanxi* networks (China), or peasant-based and tribal networks of support (Africa), it will become apparent that a feature of such networks is the extent to which they are redefined and reinvented to fit the process of modernization and economic growth (Gold et al., 2002; Michailova and Worm, 2003). *Inter alia*, this includes the ability to extend across national boundaries and to accommodate all manner of complex commercial transactions. However, to date, clan networks have tended to be much more spatially confined, with a strong linkage back to regions of origin (specific mountains, valleys, and so on), and also seemingly more capable of accommodating their form according to quite different external circumstances (Northrop, 2000; Collins, 2006). Quite simply, if *guanxi* or African tribal-based networks persist owing to the ability to reinvent tradition to suit modern purpose, the kind of clan networks encountered in Central Asian TPEs seem to be more adept at retaining original traditions; even if, at times, with a stronger priority being focused on concealment than adjustment (Northrop, 2000).

Many countries across the region have experienced national resource windfalls and are battling to escape an excessive dependency on them. Rather than using resource windfalls as a means of funding economic diversification, there has been a tendency to save the gains into a national sovereign wealth fund, and/or to fritter the gains away on vanity projects and the personal lifestyles of ruling elites. Indeed, given the challenges of sustaining national industrial bases, there has been a disturbing tendency for national economies to relapse, countenancing industrial decline as unavoidable, and/or indeed as something to be positively welcomed, given the seemingly richer gains from mining. Of course, even developed Australia fell into this trap.

A reliance on minerals brings with it not only the resource curse, but also a tendency to focus on aspirations of future minerals booms. Most notably, the oil and gas industry has a recent history of talking up oil discoveries in order to access debt capital; if they fall for such snake oil salesmanship, then national governments risk locking themselves into a cycle of suffering many of the consequences of a resource curse, without the resources to go with it (Frynas et al., 2016). Again, advances in automation mean that mining and, indeed, oil and gas, often only require far leaner labour forces than in the past (Topp, 2008). This means that there may be little trickle-down from mineral windfalls. Although some mineral-rich countries in the region have set up sovereign wealth funds, ostensibly as a device to save some of the latter for future generations, a common theme has been a great deal of opacity in how such funds are managed (Cumming et al., 2017).

A variation on the theme of foreign exchange windfalls is the case of Armenia, where a large diaspora provides the basis of inflows of investment capital and remittances. Although relations between the diaspora and the political elite have been awkward at times, the Armenian economy remains heavily reliant on the diaspora (Panossian, 2004). A risk with diaspora-driven growth is that it may lead to resource curse-like effects, with the easy foreign exchange windfalls reducing the need for sound economic policies.

CHAPTER SUMMARIES

This book is divided into three parts. Part I focuses on the transitional periphery in Central Asia. The rationale behind this part is to extend existing theories to understand the institutional set-up in the transitional periphery, particularly in clan-based economies of Central Asia. There are four chapters in this section.

In Chapter 1, Makhmadshoev contributes to the debate on the institutional perspective by examining unstable institutional settings and embedded factors that impact on firm behaviour in transitional periphery. Makhmadshoev argues that 'the neo-institutionalist approach, and in particular the North-inspired new institutional economics lens, tends to represent the most dominant approach adopted by many business and management scholars with an interest in post-socialist economies'. This chapter proposes an extension to institutional theory by integrating insights from the comparative capitalism 'varieties of transition' approach and the perspective on institutional change. The logic behind his argument for taking a more institutional change-oriented focus on institutional theory is the non-linear shape of institutional change in the transitional periphery countries. He also argues that limited attention has been paid to change agents in the transitional periphery. Therefore, he argues that integrating insights from comparative capitalism and theories of institutional change can enrich the current thinking on institutions and the firm in the transitional periphery by shedding new light on the role of actors as agents of institutional change, including the mechanisms they deploy to achieve such change.

Chapter 2 (Wood and Demirbag) seeks to examine clan-based authoritarianism and type of capitalism that has emerged in Central Asia, focusing particularly on Uzbekistan. The chapter focuses more on the theoretical aspect of transition, and aims to extend institutional theory to understand clan-based authoritarianism. Wood and Demirbag begin by examining the political context in Uzbekistan, and recent developments which highlight the main characteristics of clan-based authoritarianism and clan-based capitalism. Clan-based capitalism is characterized by strong clan networks, which makes them resilient to external shocks without making significant adjustments to the system. Wood and Demirbag also highlight implications of this emerging type of capitalism on foreign direct investment, and firm-level practices associated with the clan-based economic model in Uzbekistan. They conclude that Uzbekistan has performed better than any other post-Soviet country since 1989, which is also reflected in policy interventions used in Uzbekistan. These policy interventions encompass elements of the new (that is, the construction industry as an engine for growth) and elements of the past (most notably cotton, but also heavy engineering).

Chapter 3 (Manalsuren, Michalski and Śliwa) discusses the understandings, practices and influences upon management in contemporary Mongolia, which presents an interesting example as Mongolia is one of the poorest transitional periphery countries, largely isolated from external sources (Demirbag et al., 2005) and with relatively lower human capital development, while it has an advantageous location between two big emerging markets (Kaynak et al., 2007). Given the transitional stage of Mongolia, the research design adopted in Manalsuren et al.'s chapter is particularly meaningful and important to explore change or institutional embeddedness of management practices in the Mongolian context. The authors use a dataset of 45 in-depth interviews with three different groups of managers (socialist era, transitional era and non-native managers) to examine the managerial role in the Mongolian context. They also offer explanations for managerial practices unique to Mongolia by examining influencing factors such as the nomadic cultural heritage and the legacy of its socialist era, and the evolution and development of Mongolia's economic, legal and political system from its socialist past to its trajectory to capitalism. They weave these discussions into implications for managers and political authorities in the Mongolian context.

In Chapter 4, Usul makes the case that the clan-based economies which have emerged in the transitional periphery create different types of political risk management strategies.

Part II in this book consists of three chapters. The aim of this part is to examine developments and trends in Caucasia, in the countries of Georgia, Armenia and Azerbaijan. It expands upon and underscores themes highlighted in Part I by developing arguments on economic and social change, labour relations and human resource management in this part of the world.

In Chapter 5, Gevorkyan examines economic and social change in two countries: Armenia and Georgia. He adopts a 'five forces of change' framework and attempts to rationalize within the international business context the experiences of these two countries. The author argues that, from an institutional perspective, the experience of these two countries embodies the concept of gradualism. He weaves this into discussions of management practice, and makes a theoretical contribution in which he argues that the lesson from analysis of these two transitional periphery countries is that they should expect a dynamic evolution of macrostructures and business categories. He then proposes taking action towards developing a multifaceted analysis methodology. Gevorkyan further argues that understanding the country specifics is the starting point to understanding the evolution of business strategy in the countries included in his analysis.

In Chapter 6, Yorgun examines similarities and differences between Azerbaijan and Turkey in terms of labour relations, as these two countries have distinctly different economic and political histories. Yorgun argues that despite their distinctly different paths, there are some similarities in adopting and transforming labour relations in these two countries, one of which is clearly in the transitional periphery. Yorgun examines the impact of sudden changes and political shocks in creating changes in Turkey and Azerbaijan. He concludes that changes in industrial relations in both Turkey and Azerbaijan are ongoing processes, and that systems in both countries are not stabilized yet: the processes remain incomplete in both countries, which will continue to remain unstable for some time.

In Chapter 7, Serafini and Szamosi discuss how the national context, educational system and national labour law in transitional periphery countries affect human resources (HR) policies adopted by a United States (US) multinational corporation (MNC). The authors challenge the literature on 'Anglo-Saxonization', which assumes that US MNCs exert a homogenizing process on HR policies due to isomorphic pressure (which is also one of the arguments of the institutional theory). This is particularly important as the transitional periphery countries inherited some legacies of the Soviet era in their human resources-related policies (Sahadev and Demirbag, 2010, 2011; Wood and Demirbag, 2015). The authors adopt Whitley's definition of national features of employment and work relations, through which they examine a US MNC luxury hotel chain operating in both developing economies and transitional periphery countries in the Caucasus and Central Asia regions. They aim to address the juxtaposition of human resource management implementation according to national capitalist archetypes, namely liberal market, the coordinated market and transitional periphery economies (LMEs, CMEs, and TPEs, respectively). Serafini and Szamosi conclude that, contrary to the Anglo-Saxonization argument, in the case of transitional periphery contexts the powerful social ties resulting from deeply rooted local clan systems play a significant role. Therefore, the US MNC's adoption of home country HR policies and practices is partially institutionally rooted.

Part III also consists of three chapters. These are cases from other transitional periphery countries. Chapter 8 by Danilovich and Croucher examines investment decisions made by Belarusian firms under the conditions of institutional concentration. They point out that the reality of government–business relations is significantly different in the region in general, and in the Belarusian case in particular. Their argument builds on Makhmadshoev's analysis and complements Serafini and Szamosi's conclusions, and refers to institutional fluidity in Belarus. This chapter utilizes Zartman and Rubin's (2000) theory of power and negotiation and concludes that while the majority of individual economic actors are suppressed in the Belarusian 'pseudo-market' system, and the Soviet institutional legacy still influences state–business relations, state-controlled companies appear to exert indirect influence on the government. Danilovich and Croucher further expand their argument to how informal connections with the formal institutions enable managers to exert indirect influence on the institutions that oversee them.

Chapter 9 by Arslan, Larimo and Tarba examines the equity commitment made by multinational enterprises (MNEs) from Nordic countries at the time of market entry in transitional periphery economies. While there is a significant body of literature on MNEs' entry mode in developing countries, transitional periphery countries pose an extra layer of uncertainty and risk, hence affecting equity commitment decisions of MNEs at the market entry stage (Kaynak et al., 2007; Demirbag et al., 2008; Demirbag et al., 2010). The authors argue that, when these economies appeared to have stabilized during the 2000s, large MNEs chose high equity commitments even in transitional periphery countries. They conclude that entry mode and equity commitment decisions are influenced not only by institutional stability in these countries, but also by availability of suitable partners or target firms to acquire, as some of these countries have limited options for MNEs in the first place.

Chapter 10 is by Akbar and Kisilowski. The authors examine the 'transnational periphery' through the lens of 'nonmarket strategy' or 'corporate political strategies', through which they aim to uncover the importance of a phenomenon critical to post-Soviet countries (Demirbag et al., 1998; Demirbag and Gunes, 2000; Mellahi et al., 2012; Demirbag et al., 2015). Akbar and Kisilowski contrast their empirical findings from their research in Eastern Europe and Central Asia (EECA) countries with literature adopting Hillman and Hitt's framework in the context of Western Europe (Hillman, 2003). This is an interesting approach which uncovers limitations of Hillman and Hitt's framework (Hillman and Hitt, 1999) when applied to transitional periphery countries. Their findings are especially important given that the business environment in many of the transitional periphery countries bears a heavy legacy of the Soviet era (Demirbag et al., 2010; Zsolt et al., 2011). Therefore, Akbar and Kisilowski extend Hillman and Hitt's framework to incorporate the particularities of the EECA institutional context, focusing specifically on two other important types of nonmarket strategies, which they label as 'relational strategies' and 'procedural strategies'.

CONCLUSION

A common theme across much of the region is that the relationship between domestic governance arrangements, economic policies and growth remains tenuous. Whilst some of this may be ascribed to statistical chicanery, a great deal reflects the extent to which the relationship between formal institutions and the ad hoc solutions derived at by key actors remains tenuous. However, it is also a reflection of the extent to which market fundamentalism may be equally as unsuccessful as central planning if realities on the ground are ignored; solutions imposed in the early 1990s shared the lack of realism characteristic of their predecessors. Again, if the results of democratic elections are easily overthrown by a colour-coded revolution, then the incentives of political actors to abide by democratic rules are very slight.

It is easy to highlight institutional failures, but much more difficult to identify viable ways forward. However, what emerges from the different accounts in this volume is not only the variety of the problems experienced, but also instances – if at times fleeting – of progress and growth. Through a closer analysis of the latter, it may be possible to draw out sets of policy options that may provide more viable ways forward that are more closely in tune with realities on the ground. It is the intention of this volume not just to provide a catalogue of challenges and failures, but also to provide the basis for future debates both on how we may better theorize about the region, and on what possible solutions might prove viable, where and when.

REFERENCES

Collins, K. (2006). *Clan Politics and Regime Transition in Central Asia: Its Impact in Regime Transformation*. Cambridge: Cambridge University Press.
Cumming, D., Wood, G., Filatotchev, I., and Wood, G. (2017). Introducing

sovereign wealth funds. In Cumming, D., Wood, G., Filatotchev, I., and Wood, G. (eds), *Oxford Handbook of Sovereign Wealth Funds*, pp. 3–15. Oxford: Oxford University Press.

Demirbag, M., and Gunes, R. (2000). Political risk assessment: a case study of Turkish companies operating in Central Asian and Russian markets, in Songini, L. (ed.), *Political and Economic Relations between Asia and Europe: New Challenges in Economics and Management*, pp. 105–119. Milano: EGEA.

Demirbag, M., Gunes, R., and Mirza, H. (1998). Political risk management: a case study of Turkish companies in Central Asia and Russia. In Mirza, H. (ed.), *Global Competitive Strategies in the New World Economy: Multilateralism, Regionalization and the Transnational Firm*, pp. 283–309. Cheltenham, UK and Northampton, MA, USA: Edward Elgar Publishing.

Demirbag, M., McGuinness, M., and Altay, H. (2010). Perceptions of institutional environment and entry mode: FDI from an emerging country. *Management International Review*, 50(2), pp. 207–240, https://doi.org/10.1007/s11575-010-0028-1.

Demirbag, M., McGuinness, M., Wood, G.T., and Bayyurt, N. (2015). Context, law and reinvestment decisions: why the transitional periphery differs from other post-state socialist economies. *International Business Review*, 24(6), pp. 955–965.

Demirbag, M., Tatoglu, E., and Glaister, K. (2008). Factors affecting perceptions of the choice between acquisition and greenfield entry: the case of Western FDI in an emerging market, *Management International Review*, 48(1), pp. 5–38.

Demirbag, M., Tatoglu, E., and Oyungerel, A. (2005). Patterns of foreign direct investment in Mongolia, 1990–2003: a research note. *Eurasian Geography and Economics*, 46(4), pp. 247–259.

Demirbag, M., and Yaprak, A. (eds) (2015). *Handbook of Emerging Market Multinational Corporations*. Cheltenham, UK and Northampton, MA, USA: Edward Elgar Publishing.

Frynas, G., Wood, G., and Hinks, T. (2016). The resource curse without natural resources: expectations of resource booms and their impact. *African Affairs*. Early online at: https://academic.oup.com/afraf/article/2968106/The-resource-curse-without-natural-resources.

Gold, T., Guthrie, D., and Wank, D. (eds) (2002). *Social Connections in China: Institutions, Culture, and the Changing Nature of Guanxi*. Cambridge: Cambridge University Press.

Hall, P.A., and Soskice, D. (2003). Varieties of capitalism and institutional change: a response to three critics. *Comparative European Politics*, 1(2), pp. 241–250.

Hancke, B., Rhodes, M., and Thatcher, M. (2007). Introduction. In Hancke, B., Rhodes, M., and Thatcher, M. (eds), *Beyond Varieties of Capitalism: Conflict, Contradiction, and Complementarities in the European Economy*, pp. 3–38. Oxford: Oxford University Press.

Hillman, A. (2003). Determinants of political strategies in US multinationals. *Business and Society*, 42(4), pp. 455–484.

Hillman, A.J., and Hitt, M.A. (1999). Corporate political strategy formulation: a model of approach, participation, and strategy decisions. *Academy of Management Review*, 24(4), pp. 825–842.

Kaynak, E., Demirbag, M., and Tatoglu, E. (2007). Determinants of ownership-based entry mode choice of MNEs: evidence from Mongolia. *Management International Review*, 47(4), pp. 505–530.

Lane, C., and Wood, G. (eds) (2012). *Capitalist Diversity and Diversity within Capitalism*. London: Routledge.

Lane, D., and Myant, M. (eds) (2016). *Varieties of Capitalism in Post-Communist Countries*. London: Palgrave.

Mellahi, K., Demirbag, M., and Wood, G.T. (2012). Regulatory context and corruption: rethinking the effects of government intervention. *International Studies of Management and Organization*, 42(3), pp. 13–34.

Michailova, S. and Worm, V. (2003). Personal networking in Russia and China: blat and guanxi. *European Management Journal*, 21(4), pp. 509–519.

Nölke, A., and Vliegenthart, A. (2009). Enlarging the varieties of capitalism: the emergence of dependent market economies in East Central Europe. *World Politics*, 61(4), pp. 670–702.

Northrop, D. (2000). Languages of loyalty: gender, politics, and party supervision in Uzbekistan, 1927–41. *Russian Review*, 59(2), pp. 179–200.

Panossian, R. (2004). Homeland–diaspora relations and identity differences. In Herzing, E., and Kurkchiyan, M. (eds), *The Armenians: Past and Present in the Making of National Identity*, pp. 229–243. Abingdon: Routledge.

Sahadev, S., and Demirbag, M. (2010). A comparative analysis of employment practices among post-communist and capitalist countries in South Eastern Europe. *Employee Relations*, 32(3), pp. 248–261, https://doi.org/10.1108/01425451011038780.

Sahadev, S., and Demirbag, M. (2011). Exploring variations in employment practices in the emerging economies of Europe: assessing the impact of foreign ownership and European integration, *Human Resource Management Journal*, 21, pp. 395–414, doi:10.1111/j.1748-8583.2011.00183.x.

Topp, V. (2008). Productivity in the mining industry: measurement and interpretation, https://papers.ssrn.com/sol3/papers.cfm?abstract_id=1620243.

Wood, G., and Demirbag, M. (2012). Institutions and comparative business studies: supranational and national regulation. In Wood, G., and Demirbag, M. (eds), *Handbook of Institutional Approaches to International Business*, pp. 3–17. Cheltenham, UK and Northampton, MA, USA: Edward Elgar Publishing.

Wood, G., and Demirbag, M. (2015). Business and society on the transitional periphery: comparative perspectives. *International Business Review*, 24(6), pp. 917–920.

Wood, G., and Frynas, G. (2006). The institutional basis of economic failure: anatomy of the segmented business system. *Socio-Economic Review*, 4(2), pp. 239–277.

Wood, G., Dibben, P., and Ogden, S. (2014). Comparative capitalism without capitalism, and production without workers: the limits and possibilities of contemporary institutional analysis. *International Journal of Management Reviews*, 16(4), pp. 384–396.

Zartman, I.W., and Rubin, J.Z. (2000). The study of power and the practice of negotiation. In Zartman, I.W., and Rubin, J.Z. (eds), *Power and Negotiation*, pp. 3–28. Ann Arbor, MI: University of Michigan Press.

Zsolt, B., Demirbag, M., and Wood, G.T. (2011). Introducing governance and employment relations in Eastern and Central Europe. *Employee Relations*, 33(4), pp. 309–315, https://doi.org/10.1108/01425451111140604.

PART I

Transitional periphery: Central Asia

1. Expanding the boundaries of institutional analysis in the transitional periphery

Dilshod Makhmadshoev

INTRODUCTION

Over the last two decades, institutional theory has provided scholars from various backgrounds with powerful and effective theoretical tools to probe into the post-socialist transition economies. Researchers, particularly in the fields of international business and small business and entrepreneurship, benefited significantly by drawing on neo-institutional perspectives to explore and explain the various effects of unstable institutional settings and embedded institutional factors on firm behaviour in these environments. However, it is highlighted here that the neo-institutionalist approach, and in particular the 'new institutional economics' lens, tends to represent the most dominant approach utilized by scholars with an interest in post-socialist economies. While this perspective remains powerful and effective to this day, this chapter proposes that research in this area can potentially benefit in important ways from expanding the boundaries of institutional analysis by integrating insights from two emerging but hitherto underexploited institutional perspectives, namely the 'varieties of transition' approach (e.g., Havrylyshyn, 2006; Lane and Myant, 2007; Myant and Drahokoupil, 2011), which is an alternative to the mainstream comparative capitalism, and a more actor-centred perspective on institutional change, which is inspired by the works of Campbell (1997, 2004).

The first key observation regarding the current thinking on institutions in the context of transition economies is that it has not placed adequate emphasis on emerging variations in institutional environments among these countries. The process of transition in post-socialist states has not followed the previously anticipated linear progression towards Western models of capitalism (Makhmadshoev et al., 2015). Thus, exploring questions relating to institutional divergence becomes ever more important. Despite the popularity of institutional approaches in studying transition economies, research on the transitional periphery within business studies has remained largely silent in acknowledging the divergent transition paths and the implications of this institutional divergence on firm behaviour. The second key observation is that surprisingly little attention is paid to the role of actors as agents of institutional change, and to the mechanisms they deploy to achieve this change. Thus, it is proposed here that integrating insights from comparative capitalism and a theory of institutional change can enrich the current thinking on institutions and the firm in the transitional periphery.

This chapter will first provide an in-depth review of the new institutional economics (NIE) approach and how it is utilized in selected studies by international business (IB) and small business and entrepreneurship scholars with empirical focus on transition economies, highlighting its important explanatory capabilities. It will then introduce the two emerging institutional perspectives and highlight their relevance for the transitional periphery. In analysing the relevance of the varieties of transition (VoT) approach, it draws on some examples from empirical fieldwork conducted in Kyrgyzstan and Tajikistan. This chapter is partially based on insights obtained from this fieldwork in the Central Asian periphery, and further advances some of the conceptual ideas that were originally developed and published in contributions by Makhmadshoev et al. (2015) and Makhmadshoev and Crone (2014).

NEO-INSTITUTIONAL APPROACH (NEW INSTITUTIONAL ECONOMICS)

Institutional theory became increasingly prominent in the social sciences during the latter part of the twentieth century and has since attracted considerable attention from scholars in various fields, including economics, political science and sociology. It is widely recognized as one of the dominant approaches to understanding organizations (DiMaggio and Powell, 1983; Tolbert and Zucker, 1996; Scott, 1995). It is used in examining and explaining the importance of the wider social and cultural environments on organizational actions, organizational structures and organizational practices (Dacin et al., 2002; Kostova and Roth, 2002; Scott, 2008). Institutional thought has also revolutionized the study of economics and economic systems, and has been rigorously deployed in challenging some of the core arguments of the mainstream (neoclassical) economic theory (Coase, 1998; North, 1990).

Perhaps it is helpful to highlight that the body of knowledge regarded as institutional theory encompasses two distinctive streams: the early institutionalist approach and the neo-institutionalist approach (Furubotn and Richter, 2000; Scott, 1995). The development of institutional theory was initiated by the so-called early institutionalists (pre-1970s). However, this approach is said to have attracted increased criticism for being largely descriptive and lacking in theory (Coase, 1998; Scott, 2008). The work of early institutionalists was also strongly challenged for its inadequate focus on organizations and, crucially, for its failure to make a distinction between institutions and organizations (Scott, 1995). As a result, a new institutionalist approach (neo-institutional theory) has since emerged, which puts explicit emphasis on organizations and differentiates institutions from organizations (North, 1990; Scott, 2008). Thus, it can be argued that much of what is acknowledged today as 'institutional theory' constitutes the neo-institutionalist approach. This neo-institutionalist approach, in turn, is dominated by two major schools of thought, broadly known as: (1) the 'organizational institutionalism' – where institutions are viewed as inter- and intra-organizational forms, practices and activities that are enforced through coercive, mimetic and normative mechanisms, and which also tends to favour the terminology of regulative, normative and cognitive institutions (e.g., DiMaggio and Powell, 1983; Kostova and Roth, 2002; Scott, 1995); and (2) the 'new institutional economics' – which views institutions as 'the rules of the game' and favours the terminology of formal and informal institutions (e.g., Furubotn and Richter, 2000; North, 1990, p. 3; Williamson, 1981). It is the latter which is adopted more widely within business and management research on transition economies.

Though the new institutional economics (NIE) perspective is associated primarily with the works of Coase (1937), Williamson (1981) and North (1990), it is North who is more widely considered to have contributed significantly to bringing institutions to the forefront of economic development debate (North, 1987, 1990). Furthermore, by emphasizing the distinction between institutions (rules of the game) and organizations (players in the game) and by categorizing institutions into formal and informal types, and incorporating their enforcement mechanism into the analysis, North (1990) developed and proposed a powerful analytical framework for the study of institutional influences on economic behaviour and performance.

Moving On through the 'Rules of the Game' Metaphor

Institutions are 'the rules of the game in a society' (North, 1990, p. 3). They are forms of constraints created by humans to shape, structure and guide individual and organizational interactions and reduce uncertainties in everyday exchanges. Davis and North (1971, p. 6) define an institutional environment as 'the set of fundamental political, social and legal ground rules that establishes the basis for production, exchange and distribution'. Institutions can be formal and informal (North, 1990). Formal institutions include rules (political rules, economic rules, judicial rules and individual contracts), regulations, laws and written constitutions. Informal institutions consist of conventions, customs and social norms of behaviour, which are influenced by culture and are often distinctive to particular societies (North, 1990, 1991, 2005).

The main premise of the institutional perspective advanced by North (1990, 2005) is that institutions influence economic performance and shape economic outcomes (Furubotn and Richter, 2000; Williamson, 1998). It is by demonstrating the existence of positive transaction costs that the NIE thinking developed a strong case for challenging the mainstream (neoclassical) economic reasoning, and as a result suggested a new way of analysing economic systems and economic exchanges. North (1987, p. 419) states that 'what economists have not realized until recently is that exchange is not costless'. He goes on to assert that the cost of transacting is fundamental to the performance of economies and economic actors, including firms (North, 1987, 1990). Thus, transaction cost analysis has become a particularly important instrument in understanding how institutions influence the behaviour and performance of economic actors. 'Transaction cost' is a broad term that includes a range of costs associated with creating and operating an economic system, as well as those associated with creating and operating a new enterprise (Furubotn and Richter, 2000). Importantly, North (1990) also emphasizes that transaction costs are 'part of the costs of production' (ibid., p. 28), and include a broad range of measurable costs, such as official fees and formal expenses, as well as 'hard-to-measure costs' (ibid., p. 68), such as costs of acquiring information and a wide range of informal costs, such as bribes and informal payments.

Uncertainty and transaction costs are the two closely interconnected dimensions in the study of institutions. Some degree of uncertainty, caused by political, economic or social factors, is generally present in any environment, which in fact explains the existence of positive transaction costs (Williamson, 1997). The role of institutions, as North (1990) crucially explains, is to reduce this uncertainty and provide stability when firms engage in a particular type of economic activity. However, this may not always be the case, as institutional frameworks are dynamic and evolving in nature. For uncertainty to remain low, institutions 'must be well-designed and properly maintained' (Furubotn and Richter, 2000, p. 7). Therefore, in environments where institutions are weak or poorly implemented, uncertainty tends to be high, which in turn results in high transaction costs for economic actors. This assumption is particularly evident in the analysis of the institutional environments of the former communist countries, including those in the periphery (Makhmadshoev and Crone, 2014; Peng and Heath, 1996; North, 1990, 1997).

North (1987, 1990) draws particular attention to growth benefits gained from participation in trade, but more importantly provides an explanation as to how institutional frameworks influence the process of participation in trade. The NIE argues that the idea of perfect market information is highly abstract, thus competition in markets (or in an economy) may not always be perfect or fair (Furubotn and Richter, 2000). Institutional frameworks, largely through formal state policies and regulatory mechanisms, play an important role in establishing and maintaining competitive conditions in markets. However, institutions differ from country to country, therefore in societies where the rules of competition are not well established or not properly administered, firms may face high transaction costs and limited opportunities for growth and expansion. This provides a partial explanation as to why some countries and their firms are more competitive and more successful when participating in international trade (Hall and Soskice, 2001).

The broader conceptualization of the institutional environment also encompasses the role of organizations (that is, non-firm organizations). Analysing organizations in this way, however, does not suggest disregarding the all-important distinction made between institutions (as the rules of the game) and organizations (as players of the game). North (1990) emphasizes the importance of conceptually distinguishing institutions from organizations. However, he further clarifies that this should not necessarily exclude organizations from the analysis, for sometimes it may be unreasonable to separate the analysis of the rules of the game from different organizations, agencies and associations that enforce, monitor and facilitate these rules. North (1990, p. 4) states that 'when we examine the costs that arise as a consequence of the institutional framework we see they are a result not only of that framework, but also of the organizations that have developed in consequence of that framework'. Thus, the analysis of institutional environments needs to focus not only on specific rules and norms, but can also include organizations that provide institutional support to economic actors in achieving their objectives and those that act as enforcers of rules and regulations.

One of the main shortcomings of the North-inspired institutional approach relates to its conceptualization of informal institutions. North recognizes certain difficulties in providing a clear-cut definition of informal institutions, mainly because the understanding of informal institutions in the NIE often overlaps with the sociological perspectives on network theory (Granovetter, 1973; Murdoch, 2000) and social capital (Coleman, 1988; Granovetter, 1985; Woolcock, 1998). This chapter adheres to the understanding of informal institutions informed by the NIE, as it is deemed more appropriate in identifying specific informal institutions at the national level, particularly in transition economies, and understanding how they influence firm behaviour. What North's and his NIE associates' contributions to the wider institutional theory suggest is that institutional environments of countries are a mix of economic, political and social structures that define and enforce the fundamental rules of production, interaction and exchange. This may include conditions of access to means of production as well as the more specific regulations concerning international trade and entry into specific industries. Thus, institutions not only influence the nature of activities of firms, but at a more fundamental level also affect the various opportunities available to them.

Utility of NIE in IB and SME and Entrepreneurship Research on Transition Economies

The North-inspired institutional approach has established itself as a dominant analytical tool for understanding the effects of institutions in transition economies and analysing economic activities of firms in these environments. The distinction of formal and informal institutions has been particularly pertinent in this respect. The institutional approach states that economic activities of firms are influenced not only by formal rules, but also by a range of informal rules (North, 1990; Peng, 2003). It also suggests that when formal rules are weak and inefficient, informal rules become more influential and gradually replace formal rules. Given that transition economies are undergoing a radical structural and institutional change, especially in terms of formal institutions, it is informal institutions that often take over and govern economic activities in such environments (North, 1990; Peng and Heath, 1996). The application of an institutional approach focuses attention on how the lack of formal rules may lead to increased uncertainty, and thus to high transaction costs for firms (North, 1990).

In recent years, institutions (or 'an institution-based view') have become a major focus in the IB and strategic management research community, alongside the more established industry-based and resource-based views of (international) strategy (Dunning, 2004; Meyer and Peng, 2005; Mudambi and Navarra, 2002; Peng, 2004; Peng et al., 2008). This can be observed from a growing number of Special Issues on the topic of institutions and IB in top-ranking academic journals (notable examples include the *Journal of International Business Studies* Special Issues in 2008, Vol. 39

and 2010, Vol. 41; and the *Journal of International Management* Special Issue in 2008, Vol. 14, with specific empirical focus on transition economies) and edited books dedicated to the topic (a notable example Wood and Demirbag, 2012). Several reasons have been proposed as to why IB scholars should make more efforts in integrating institutional perspectives in their research. Firstly, it is argued that focusing on institutions could help to answer one of the major questions in IB research, which is, 'what determines the international success and failure of firms?' (Peng, 2004, p. 106). Secondly, scholars acknowledge that much of the IB and strategic management research in the past has not been particularly interested in institutions, largely because the influence of institutions on firm activities and performance was not considered significant (Meyer and Peng, 2005). Considerable differences in institutional environments between developed, emerging and transition economies have been observed, which in turn led scholars to believe that 'institutions are much more than background conditions, and that institutions directly determine what arrows a firm has in its quiver as it struggles to formulate and implement strategy and to create competitive advantage' (Meyer et al., 2009, p. 61; see also Meyer and Peng, 2005; Peng et al., 2008).

The current stream of research within IB emphasizing institutions in the context of transition economies has focused largely on internationalization of Western-based multinational enterprises (MNEs) into transition economies (Bevan et al., 2004; Cuervo-Cazurra, 2008; Gelbuda et al., 2008; Hitt et al., 2004; Jackson and Deeg, 2008; Makhmadshoev et al., 2015; Meyer, 2001; Meyer and Peng, 2005; Meyer and Vo Nguyen, 2005; Meyer et al., 2009; Peng et al., 2008). The primary empirical focus thus far has been on some transition economies, such as Russia, China, and those in Central and Eastern Europe (Gelbuda et al., 2008; Meyer, 2001; Meyer et al., 2009; Meyer and Peng, 2005; Peng et al., 2008). Other relatively under-researched and somewhat peripheral transition economies, such as those in Central Asia, the Caucasus and the Balkans, are yet to be given adequate research attention. More importantly, perhaps, it is observed that while the growing scholarly interest in institutions and institutional approaches within the field of IB is a positive sign, the North-inspired NIE approach has been the main institutional perspective adopted by this stream of research in probing into the post-socialist transition economies.

A similar trend is also observed in the stream of research on entrepreneurship and small and medium-sized enterprise (SME) development in transition economies, where the North-inspired NIE approach appears to be the dominant institutional framework adopted (e.g., Aidis, 2005; Estrin et al., 2008; Puffer et al., 2010; Smallbone and Welter, 2012; Williams and Vorley, 2017). It is argued that the development of small firms is influenced not only by a range of internal firm characteristics, such as 'creativity, drive and commitment of individuals', but also to a great extent by external factors created by the environments in which firms evolve and develop (Smallbone and Welter, 2001b, p. 64). External factors are considered especially influential for small firm development in transition economies, because of their weak and often ineffective institutional environments. For example, Smallbone and Welter (2001a, p. 260) state that 'in transition economies, the dominant feature influencing the nature and pace of entre-preneurship and small business development is the external environment, which, in some cases, appears hostile in social, economic and political terms'.

The adoption of North's (1990) framework has allowed some studies to distinguish between formal and informal institutional barriers. For exam-ple, barriers relating to general regulatory environments, which include tax rates and changes to tax regulations, are categorized as formal barriers (barriers created by formal institutions), whereas barriers relating to lack of law enforcement, corruption and unfair competition are categorized as informal barriers (barriers created by informal institutions) (Aidis, 2005; Smallbone and Welter, 2012). Some studies also categorize social con-nections and networking practices as important features of the informal institutional environment in transition economies (Aidis, 2005; Estrin et al., 2008; Makhmadshoev and Crone, 2014; Smallbone and Welter, 2012), and suggest that the prevalence of these practices indicates 'the absence of a well-functioning formal institutional framework' (Estrin et al., 2008, p. 28). However, their impact on entrepreneurship and firm growth is viewed not only as adverse (for example, in the Russian environment) but also as favourable (in the Chinese environment) (Estrin et al., 2008), which suggests that it can be misleading to attribute informal institutional factors as barriers only. Informal institutions are indeed gaining more attention in this research area, as demonstrated in a review study by Manev and Manolova (2010), who call for more studies to focus on understanding informal institutional environments and their impact on entrepreneurship in transition economies.

The discussions above illustrate that the neo-institutionalist approach, and in particular the North-inspired NIE perspective, continues to provide researchers in the IB and the SME and entrepreneurship fields with a pow-erful tool to unpack the various complexities of the transitional context and grasp their varying implications on firms. It is argued here that this current institutional thinking on transition economies can be potentially further enhanced and enriched by infusing and integrating insights from the two relatively underexploited institutional approaches on institutional divergence and institutional change. In the sections that follow I attempt to demonstrate their compatibility with the dominant NIE approach, as well as their utility for the transitional periphery.

INSTITUTIONAL DIVERGENCE AND VARIETIES OF TRANSITION

A key argument advanced by this stream of research is that not only institutions matter, but so do differences in institutions. While the neo-institutional approach continues to be influential and effective, recent contributions from other social science disciplines, particularly political economy and economic sociology, have drawn attention to the widening institutional divergence among transition economies. It is one of the main aims of this chapter to emphasize the divergent paths of transition experienced in some countries in transitional periphery and point to this embryonic varieties of transition (VoT) approach, also referred to as the 'varieties of post-socialism' or 'varieties of capitalism in post-communist countries', which places emphasis on understanding the implications of institutional divergence in the former socialist economies on economic and social behaviour.

The VoT takes its roots from the 'varieties of capitalism' (VoC) debate. The latter was originated by political economists (Amable, 2003; Hall and Soskice, 2001) and represents a dominant approach to comparative capitalism (CC) adopted in business and management literature. This approach helps to understand not only the differences in institutional structures across countries with capitalist systems (Hall and Soskice, 2001), but also the internal diversity within national contexts (Lane and Wood, 2009). Amable (2003) states that the VoC thinking was originally triggered by observed differences in macroeconomic performances among the group of developed countries (notably the United States, European countries and Japan). A key feature of this literature is the notion of institutional complementarity. According to Hall and Soskice (2001, p. 17), 'two institutions can be complementary if the presence (or efficiency) of one increases the returns from (or efficiency of) the other'. The extent of institutional complementarity may serve as an indicator of the diversity in institutional frameworks between different forms of market economies (Hall and Soskice, 2001). This work has delineated distinct national models of capitalism among developed economies, such as Hall and Soskice's (2001) division of liberal versus coordinated market capitalism. In this way, the CC literature draws the attention of researchers to the complex and diverse 'topography of institutional landscapes' (Jackson and Deeg, 2008, p. 541) and suggests the need to incorporate a more sophisticated and contextually rich characterization of institutional environments (Michailova, 2011; Redding, 2005).

Yet, when it comes to considering the institutional environments of transition economies, this dominant CC literature is silent (Makhmadshoev et al., 2015). Indeed, the relevance and applicability of the established CC frameworks to transition economies have been questioned (Havrylyshyn, 2006; Myant and Drahokoupil, 2012). Scholars observe that the CC literature tends to assume that institutional configurations are permanent or subject to only gradual change, whereas transition economies are, by their nature, subject to continuous institutional change and uncertainty (Myant and Drahokoupil, 2012). Furthermore, in the case of the former Soviet Union and especially the transitional periphery, it is observed that the transition process has not followed the linear progression towards the established models of capitalism, which was initially anticipated by policy-makers and scholars alike. Thus, as an alternative to the mainstream CC literature discussed above, Makhmadshoev et al. (2015) identified a distinct and emergent strand of work, though dominated by political scientists and economic sociologists to date, that seeks to identify, classify and accentuate varieties of capitalism in post-communist or transition countries (Feldmann, 2006; Lane and Myant, 2007).

This approach basically argues that the process of transforming planned economies into well-functioning market economies has taken a distinct trajectory in each country, and one that may be characterized by path-dependence. As a result, these divergent paths of transition have resulted in an institutional diversity among the former Soviet republics (Blackmon, 2007; Havrylyshyn, 2006). Thus, borrowing from the CC approach, the VoT camp identifies a number of different emerging models of capitalism in transition economies. For instance, Lane (2007) proposes a threefold typology comprising state-led capitalism, hybrid state/market uncoordinated capitalism, and the transition laggards characterized by statist economies (see Table 1.1). Similarly, Havrylyshyn (2006) identifies four types of transition currently prevailing in post-communist states, namely liberal societies, intermediate regimes, captured states and lagging reformers (see Table 1.2). Furthermore, Myant and Drahokoupil (2011) propose the following fivefold typology of the 'varieties of capitalism in transition': foreign direct investment (FDI)-based market economies; peripheral market economies; oligarchic or clientelistic capitalist economies; order states; and remittance- and aid-dependent countries (see Table 1.3).

This literature also questions the general assumption that the former communist countries embarked on the process of transition from similar starting points. This is because from an economic point of view some countries were significantly better than others before the collapse of

Table 1.1   Typology of emerging capitalisms in post-communist states, as per Lane

Post-communist states	Typology
State-led capitalism: Slovenia, Czech Republic, Poland, Hungary, Slovakia, Estonia, Lithuania, Croatia, Latvia, Romania, Bulgaria	Closest to 'Continental' form of market capitalism; levels of marketization and privatization comparable to Organisation for Economic Co-operation and Development (OECD) states; high exposure to the global economy and large private sectors; embedded welfare states make them comparable to continental European model of capitalism; some have greater state coordination, but all have developed economic, political and societal preconditions of capitalism. Extent of transition: transition almost complete.
Hybrid state/market uncoordinated capitalism: Russian Federation, Ukraine, Kazakhstan, Georgia, Moldova	Economically poorer group, with high levels of poverty, inflation and unemployment; weak governing institutions led to 'unsuccessful' period of transition and a period of 'chaotic capitalism'; pursued privatization, but exposure to the global economy remains low; have low levels of domestic investment; contexts characterized by high institutional uncertainty, corruption, and rent-seeking entrepreneurs; all countries lack psychological, political and societal preconditions to support modern capitalism. Extent of transition: only group to assume a 'transitionary' status.
Transition laggards or statist economies: Uzbekistan, Turkmenistan, Belarus	Countries in the group deemed not to have made breakthrough to a capitalist system; contexts characterized by high levels of state coordination and bureaucratic control, and low levels of private ownership and exposure to the global economy; key economic functions, internal and external, continue to be controlled by the state or state-owned corporations. Extent of transition: no significant progress toward the transition.

Source: Complied by author from Lane (2007, pp. 35–37).

the communist regime. For instance, Central and Eastern European countries (CEECs) already had higher levels of industrialization compared to many smaller countries, which had significantly weaker levels of industrialization and served primarily as producers and suppliers of

Table 1.2   Variation in transition outcomes in post-communist states, as per Havrylyshyn

Post-communist states	Key characteristics
Liberal societies: Estonia, Latvia, Lithuania, Czech Republic, Hungary, Poland, Slovenia, Slovakia, Croatia, Bulgaria, Romania	Developed and well-functioning market economies; liberal democratic systems; avoided development of oligarchic tendencies; high performance on economic and social indicators; most countries achieved European Union (EU) membership; transition is complete in most countries.
Intermediate regimes: Albania, Macedonia, Bosnia-Herzegovina, Serbia, Georgia, Ukraine, Kyrgyzstan	Significant degree of rent-seeking and oligarchic tendencies in the economy and state policy, but receding; mid-range performance on economic and social indicators; future EU membership gives reform incentive to some; gradually but firmly moving towards liberal states.
Captured states: Russian Federation, Kazakhstan, Azerbaijan, Moldova, Armenia, Tajikistan	Existence of powerful 'economic oligarchy'; low levels of competition in economy and state policy; insufficient evolution toward market institutions; economic and social indicators on the lower end of scale; transition very slow and sluggish in most cases.
Lagging reformers: Belarus, Turkmenistan, Uzbekistan	Limited progress in terms of market reforms; insignificant liberalization and privatization; role of state in the economy and polity remains dominant; transition in all of these countries 'has barely started'.

Source: Compiled by author from Havrylyshyn (2006, pp. 261–263).

raw materials during the Soviet rule. In addition, there are countries in the Commonwealth of Independent States (CIS) that were significant oil and gas producers and possessed vast reserves of natural resources. This means that smaller countries with weak industrial capacities and insignificant oil and gas resources faced a tougher transition path compared to the other two groups (Myant and Drahokoupil, 2011, p. xix). Subsequent divergence in transition paths was further influenced by a broad policy approach adopted by major international institutions that somewhat erroneously assumed that a generic policy package, consisting of two opposing methods of 'shock-therapy' and 'gradualism', would be appropriate to all transition countries (ibid.). They failed to consider

Table 1.3   Varieties of capitalism in transition economies, as per Myant and Drahokoupil

Varieties of capitalism	Key characteristics
FDI-based market economies: Central-Eastern European countries	Democratic political systems and EU integration; strong export structures built around inbound FDI; second-rank positions within global value chains; sound domestic environments for private sector growth.
Peripheral market economies: The Baltics and South-Eastern European countries	Democratic political systems and EU membership; conducive institutions for private sector development; less stable export structure based on manufacturing; weak domestic economies and open to external shocks; dependence on remittances and lower welfare provisions.
Oligarchic or clientelistic capitalism: Most countries in the CIS	Close ties between business and politics; weakly developed environment for new businesses; levels of social and employment protection are low; weak exports and low levels of domestic investment; 'relatively authoritarian political systems'.
Order state capitalism: CIS countries with limited reforms	Some degree of integration into the global economy; prevalence of state ownership and control of economy; exports dominated by commodities and raw materials; also characterized by 'authoritarian political systems'.
Remittance- and aid-based economies Low-income CIS and Eastern European states	Weak bases for economic transformation; weak environments for private sector development; adversely affected by peripheral geographical locations; dominated by domestic-oriented entrepreneurship; potential to develop into MNE subcontracting locations.

Source: Compiled by author from Myant and Drahokoupil (2011, pp. 310–312).

specific policy needs of individual countries and instead focused on the agenda to prioritize speedy implementation of different transitional requirements, such as liberalization of prices, international trade and banking activities, legalization of private enterprise, privatization, and sharp minimization in state intervention. While this approach indeed benefited some countries, it did not produce expected results in countries with weaker capacities to absorb and implement the suggested policy package, thereby necessarily affecting the outcomes of the transition process in these countries.

Whilst many of these states continue to be collectively labelled as transition economies, and may be deemed to have similar political economies, the aforementioned literature highlights the significant divergence that has taken place in the nature and direction of transition among the group. The tables and their classifications suggest that the nature and outcomes of transition appear to vary significantly; authors report that whilst many countries have completed the process, and many others are in the process of transformation, there are also a number of countries where the transition has barely commenced. Further, it is noted here that this diversity of transition shapes the process of institutional development and influences the specific type of market economic system that is being constructed in particular countries (Myant and Drahokoupil, 2012). This implies significant variation in these countries' (emerging) institutional contexts. It is important to acknowledge that attempts have been made in the aforementioned business and management literature to emphasize the heterogeneity in institutional contexts. For instance, IB scholars distinguish between the 'big bang' versus the more gradual model of transition adopted by the larger economies of Russia and China, respectively (Buck et al., 2000; Hitt et al., 2004; Tsang, 1996), while the SME and entrepreneurship scholars distinguish between transition economies with more advanced and less advanced market reforms (Smallbone and Welter, 2001b, 2012). However, it is observed that no corresponding attention has been paid to smaller post-Soviet economies in the periphery, and more importantly, no conceptual link has been made to this particular strand of comparative institutionalism literature, which places emphasis on the direction and nature of the transition process, in addition to the speed of transition (Makhmadshoev et al., 2015). This suggests a need to better understand the implications of the varieties of transition on firm behaviour. This observation is particularly timely, given that the comparative institutionalism approach is rapidly gaining ground within wider business and management literature (Jackson and Deeg, 2008; Hall and Soskice, 2001; Hotho and Pedersen, 2012).

Utility of the VoT for the Transitional Periphery: Some Empirical Evidence

As stated in the previous section, a key argument of the VoT approach is that the formerly planned economies may be developing diverse national institutional environments as a result of experiencing divergent paths to the transition process. By drawing upon insights obtained through original fieldwork in Central Asia and integrating these with empirical evidence gathered from publicly available sources, this section demonstrates the usefulness of this argument and further cautions researchers that it may be erroneous to attribute countries in the transitional periphery, and indeed transitional countries in general, as a homogeneous category in relation to their institutional configurations (Makhmadshoev et al., 2015).

One of the key and somewhat unanticipated findings of the fieldwork conducted in the Central Asian countries of Kyrgyzstan and Tajikistan was that despite their similarities and common Soviet heritage, the institutional environments of the two countries were found to be similar but different. This partly accounted for differences in the impact of institutional contexts on firm behaviour in the two countries. Tajikistan gained independence in September 1991 following the break-up of the Soviet Union and almost immediately entered a state of civil war, which ended only in 1997 (Heathershaw, 2009). This political reality effectively delayed, and perhaps even derailed, the start of the transition process, and the country was unable to fully initiate the programme of structural reforms until the end of the crisis (EBRD, 2002; Rakhimov et al., 2003). In contrast, Kyrgyzstan avoided any major internal conflicts after gaining independence. With the West-oriented, liberal-minded Askar Akayev elected as its first President, Kyrgyzstan rapidly adopted a radical transition programme promoted by major international organizations such as the International Monetary Fund (IMF) and the World Bank, which in turn was informed by the so-called Washington Consensus (Myant and Drahokoupil, 2011, p.xx), and focused on pursuing important measures to stabilize the macroeconomic and financial situation, liberalize prices and commercial activity, and promote privatization and denationalization (Dabrowski and Antczak, 1995; Jermakowicz et al., 1995). Subsequently, in 1993, it became the first of the CIS countries to introduce its own currency (Slay, 1995), and one of the first to liberalize its foreign trade (Dabrowski and Antczak, 1995). Success in economic reforms soon resulted in Kyrgyzstan becoming the first of all former Soviet republics to gain membership in the World Trade Organization (WTO), in 1998, an important milestone for the economic (re)integration of Kyrgyzstan with the outside world.

Tajikistan, at least initially, has been included in the category of 'slow reformers' along with the likes of Belarus, Turkmenistan and Uzbekistan (EBRD, 2002, p.79). According to the World Bank (2013a), which provides one of the widely used indicators for regulatory reforms, Tajikistan's business regulations are one of the least favourable amongst the former Soviet republics, including those in the transitional periphery (see Table 1.4).

Table 1.4 *Indicators of the institutional environment for countries in transitional periphery*

Doing Business indicators	Ease of doing business ranking		Starting a business ranking		Getting credit ranking		Paying taxes ranking		Trading across borders ranking	
Year	2007	2017	2007	2017	2007	2017	2007	2017	2007	2017
Case study countries										
Tajikistan	133	128	166	85	143	118	154	140	163	144
Kyrgyzstan	90	75	41	30	65	32	150	148	173	79
Rest of Central Asia										
Kazakhstan	63	35	40	45	48	75	66	60	172	119
Uzbekistan	147	87	70	25	159	44	155	138	169	165
Turkmenistan	n/d	n/d	n/d	n/d	n/d	n/d	n/d	n/d	n/d	n/d
Caucasus										
Armenia	34	38	46	9	65	20	148	88	119	48
Azerbaijan	99	65	96	5	21	118	136	40	158	83
Georgia	37	16	36	8	48	7	104	22	95	54

Notes:
2007 ranking (1–175); 2017 ranking (1–190).
n/d = no data.
Ease of Doing Business, Starting a Business, Getting Credit, Paying Taxes and Trading Across Borders are rankings of up to 190 countries and examine business regulations as they apply to local firms.

Sources: All indicators from World Bank 'Doing Business' reports, http://www.doingbusiness.org (accessed 8 March 2017).

It stands at 128 in the overall ranking of 190 countries on Ease of Doing Business, which does not compare favourably with other countries in the transitional periphery. However, in terms of reforms relating to economic integration, some important and positive steps have been taken in order to liberalize foreign trade, remove cross-border barriers to trade, and attract foreign direct investment (FDI). For example, a resolution was adopted by the government on foreign trade liberalization in 1995 (UNESCAP, 2001); export duties were abolished to facilitate foreign trade; and new legislation on foreign investment was adopted in 1992 to attract FDI and encourage foreign investors to participate in privatization. With the introduction of a new law on investments in 2007, significant legal improvements were made in protecting the rights of investors (World Bank, 2013b). In addition, Tajikistan applied for membership of the WTO in 2001, and after many years of negotiations was accepted as a member in 2013, becoming only the second country in Central Asia, following the Kyrgyz Republic, to achieve this (Kazakhstan also joined later in 2015).

According to various observers, Kyrgyzstan's business regulations are some of the most favourable amongst the former Soviet republics, and considerably more favourable when compared to other countries in the Central Asian periphery (perhaps excluding Kazakhstan, which has moved up the World Bank rankings in recent years). It appears to have achieved the most progress in reforms among its Central Asian neighbours in accordance with the European Bank for Reconstruction and Development (EBRD)'s transition indicators, and its average score of the six indicators suggests that its progress has been almost comparable to Armenia and Georgia, making them the three leading countries in terms of reforms in the transitional periphery (see Table 1.5). A number of key regulatory improvements have been made in Kyrgyzstan in areas of taxation and foreign trade, which have had a positive impact on domestic and international activities of firms. Further to abolishing export duties in the early 1990s, and reducing the number of export documents (World Bank, 2013c), in 2008 the implementation of the Single Window project commenced in Kyrgyzstan, which was aimed at facilitating foreign trade by means of simplifying customs procedures and reducing various inefficiencies and costs associated with imports and exports.

Also worthy of discussion are the observed differences in the political sphere that may have acted as an important factor behind the divergent transition processes in the two countries, and which may have contributed to the development of potentially different institutional environments for firms (see, e.g., Makhmadshoev and Crone, 2014; Makhmadshoev et al., 2015). In particular, Kyrgyzstan's unprecedented changes in its political landscape over the last decade have cemented a certain revolutionary

Table 1.5 EBRD transition indicators for countries in transitional periphery

Transition indicators	LSP		SCP		G&ER		PL		T&FS		CP		Average of six indicators	
Year	1991	2014	1991	2014	1991	2014	1991	2014	1991	2014	1991	2014	1991	2014
Case study countries														
Tajikistan	1.0	2.3	1.0	4.0	1.0	2.0	1.0	4.0	1.0	3.7	1.0	1.7	1.0	2.95
Kyrgyzstan	1.0	3.7	1.0	4.0	1.0	2.0	1.0	4.3	1.0	4.3	1.0	2.0	1.0	3.38
Rest of Central Asia														
Kazakhstan	1.0	3.0	1.0	4.0	1.0	2.0	1.0	3.7	1.0	3.7	1.0	2.0	1.0	2.9
Uzbekistan	1.0	2.7	1.0	3.3	1.0	1.7	1.0	2.7	1.0	1.7	1.0	1.7	1.0	2.3
Turkmenistan	1.0	1.0	1.0	2.3	1.0	1.0	1.0	3.0	1.0	2.3	1.0	1.0	1.0	1.76
Caucasus														
Armenia	1.0	3.7	1.0	4.0	1.0	2.3	1.0	4.0	1.0	4.3	1.0	2.3	1.0	3.43
Azerbaijan	1.0	2.0	1.0	3.7	1.0	2.0	1.0	4.0	1.0	4.0	1.0	1.7	1.0	2.9
Georgia	1.0	4.0	1.0	4.0	1.0	2.3	1.0	4.3	1.0	4.3	1.0	2.0	1.0	3.48

Notes:
LSP – large-scale privatization; SCP – small-scale privatization; G&ER – governance and enterprise restructuring; PL – price liberalization; T&FS – trade and foreign exchange system; CP – competition policy.
The measurement scale for the indicators ranges from 1 to 4+, where 1 represents little or no change from a rigid centrally planned economy and 4+ represents the standards of an industrialized market economy. The last column shows a simple average of six EBRD indicators.

Source: Author's calculations based on EBRD transition indicators data, http://www.ebrd.com/pages/research/economics/data (accessed 8 March 2017).

culture in the country, indicating the apparent determination of its people to reject authoritarianism and instead push further towards democracy and economic freedom. Indeed, Kyrgyzstan, unlike many of its post-Soviet neighbours, followed a more liberal and a more democratic path to transition (Matveeva, 2009). Askar Akayev, the first president elected after independence, became a popular figure in the West for his open and liberal views, and was famously described as a 'Jeffersonian democrat in the heart of Asia' (Merry, 2004, p. 296). However, a series of 'authoritarian moves' by Akayev in the late 1990s and early 2000s, such as stricter control of mass media, election rigging and increasing nepotism, led to the Tulip revolution in 2005, which saw the dramatic overthrow of his regime (Collins, 2009; Tudoroiu, 2007, p. 331). Despite such an extraordinary end to his rule, many still consider Akayev, formerly a member and head of the Kyrgyz Academy of Sciences, a key architect of Kyrgyzstan's more liberal and progressive transition course. This historic event, the first of its kind in the post-Soviet Central Asia, set the stage for the subsequent overthrow in 2010 of Akayev's successor, Kurmanbek Bakiev, who was overthrown for reasons similar to his predecessor. In 2010 Roza Otunbayeva became an interim president, until Almazbek Atambayev became the newly elected president of the Kyrgyz Republic in December 2011. In accordance with the Constitution, the country elected a new president in October 2017, Sooronbay Jeenbekov, and for the first time in post-Soviet Central Asia power was transferred peacefully from one elected president to another.

In neighbouring Tajikistan, by contrast, the government vowed to undertake structural changes and implement market reforms in the early years of transition, and thereby appealed for technical and financial assistance from foreign governments and international organizations. Yet, almost three decades into the transition, some core features of the planned economy remain widespread, such as the state monopoly of economically important sectors, control over exchange and interest rates, and state intervention in the banking sector (EBRD, 2010, 2012). Coupled with hesitation by the state over taking on the implementation of market reforms more rigorously, it is likely that instead of a market system Tajikistan may be heading towards some form of state capitalism, if any form of capitalism at all. Thus far the nature of transition in Kyrgyzstan has been fundamentally different to any of the countries in the Central Asian periphery, but comparable to that of Georgia in the Caucasus, where a similar Rose revolution took place in 2003 which saw the fall of the Shevarnadze regime (Tudoroiu, 2007). This served as a basis for implementing liberal market reforms, opening the economy to competition and investment, and fostering stronger ties with the West. The parallels that can be drawn between the transition experiences of Georgia and Kyrgyzstan suggest that their national institutional environments, and subsequently their effects on firms, are bound to be different when compared to other countries in the transitional periphery. This chapter's analysis and the empirical evidence provided in the tables also suggest that countries in the transitional periphery are, in effect, moving from institutional convergence to institutional divergence.

Table 1.6, which is a summary of fieldwork responses to how firms in Tajikistan and Kyrgyzstan perceive their national institutional environments, supports the VoT argument on the existence of divergence in the outcomes of transition. In particular, analysis of the findings suggests that formal institutions in Kyrgyzstan are generally more advanced (that is, better designed) from a regulatory point of view. This was found to have a positive influence on firm behaviour (note that the firms studied were SMEs in the cotton, textile and garment sectors in the two countries). It was also suggested that formal institutions have a positive impact on firm activity because they help to reduce formal and informal transaction costs. Firms in Kyrgyzstan were observed to incur lower transaction costs because more developed formal institutions, in principle, suggest more efficient transactions. Accordingly, a more advanced formal institutional environment in Kyrgyzstan suggests a more successful transition to the market mechanism and, thus, lower transaction costs for firms. North (1990) indicates that the underlying institutional frameworks in the society can either reinforce or discourage firms from engaging in economic activity. Research findings on formal institutions seem to reflect this assumption. Formal institutions in Tajikistan act to increase transaction and production costs, create a range of regulatory obstacles to exporting, and provide few (if any) incentives for firms; whereas in Kyrgyzstan, formal institutions generally act to reduce transaction costs and export-related regulatory barriers and, in addition, provide certain incentives for firms to engage in the production and exports of textiles and garments. This comparative example clearly illustrates diversity in formal institutional contexts, as well as how institutions can both constrain and facilitate firms' economic activities.

In understanding the variation in the influence of informal institutions between the two countries, the key explanation lies, at least partly, with the quality of formal institutions and the mechanism of their enforcement and implementation, which according to the CC and VoT theorists amounts to institutional complementarity. In this study, formal institutions were found to be more advanced and more effectively enforced in Kyrgyzstan compared to Tajikistan. For instance, lower tax rates and the simplified system of tax calculation in the Kyrgyz case signal more optimal tax rules, and thus more advanced formal institutions. This shows the intent of the

Table 1.6   Comparative analysis of fieldwork data highlighting differences in institutional contexts in two countries in the transitional periphery

	Perception of formal institutional context	Perception of informal institutional context	Representative quotes from fieldwork
Country A: Tajikistan	Regulative environment in general is unpredictable and complex. Tax rules change frequently and compliance with tax rules is complex and costly. Frequent and unannounced visits by state inspectors (i.e., taxation, standardization, fire and other state agencies and bodies). Process of exporting is complicated and time-consuming. Process of obtaining export-related documents is difficult and lengthy. Firms' overall view of the formal institutional environment is largely negative, with little optimism for tangible improvements.	Informal (personal) relations play an important role in business survival. Informal relations play an important role in facilitating exporting and reducing bureaucratic hurdles associated with it. Informal relations play an important role in gaining privileged access to resources and protecting property. Informal costs of doing business are unnecessarily high for private firms. Firms without (personal) informal relationships have fewer chances of survival and success compared to those with strong connections.	'Theoretically speaking, the legal framework is not bad . . . the government is taking certain steps to improve the legislation to help SMEs grow, but the actual implementation of new laws and policies is poor in practice.' 'The main problem is with the practical side of it – the operating mechanism of the taxation system.' '. . .having close relationships, for example with the governor of the region, helps you immensely . . . such contacts are absolutely important [for firm survival and success]'
Country B: Kyrgyzstan	Regulative environment is more predictable. Norms and practices of tax inspection regime are more conducive to firms, with fewer	Informal personal relations are notably less important (than before, and compared to Tajikistan) for business survival and success, but play some role.	'. . .we don't have any problems with the taxation system. Tax rates in my opinion are OK. I mean, we don't pay too many types of taxes, just three or four'

32

visits by tax inspectors and lower informal costs.	Informal relations are less important in facilitating exporting.	'…since several years ago, I think since 2008, the legal framework has become more or less positive and unproblematic for firms'
Rules of paying and calculating taxes are improving and less constraining than in past (and compared to Tajikistan).	Informal relations are important in a similar way as in Tajikistan in gaining access to key resources and protecting property.	'Informal connections were important in the past, because the regulation was complex…. But it is no longer like this…. I guess it is good for you if you have connections and influential relatives, but I am not sure it can help your business as much [as in the past].'
Process of exporting is relatively simpler and less burdensome than in past (and compared to Tajikistan).	Informal costs lower than in Tajikistan, due to enhanced tax and export regulations.	
Experience of obtaining export-related documentation is relatively easy and fast, and not very costly.	Possible for firms without strong informal connections to survive and succeed, due to the diminishing nature of informality in the country, which is partly the result of unprecedented political changes.	
Firms' overall view of the formal institutional environment is largely positive, with more optimism for further improvements.		

Sources: Own fieldwork; adapted from Makhmadshoev and Crone (2014) and Makhmadshoev et al. (2015).

Kyrgyz state to create a regulatory environment which encourages competition (by enabling more firms to enter the private sector) and discourages state intervention (by reducing the influence of tax inspectors on firms), thereby making the regulatory environment more in line with the principles of the market economy (Furubotn and Richter, 2000). The relatively strong implementation of this law has added more transparency in interactions between state officials and businesses and, importantly, resulted in a significant decline of the level and frequency of informal payments made by firms to tax officials. This example demonstrates how more advanced formal institutions have contributed to reforming undesirable informal institutions by making the latter less prevalent, and thus less constraining for firms. This portrays a contrasting yet analytically consistent picture with regard to the case of Tajikistan, where the reverse line of argumentation (that is, weak formal institutions contributed to informal institutions becoming more prevalent, and thus more constraining for firms) was found to be applicable. Indeed, it was one of the key emerging findings of the fieldwork that institutions have developed, and therefore function, differently in the two seemingly similar post-Soviet states; consequently, their influence on firm behaviour appears to vary also.

ACTOR-CENTRED PERSPECTIVE ON INSTITUTIONAL CHANGE

Though I do not offer empirical evidence to support the utility of this institutional perspective, I argue conceptually for its importance and relevance in furthering the current thinking on institutions and the firm in the transition periphery. An increasing number of scholars have recently called for more attention to be given to better understanding the role of economic actors, as well as the mechanisms they deploy, in shaping the process of institutional change in transition economies (Kalantaridis, 2007; Puffer et al., 2010; Welter and Smallbone, 2011). This can be seen as part of the broader debate to give greater emphasis to agency in institutional research, which is described by Carney et al. (2009, p. 361) as 'the second movement in institutional theory'. In response to this call, one can point to the pertinence of an emerging yet hitherto underexplored perspective on institutional change, which is informed by the works of Campbell (1997, 2004) in the areas of rational choice institutionalism and institutional economics. Though the neo-institutional perspective discussed earlier, and in particular the seminal work of North (1990), places considerable emphasis on understanding the process of institutional change and its importance for economic development (North, 2005), a key limitation of this approach is that the mechanisms through which institutional change may be manifested are, arguably, poorly specified (Campbell, 2004). Indeed, as the review of this approach earlier demonstrated, emphasis is placed predominantly on unpacking the meaning of institutions and analysing how they interact and change at a macro level. Thus, Campbell (2004, p. 88) argues that 'any account of how institutions are built or affect social behaviour requires a micro-level account of actors as causal agents'. Examining the utility of the approach which places more emphasis on actors or firms as institutional players in probing into the transition economies, albeit conceptually, fits well with the broader objective of this book, which is to advance more firm-centred perspectives.

It has been suggested by a number of institutionally focused scholars that the emergence of capitalist institutions in the former planned econo- mies follows a certain path-dependent or evolutionary process (Campbell, 2004; Smallbone and Welter, 2006; Welter and Smallbone, 2011). This is reflected in the reality where the formal institutions in many transition economies are being replaced and redesigned, but the informal institutions developed during the Soviet times and entrenched in norms and traditions continue to dominate economic and social behaviours, including those of the firm (Peng and Heath, 1996). While scholars use the concept of path- dependence to examine the development of economic institutions in post communist countries (Manolova et al., 2010; Smallbone and Welter, 2012; Stark and Bruszt, 1998; Zweynert, 2006), what has often been missing in such analyses is elaboration of the specific mechanisms through which path-dependent institutional change could be manifested and explained (Kalantaridis, 2007). As Campbell (2004, p. 66) states in this regard, 'the difficulty is that the mechanisms whereby path-dependent effects occur are often poorly specified, if not completely neglected'. To address this limitation, the concept of 'bricolage' is identified, which is underexploited in institutional studies (with the exception of some, including Carney et al., 2009; Lanzara, 1998; Phillips and Tracey, 2007), yet represents a notion well suited to enhancing our understanding of path-dependent evolution- ary institutional change: the type that prevails in countries transitioning from communism to capitalism (Campbell, 2004). This section now turns to analysing the pertinence of bricolage.

Bricolage

Originally introduced by anthropologist Claude Levi-Strauss, the term 'bricolage' characterizes a certain way of acting in the society whereby actors use existing resources and instruments, or 'whatever is at hand', to make do (Levi-Strauss, 1966, p. 17). Baker and Nelson's (2005) seminal paper is widely viewed to have laid the foundations for building the theory of bricolage in entrepreneurship and wider management research. They define bricolage as 'making do by applying combinations of the resources at hand to new problems and opportunities' (Baker and Nelson, 2005, p. 333). According to this definition, 'making do' refers to a specific attitude of actors in refusing to accept the various institutional limitations imposed by their operating environments. Instead, they focus on combining a variety of existing resources available cheaply or freely – including skills, capabilities, financial and physical resources – to create new solutions to problems or to explore new business opportunities. Stinchfield et al. (2013) posit that resources at hand may include 'physical, artifacts, skills or ideas' that actors can draw upon when faced with opportunities or obstacles. Baker and Nelson (2005) further suggest that actors can engage in bricolage across five areas or domains, namely physical inputs, labour inputs, skills inputs, customers and markets, and institutional and regulatory environment.

Thus, actors can make do not only by redesigning and reapplying physical and social resources, but also by reshaping a variety of institutional and regulatory elements available at hand. Indeed, a growing number of studies have emphasized the institutional utility of bricolage (DiDomenico et al., 2010; Fisher, 2012; Phillips and Tracey, 2007). Among these are Carney et al. (2009), who suggest that the concept is highly relevant in understanding the process whereby actors combine different institutional elements to develop new types of institutions or reconfigure existing ones to address new challenges. In a similar spirit, Desa (2012) and Mair and Marti (2009) have also demonstrated how actors engage in bricolage to fill various voids in resource-depleted and institutionally challenging environments. The former, for instance, noted that 'bricolage acts as an entrepreneurial response mechanism that reconfigures macro institutional environments' (Desa, 2012, p. 743).

Importantly, scholars also suggest that bricolage as a mechanism is not just about creating something from resources available at hand, or bringing together different institutional elements to address a certain problem, but is also about shaping the process of institutional development (Carney et al., 2009; Campbell, 2004; Desa, 2012; Mair and Marti, 2009; Phillips and Tracey, 2007). For instance, Desa (2012, p. 730) states that actors who engage in bricolage are also participants of 'a process of actor-initiated institutional change'. Campbell (2010, p. 98) who advocates bricolage specifically as a mechanism of path-dependent, incremental institutional change, describes it as the process or mechanism through which institutional change may involve 'the rearrangement or recombination of institutional principles and practices in new and creative ways'.

Through engagement in bricolage actors can change existing institutions or create new ones by infusing elements of their old and newly imported institutional systems (Campbell, 2004). Thereby, bricolage can be seen as an appropriate, firm-centred perspective with great potential to enhance our understanding of the behaviour, activity and creativity of economic actors and firms in the context of transition economies, where institutions are, by definition, in a state of flux and where such actors can play a significant role in the formation and co-creation of institutional systems (Tracey and Phillips, 2011). In other words, the concept has potential to offer an appropriate micro-level perspective on how economic actors can influence institutions, thereby complementing the established macro-level perspective discussed earlier in the chapter on how institutional structures influence economic actors. In this way, exploring the notion of bricolage can shed fresh light on the duality between institutions and actors, and thereby contribute to furthering the current thinking on institutions and the firm in the transitional periphery.

CONCLUSION

This chapter has argued that researchers in recent years have benefited significantly by drawing on institutional theory to explore and explain the various effects of unstable institutional settings and embedded institutional factors on firm behaviour in transitional environments. It has highlighted that the neo-institutionalist approach, and in particular the North-inspired new institutional economics lens, tends to represent the most dominant approach adopted by many business and management scholars with an interest in post-socialist economies. While acknowledging that this perspective remains powerful and effective to this day, the chapter has proposed that research in this area can potentially benefit in important ways by integrating insights from two emerging, but hitherto underexploited institutional perspectives, namely comparative capitalism's varieties of transition approach and the more actor-centred perspective on institutional change. In other words, the conceptual and empirical analyses, and the suggestion to integrate insights from the two emerging institutional approaches, signify that the nature of questions asked within the literature on institutions and the firm in transition economies can, and perhaps should, be broadened to include not only various deterministic questions relating to how institutions influence the behaviour of the firm, but also what are the implications of institutional diversity on firm behaviour and what is the firm's role, if any, as a creative and rational actor in influencing the process of institutional change in these transitional environments.

More than 25 years after the collapse of the Soviet regime, it becomes apparent that the process of transition in former Soviet republics has not followed the intended progression towards Western models of capitalism; to the contrary, various paths have emerged, resulting in the varieties of capitalism in transition economies. Literature suggests that only the Baltic states and countries of the former Communist bloc of Eastern and Central Europe can be considered to have completed the process of transition, whilst many others, including those in the periphery, have mostly stalled, stagnated or derailed. The varieties of transition approach points out that this divergence in the transition process among the former communist states translates into a great number of institutional configurations at national levels. This institutional divergence is likely to widen, resulting in further variation between national institutions, which in turn obliges researchers to start asking not only how institutions matter in transition economies, but also how differences in institutions matter. Thus, exploring the heterogeneity of institutional contexts, and placing more emphasis on understanding the increasingly important role of economic actors in influencing the process of institutional transformation, can lead researchers to important new insights on the relationship between institutions and the firm in the transitional periphery.

REFERENCES

Aidis, R. (2005), 'Institutional barriers to small- and medium-sized enterprise operations in transition countries', *Small Business Economics*, 25 (4), 305–318.

Amable, B. (2003), *The Diversity of Modern Capitalism*, New York: Oxford University Press.

Baker, T. and R.E. Nelson (2005), 'Creating something from nothing: resource construction through entrepreneurial bricolage', *Administrative Science Quarterly*, 50 (3), 329–366.

Bevan, A., S. Estrin and K. Meyer (2004), 'Foreign investment location and institutional development in transition economies', *International Business Review*, 13 (1), 43–64.

Blackmon, P. (2007), 'Divergent paths, divergent outcomes: linking differences in economic reform to levels of US foreign direct investment and business in Kazakhstan and Uzbekistan', *Central Asian Survey*, 26 (3), 355–372.

Buck, T., I. Filatotchev, P. Nolan and M. Wright (2000), 'Different paths to economic reform in Russia and China: causes and consequences', *Journal of World Business*, 35 (4), 379–400.

Campbell, J.L. (1997), 'Mechanisms of evolutionary change in economic governance: interaction, interpretation and bricolage', in L. Magnusson and J. Ottosson (eds), *Evolutionary Economics and Path Dependence*, Cheltenham, UK and Northampton, MA, USA: Edward Elgar Publishing, pp. 10–32.

Campbell, J.L. (2004), *Institutional Change and Globalisation*, Princeton, NJ: Princeton University Press.

Campbell, J.L. (2010), 'Institutional reproduction and change', in G. Morgan, J.L. Campbell, C. Crouch, O.K. Pedersen and R. Whitley (eds), *The Oxford Handbook of Comparative Institutional Analysis*, New York: Oxford University Press, pp. 87–116.

Carney, M., E. Gedajlovic and X. Yang (2009), 'Varieties of Asian capitalism: toward an institutional theory of Asian enterprise', *Asia Pacific Journal of Management*, 26, 361–380.

Coase, R.H. (1937), 'The nature of the firm', *Economica*, 4 (16), 386–405.

Coase, R. (1998), 'The new institutional economics', *American Economic Review*, 88 (2), 72–74.

Coleman, J.S. (1988), 'Social capital in the creation of human capital', *American Journal of Sociology*, 94, S95–S120.

Collins, K. (2009), 'Economic and security regionalism among patrimonial authoritarian regimes: the case of Central Asia', *Europe-Asia Studies*, 61 (2), 249–281.

Cuervo-Cazurra, A. (2008), 'Better the devil you don't know: types of corruption and FDI in transition economies', *Journal of International Management*, 14, 12–27.

Dabrowski, M. and R. Antczak (1995), 'Economic reforms in Kyrgyzstan', *Russian and East European Finance and Trade*, 31 (6), 5–30.

Dacin, M.T., J. Goodstein and W.R. Scott (2002), 'Institutional theory and institutional change: introduction to the Special Research Forum', *Academy of Management Journal*, 45 (1), 45–57.

Davis, L.E. and D.C. North (1971), *Institutional Change and American Economic Growth*, Cambridge: Cambridge University Press.

Desa, G. (2012), 'Resource mobilization in international social entrepreneurship: bricolage as a mechanism of institutional transformation', *Entrepreneurship Theory and Practice*, 36 (4), 727–751.

DiDomenico, M.L., H. Haugh and P. Tracey (2010), 'Social bricolage: theorizing social value creation in social enterprise', *Entrepreneurship Theory and Practice*, 34 (4), 681–703.

DiMaggio, P.J. and W.W. Powell (1983), 'The iron cage revisited: institutional isomorphism and collective rationality in organisational fields', *American Sociological Review*, 48 (2), 147–160.

Dunning, J.H. (2004), 'An evolving paradigm of the economic determinants of international business activity', in J. Cheng and M. Hitt (eds), *Managing Multinationals in a Knowledge Economy: Economics, Culture and Human Resources*, Advances in International Management, Vol. 15, Elsevier: Oxford, pp. 3–27.

EBRD (2002), *Transition Report 2002: Agriculture and Rural Transition*, London: European Bank for Reconstruction and Development.

EBRD (2010), *Transition Report 2010: Recovery and Reform*, London: European Bank for Reconstruction and Development.

EBRD (2012), *Commercial Laws of Tajikistan, April 2012: An Assessment by the EBRD*, London: European Bank for Reconstruction and Development.

Estrin, S., K.E. Meyer and M. Bytchkova (2008), 'Entrepreneurship in transition economies', in A. Basu, M. Casson, N. Wadeson and B. Yeung (eds), *The Oxford Handbook of Entrepreneurship*, Oxford: Oxford University Press, pp. 693–725.

Feldmann, M. (2006), 'Emerging varieties of capitalism in transition countries: industries relations and wage bargaining in Estonia and Slovenia', *Comparative Political Studies*, 39 (7), 829–854.

Fisher, G. (2012), 'Effectuation, causation, and bricolage: a behavioral comparison of emerging theories in entrepreneurship research', *Entrepreneurship Theory and Practice*, 36 (5), 1019–1051.

Furubotn, E.G. and R. Richter (2000), *Institutions and Economic Theory: The Contribution of the New Institutional Economics*, Ann Arbor, MI: University of Michigan Press.

Gelbuda, M., K.E. Meyer and A. Delios (2008), 'International business and institutional development in Central and Eastern Europe', *Journal of International Management*, 14 (1), 1–11.

Granovetter, M.S. (1973), 'The strength of weak ties', *American Journal of Sociology*, 78 (6), 1360–1380.

Granovetter, M.S. (1985), 'Economic action and social structure: the problem of embeddedness', *American Journal of Sociology*, 91 (3), 481–510.

Hall, P.A. and D. Soskice (2001), 'An introduction to varieties of capitalism', in P.A. Hall and D. Soskice (eds), *Varieties of Capitalism: The Institutional Foundations of Comparative Advantage*, Oxford: Oxford University Press, pp. 1–68.

Havrylyshyn, O. (2006), *Divergent Paths in Post-Communist Transformation: Capitalism for All or Capitalism for the Few?*, Basingstoke: Palgrave Macmillan.

Heathershaw, J. (2009), *Post-Conflict Tajikistan: The Politics of Peacebuilding and the Emergence of Legitimate Order*, London: Routledge.

Hitt, M.A., D. Ahlstrom, M.T. Dacin, E. Levitas and L. Svobodina (2004), 'The institutional effects on strategic alliance partner selection in transition economies: China vs. Russia', *Organisation Science*, 15 (2), 173–185.

Hotho, J.J. and T. Pedersen (2012), 'Beyond the "rules of the game": three institutional approaches and how they matter for international business', in G. Wood and M. Demirbag (eds), *Handbook of Institutional Approaches to International Business*, Cheltenham, UK: Edward Elgar Publishing, pp. 236–273.

Jackson, G. and R. Deeg (2008), 'Comparing capitalism: understanding institutional diversity and its implications for international business', *Journal of International Business Studies*, 39, 540–561.

Jermakowicz, W.W., J. Pankow and G. Soros (1995), 'Privatization in the Kyrgyz Republic', *Russian and East European Finance and Trade*, 31 (6), 31–72.

Kalantaridis, C. (2007), 'Institutional change in post-socialist regimes: public policy and beyond', *Journal of Economic Issues*, 41 (2), 435–442.

Kostova, T. and K. Roth (2002), 'Adoption of organisational practice by subsidiaries of multinational corporations: institutional and relational effects', *Academy of Management Journal*, 45 (1), 215–233.

Lane, D. (2007), 'Post-state socialism: a diversity of capitalisms?', in D. Lane and M. Myant (eds), *Varieties of Capitalism in Post-Communist Countries*, Basingstoke: Palgrave Macmillan, pp. 13–39.

Lane, D. and M. Myant (eds) (2007), *Varieties of Capitalism in Post-Communist Countries*, Basingstoke: Palgrave Macmillan.

Lane, C. and G. Wood (2009), 'Capitalist diversity and diversity within capitalism', *Economy and Society*, 38 (4), 531–551.

Lanzara, G.F. (1998), 'Self-destructive processes in institution building and some modest countervailing mechanisms', *European Journal of Political Research*, 33, 1–39.

Levi-Strauss, C. (1966), *The Savage Mind*, Chicago, IL: University of Chicago Press.

Mair, J. and I. Marti (2009), 'Entrepreneurship in and around institutional voids: a case study from Bangladesh', *Journal of Business Venturing*, 24, 419–435.

Makhmadshoev, D. and M. Crone (2014), 'Exploring the influence of the national institutional environment on SME exporters: comparative evidence from Tajikistan and the Kyrgyz Republic', in M.T.T. Thai and E. Turkina (eds), *Internationalisation of Firms from Economies in Transition: The Effects of a Politico-Economic Paradigm Shift*, Cheltenham, UK and Northampton, MA, USA: Edward Elgar Publishing, pp. 303–331.

Makhmadshoev, D., K. Ibeh and M. Crone (2015), 'Institutional influences on SME exporters under divergent transition paths: comparative insights from Tajikistan and Kyrgyzstan', *International Business Review*, 24 (6), 1025–1036.

Manev, I.M. and T.S. Manolova (2010), 'Entrepreneurship in transitional economies: review and integration of two decades of research', *Journal of Developmental Entrepreneurship*, 15 (1), 69–99.

Manolova, T.S., I.M. Manev and B.S. Gyoshev (2010), 'In good company: the role of personal and inter-firm networks for new venture internationalization in a transition economy', *Journal of World Business*, 45, 257–265.

Matveeva, A. (2009), 'Legitimising Central Asian authoritarianism: political manipulation and symbolic power', *Europe-Asia Studies*, 61 (7), 1095–1121.

Merry, E.W. (2004), 'Governance in Central Asia: national in form, Soviet in content', *Cambridge Review of International Affairs*, 17 (2), 285–300.

Meyer, K.E. (2001), 'Institutions, transaction costs, and entry mode choice in Eastern Europe', *Journal of International Business Studies*, 32 (2), 357–367.

Meyer, K.E. and M.W. Peng (2005), 'Probing theoretically into Central and Eastern Europe: transaction, resources, and institutions', *Journal of International Business Studies*, 36 (6), 600–621.

Meyer, K.E. and H. Vo Nguyen (2005), 'Foreign investment strategies and sub-national institutions in emerging markets: evidence from Vietnam', *Journal of Management Studies*, 42 (1), 63–93.

Meyer, K.E., S. Estrin, S.K. Bhaumik and M.W. Peng (2009), 'Institutions, resources, and entry strategies in emerging economies', *Strategic Management Journal*, 30, 61–80.

Michailova, S. (2011), 'Contextualizing in international business research: why do we need more of it and how can we be better at it?', *Scandinavian Journal of Management*, 27, 129–139.

Mudambi, R. and P. Navarra (2002), 'Institutions and international business: a theoretical overview', *International Business Review*, 11, 635–646.

Murdoch, J. (2000), 'Networks – a new paradigm of rural development?', *Journal of Rural Studies*, 16 (4), 407–419.

Myant, M. and J. Drahoupil (2011), *Transition economies: Political Economy in Russia, Eastern Europe, and Central Asia*, Hoboken, NJ: Wiley-Blackwell.

Myant, M. and J. Drahoupil (2012), 'International integration, varieties of capitalism and resilience to crisis in transition economies', *Europe-Asia Studies*, 64 (1), 1–33.

North, D.C. (1987), 'Institutions, transaction costs and economic growth', *Economic Inquiry*, 25 (3), 419–428.

North, D.C. (1990), *Institutions, Institutional Change and Economic Performance*, Cambridge: Cambridge University Press.

North, D.C. (1991), 'Institutions', *Journal of Economic Perspectives*, 5 (1), 97–112.

North, D. (1997), 'The contribution of the new institutional economics to an understanding of the transition problem', UNU World Institute for Development Economics Research (WIDER), Annual Lectures 1, Helsinki.

North, D.C. (2005), *Understanding the Process of Economic Change*, Princeton, NJ: Princeton University Press.

Peng, M.W. (2003), 'Institutional transitions and strategic choices', *Academy of Management Review*, 28 (2), 275–296.

Peng, M.W. (2004), 'Identifying the big question in international business research', *Journal of International Business Studies*, 35 (2), 99–108.

Peng, M.W. and P.S. Heath (1996), 'The growth of the firm in planned economies in transition: institutions, organisations, and strategic choice', *Academy of Management Review*, 21 (2), 492–528.

Peng, M.W., D.Y.L. Wang and Y. Jiang (2008), 'An institution-based view of international business strategy: a focus on emerging economies', *Journal of International Business Studies*, 39, 920–936.

Phillips, N. and P. Tracey (2007), 'Opportunity recognition, entrepreneurial capabilities and bricolage: connecting institutional theory and entrepreneurship in strategic organization', *Strategic Organization*, 5 (3), 313–320.

Puffer, S.M., D.J. McCarthy and M. Boisot (2010), 'Entrepreneurship in Russia and China: the impact of formal institutional voids', *Entrepreneurship Theory and Practice*, 34 (3), 441–467.

Rakhimov, R., N. Kaiumov, M. Nurmakhmadov, O. Boboev, M. Kabutov and D. Kodirov (2003), 'The social policy of Tajikistan in a transition economy', *Sociological Research*, 42 (4), 6–37.

Redding, G. (2005), 'The thick description and comparison of societal systems of capitalism', *Journal of International Business Studies*, 36 (2), 123–155.

Scott, W.R. (1995), *Institutions and Organisations*, Thousand Oaks, CA: SAGE Publications.

Scott, W.R. (2008), *Institutions and Organisations: Ideas and Interests*, Thousand Oaks, CA: SAGE Publications.

Slay, B. (1995), 'Editor's introduction', *Russian and East European Finance and Trade*, 31 (3), 3–4.

Smallbone, D. and F. Welter (2001a), 'The distinctiveness of entrepreneurship in transition economies', *Small Business Economics*, 16 (4), 249–262.

Smallbone, D. and F. Welter (2001b), 'The role of government in SME development in transition economies', *International Small Business Journal*, 19, 63–77.

Smallbone, D. and F. Welter (2006), 'Conceptualising entrepreneurship in a transition context', *International Journal Entrepreneurship and Small Business*, 3 (2), 190–206.

Smallbone, D. and F. Welter (2012), 'Entrepreneurship and institutional change in transition economies: the Commonwealth of Independent States, Central and Eastern Europe and China compared', *Entrepreneurship and Regional Development*, 24 (3/4), 215–233.

Stark, D. and L. Bruszt (1998), *Postsocialist Pathways: Transforming Politics and Property in East Central Europe*, New York: Cambridge University Press.

Stinchfield, B.T., R.E. Nelson and W. Wood (2013), 'Learning from Levi-Strauss' legacy: art, craft, engineering, bricolage, and brokerage in entrepreneurship', *Entrepreneurship Theory and Practice*, 37 (4), 889–921.

Tolbert, P.S. and L.G. Zucker (1996), 'The institutionalization of institutional theory', in S.R. Glegg, G. Hardy and W. Nord (eds), *Handbook of Organisation Studies*, Thousand Oaks, CA: SAGE Publications, pp. 175–190.

Tracey, P. and N. Phillips (2011), 'Entrepreneurship in emerging markets: strategies for new venture creation in uncertain institutional context', *Management International Review*, 51 (1), 23–39.

Tsang, S. (1996), 'Against "big bang" in economic transition: normative and positive arguments', *Cambridge Journal of Economics*, 20 (2), 183–193.

Tudoroiu, T. (2007), 'Rose, Orange, and Tulip: the failed post-Soviet revolutions', *Communist and Post-Communist Studies*, 40, 315–342.

UNESCAP (2001), *Accession to the World Trade Organization: Issues and Recommendations for Central Asian and Caucasian Economies in Transition*, Studies in Trade and Investment No. 48, United Nations Economic and Social Commission for Asia and the Pacific, New York.

Welter, F. and D. Smallbone (2011), 'Institutional perspectives on entrepreneurial behaviour in challenging environments', *Journal of Small Business Management*, 49 (1), 107–125.

Williams, N. and T. Vorley (2017), 'Fostering productive entrepreneurship in post-conflict economies: the importance of institutional alignment', *Entrepreneurship and Regional Development*, 29 (5/6), 444–466.

Williamson, O.E. (1981), 'The economics of organisation: the transaction cost approach', *American Journal of Sociology*, 87 (3), 548–577.

Williamson, O.E. (1997), 'Hierarchies, markets and power in the economy: an economic perspective', in C. Menard (ed.), *Transaction Cost Economics: Recent Developments*, Cheltenham, UK and Northampton, MA, USA: Edward Elgar Publishing, pp. 1–29.

Williamson, O.E. (1998), 'The institutions of governance', *American Economic Review*, 88 (2), 75–79.

Wood, G. and M. Demirbag (eds) (2012), *Handbook of Institutional Approaches to International Business*, Cheltenham, UK and Northampton, MA, USA: Edward Elgar Publishing.

Woolcock, M. (1998), 'Social capital and economic development: towards a theoretical synthesis and policy framework', *Theory and Society*, 27 (2), 151–208.

World Bank (2013a), *Doing Business 2013: Smarter Regulations for Small and Medium-Size Enterprises*, Washington, DC: World Bank.

World Bank (2013b), *Doing Business 2013: Economy Profile for Tajikistan*, Washington, DC: World Bank.

World Bank (2013c), *Doing Business 2013: Economy Profile for Kyrgyz Republic*, Washington, DC: World Bank.

Zweynert, J. (2006), 'Economic ideas and institutional change: evidence from Soviet economic debates 1987–1991', *Europe-Asia Studies*, 58 (2), 169–192.

2. Uzbekistan: autocracy, development and international firms

Geoffrey Wood and Mehmet Demirbag

INTRODUCTION

This chapter seeks to develop our understanding of both transitional peripheral economies, and the consequences of clan-based authoritarianism, through looking more closely at the type of capitalism that has emerged in Central Asia, the dominant growth regime and the type of firm-level practices associated with this, focusing in particular on the case of Uzbekistan. The chapter highlights and draws out the implications for foreign direct investment. Uzbekistan is characterized by strong clan networks and, indeed, by the ability of the clans to adapt to all manner of external shocks without significant adjustment (Northrop, 2000; Collins, 2002; McGlinchey, 2009). As Pomfret (2000a) notes, it has combined slow reform with – in regional terms – relatively strong economic performance. Although it is fashionable for Western economic commentators to dismiss the country for poor economic performance, in fact it has performed better than any other post-Soviet country since 1989 (Popov, 2013). This has reflected a combination of policy interventions, which have encompassed both elements of the new and elements of the past. The former would include the prominence of the construction industry as an engine for growth and development, and the attracting of foreign automotive firms. The latter would include the sustanance of traditional areas of industry, most notably cotton, but also heavy engineering (see Pomfret, 2000b).

THE UZBEK POLITICAL CONTEXT

In 1991, the failure of the anti-Gorbachev coup led to a number of former Soviet republics, including Uzbekistan, declaring independence; the old Communist Party was rebranded as the People's Democratic Party of Uzbekistan (PDPRU) under the leadership of Islam Karimov. The main opposition party was subsequently rendered illegal, amid widespread allegations that the PDPRU had rigged the election in its favour (Akbarzadeh, 2015). Karimov subsequently entrenched his power, presenting himself to the international community as a bulwark against Islamic fundamentalism (Luhn, 2015; Starr, 1996). The teaching of political science was banned in 2015, given the government objections to the concept of an authoritarian state (Luhn, 2015).

In 2016, Karimov died following a brain haemorrhage. According to Amnesty International, his rule was characterized by proliferating corruption scandals and human rights violations (Amnesty International, 2015; Ambrosio, 2015). There were many cases of these being linked: whistle-blowers or those obstructing corruption faced arbitrary arrest and worse (ibid.); it is alleged that there is still no evidence that these abuses have ceased following his death (Ambrosio, 2015; Human Rights Watch, 2016).

In later years, his rule was also characterized by bitter squabbles within his family, between his wife and one of his daughters and another daughter who had been previously favoured, Gulnara (Boonstra and Laruelle, 2014; Pannier, 2012). Whether due to this fight, or because of her serial involvement in alleged corruption scandals, Gulnara was placed under house arrest and subsequently disappeared (Malashenko, 2014; *The Economist*, 2016). It was later revealed that she was convicted of fraud and embezzlement in 2015, and the Uzbek government has sought to recover $1.5 billion of assets she allegedly held abroad (*Guardian*, 2017).

At the time of his death, the equivalent of roughly 7 per cent of the entire national budget in the form of national assets abroad were frozen, following investigations by the United States (US) Department of Justice (Ilkhamov, 2016). In a subsequent election, his chosen successor and sometime Prime Minister, Shavkat Mirziyoyev, was elected President with almost 90 per cent of the vote (*The Economist*, 2016; Rodriguez, 2016). At the time of Karimov's death, a lack of jobs at home led to some 2 million Uzbeks working abroad. As noted elsewhere in this book, large diasporas ensure that no matter how bad mismanagement is at home, money continues to flow in; indeed, the larger the diaspora, the greater the inflows.

THE DISCREDITING OF DEMOCRACY AND THE MARKET

The collapse of the Soviet Union led to many successor states experiencing the dual shocks of rapid marketization and democratization (Gerber and Hout, 1998). Yet, both processes were rendered unmanageable through the opportunism of external and internal agents (ibid.; Tikhomirov, 2018; Spechler, 2007). In the case of the former, interventions ranged from bungled efforts to micro-manage transitions, to the promotion of hasty privatizations that amounted to the outright looting of state assets (MacWilliam and Rafferty, 2017). There is little doubt that, in part, this was motivated by a desire to damage post-Soviet institutions so severely as to make their reconstruction unfeasible. However, as Klein (2007) notes, a feature of neoliberal reforms is that they also have often been prompted by a desire to completely destroy established institutions, on the assumption that disorder creates opportunities for markets: the notion that capitalism thrives through creative destruction. In practice, post-state socialist transitions often opened opportunities for kleptocratic elites and for the primitive expropriation of publicly owned resources (Tichomirov, 2018; Spechler, 2007). Such reforms also led to large-scale job losses, the collapse of core industries and the impoverishment of both workers and the elderly. In the short term, this led to rapid economic decline (Gerber and Hout, 1998). In turn, this convinced rulers of post-state socialist countries that had been slow in implementing radical neoliberal reforms that their initial reluctance had been proved well founded. This is not to suggest that such rulers were necessarily less corrupt than the oligarchs who attained dominance in those countries that had undertaken radical market reforms. At the same time, it soon became clear that countries which held off from radical market reforms often remained in economically better shape than those who had fallen for the siren call of radical neoliberalism.

In the case of Uzbekistan, initial moves to democratization soon degenerated into personal authoritarianism (McGlinchey, 2009). Whilst it would be easy to blame this solely on the difficulties of building and embedding democratic institutions, or on the choices made by powerful individuals, it should also be noted that democracy is unlikely to be secured if democratic institutions are completely lacking in credibility. Not only did many elected governments in the post-Soviet world show themselves completely incapable of providing basic security and prosperity for their citizens, but the colour-coded revolutions – many of which were clearly fanned and orchestrated by well-organized external interests and non-governmental organizations – reduced the incentives for indigenous politicians to play by democratic rules. What the latter showed was that if politicians espoused the 'wrong' policies or drifted too closely back to the Russian orbit, they risked being ejected by tightly organized groups of often middle-class protesters, no matter their democratic mandate or how recently they were elected; if all democracy is conditional, it pays to actively work on setting the conditions (Averre, 2007; Delcour and Wolczuk, 2015). In turn, as democracy and the market were often conflated, this led to both being discredited. Given the risks of engaging with the West (and, in particular, the risks of having unpopular economic policies and/or colour-coded revolutions foisted on a country), the Uzbek government has concluded that its domestic survival is contingent on close ties with Russia (Anceschi, 2010). Again, a key feature of Uzbekistan is the selective disbursement of political patronage of clan-based neo-patrimonial lines (Ilkhamov, 2016).

ANTIQUARIANISM

In a landmark 2016 book, Jens Beckert notes not only that expectations play a major role in economic behaviour, but also that what may happen in the future is unclear (Beckert, 2016). People try to create and sustain fictions as to how matters may be as a basis for economic decision-making. In other words, it is impossible to make any economic decision without some idea of what may happen; and as knowledge is imperfect, the gap is filled in some manner with imagined hope or despair (Beckert, 2016). In the case of Central Asia, Russian colonial rule has cast lasting legacies, but for at least a very large proportion of the indigenous population, this is not something that they would necessarily return to, even if some aspects – above all, basic employment, income and retirement security – were deeply treasured and fondly remembered. On the one hand, imagination as to the future has to have some basis of material knowledge. On the other hand, the more benign aspects of authoritarian rule need to be sanitized from the inherent contamination of the colonial. The alternative building material for an imagined future – Western democracy and its associated prosperity – is compromised, because of the failure of untrammelled markets to deliver an improvement, or even to maintain, material conditions for the bulk of the population, and because democratic experiments were always conditional on people voting the right way.

In short, both as an ideology to serve the political status quo, and to provide a narrative on future prosperity, there was a need for a common understanding of what things were, are and could be. This has led the Uzbek government to promote an ideology and narrative of antiquarianism. This may be defined as the promotion of a particular period of past glory, both as a core feature of national identity, and as the basis for present and future life. The future is seen as centred not only on order, predictability and prosperity, but also on the assumption that there is an inherent national capacity for greatness. Antiquarianism is an ideology most commonly associated with the Internal Macedonian Revolutionary Organization, and has served as the driver for a particular path of development in the Macedonian Republic (Dimova, 2012; Lomonosov, 2012). Hardly surprisingly, it centres on the personage of Alexander the Great; in turn, this continues to sour relations with Greece, with contending interpretations of his ethnic and national origins (Lomonosov, 2012). What the case of Macedonia tells us is that antiquitarianism may provide a powerful ideological justification for a particular national trajectory, but that this is inward- rather than outward-looking, and comes at the cost of inclusiveness.

In the case of Uzbekistan, the golden age is that of Timur the Great (Tamburlaine) and his immediate descendants. As is the case with Macedonia, the official antiquarianism emphasizes the splendours of the past, direct links between it and the present, a need for unity and order, and an inherent capacity for national greatness. However, it also is an approach that, at first glance, discounts economics: it is suggested that political vision and what is inherent in the nation can solve structural economic problems. In practice, however, as with a number of other contemporary authoritarian ideologies encountered in emerging markets, antiquarianism relies on economic growth as a basis for ideological legitimation: stable economic growth is seen as a way of solving political problems. This is, of course, the inverse of President Trump's United States and Prime Minister May's United Kingdom, where populist ideologies are used as a way of distracting from structural economic problems, which are used as an open-ended justification for ever more extremist right-wing policies.

GROWTH REGIMES: NATURAL RESOURCES, CONSTRUCTION AND BEYOND

A feature of the contemporary global political economy has been the concentration of manufacturing in a relatively small number of super-exporters, most notably Germany and China. This has challenged the basis of economic diversification in many emerging markets. Owing to the difficulties in autonomously developing a tariff regime to support industrialization, and the demands of the international financial institutions and the World Trade Organization, it is in most instances unfeasible for such economies to follow the traditional recipe of inward-led industrialization as a path to national development. Unlike many post-Soviet economies, Uzbekistan has managed to preserve a significant industrial base, but one that, on its own, is insufficient to provide the basis of national growth and prosperity (Dadabaev, 2005).

Historically, Uzbekistan was a significant oil and gas producer, generating some 200 000 barrels/day (b/d) as recently as the late 1990s. However, oil production rapidly declined in the early 2000s, and is now barely sufficient to serve domestic needs (World Energy Council, 2017). Industry sources ascribe the decline to underinvestment (ibid.), but the industry is well known for over-hyping reserves worldwide. At the same time, the government has opened up the industry to foreign investment (EIA, 2017); however, given the present price volatility, the interest of the industry in potentially marginal regions of the world has somewhat waned.

The country has sizeable reserves of other minerals, most notably gold and uranium: it has the world's fourth-largest gold reserves. Subsoil reserves are owned by the government, but mining firms may get time-specific licences to exploit them. Although the licences may be expropriated by the government, there is legal protection of investment and privately owned mining equipment (Jabbarov, 2014). However, given corruption and unrestrained government power, the country is judged to be a poor and risky investment environment (EBRD, 2007).

Another major primary export has been cotton (Pomfret, 2000b). Indeed, access to cheap Uzbek cotton fuelled the rise of cheap clothing exports from China in the 1990s and early 2000s. However, the widespread usage of child labour and other categories of vulnerable labour in the industry meant that any national benefits were concentrated in the hands of a few (Bhat, 2015). Many Uzbeks, from schoolchildren to doctors, have been forced to work for up to two months in the fields at annual harvest time (Bhat, 2015; Bishkek, 2013). The large-scale cultivation of cotton requiring heavy irrigation caused large-scale environmental degradation in the Soviet era, and in large areas of the country there is now a risk of full-blown environmental collapse (Forkutsa et al., 2009). Although cotton remains an important export, there is little doubt that it can no longer serve as a vehicle for driving national growth.

Yet, as noted above, the ruling elite have staked their fortunes on an ability to continue to deliver economically. As regulation theory reminds us, at a particular time and place, national economies rely on a particular dominant production paradigm and associated supportive regulatory institutions. This, in turn, can provide the basis for a specific growth regime. All growth regimes are spatially and temporarily confined, but by definition are capable of sustaining themselves over a particular area for a sustained period of time.

As with a number of emerging markets, the Uzbek government has sought to provide at least some foundation for growth through promoting and sponsoring construction activity (see Ruddock and Lopes, 2006). This centres not only on large-scale infrastructural works – the high-speed railway between Tashkent and Samarkand being a notable example – and postmodern-styled office buildings, but also the development of new residential accommodation. The latter replaces traditional and Soviet-era housing, and is sold to citizens, with finance being provided by state loans. In essence, what has happened is that the state converts part of the public debt, run up to fund large-scale construction works, into private debt.

Whilst the process of relocation is sometimes traumatic, with arbitrary expropriation of traditional residences, the new housing provides more modern facilities for a relatively modest cost. In essence, rather than relying on private finance to provide loan funding for public works, as per the public–private partnership model that was widely deployed in the United Kingdom (UK) in the early to mid-2000s, the Uzbek model uses public finance to provide private individuals with loans to buy what becomes their personal property. Whilst the government runs the risk of accumulating a large amount of bad debt, it also has the potential to secure a future revenue stream, whilst relieving present political pressures through the economic growth generated by large-scale public spending on construction. It cannot be concluded that the construction-centred model as yet constitutes a full-fledged growth regime; it is difficult to anticipate how long a wave of large-scale building works can be sustained (Raupova et al., 2014).

MANUFACTURING

It is an undeniable achievement that Uzbekistan has managed to retain and develop a significant industrial base. In the case of the automotive industry, a joint venture with Turkish interests led to the development of the SamKocauto bus and truck plant, which was founded in 1996; it produces Nissan and Isuzu vehicles. Another 2009 joint venture with MAN led to the opening of a plant to assemble MAN CKD truck kits (Sotivoldiyev, 2014). Subsequently, MAN became engulfed in a bribery scandal involving operations elsewhere in Central Asia, and rumours surfaced that there was an Uzbekistan link (see Letzien, 2014).

A new automotive plant was constructed in the Fergana valley, as a joint venture with then Korean car manufacturer Daewoo in 1996. Following the Asian financial crisis, Daewoo was subsumed into GM, but the plant has continued to assemble both CKDs and SKDs from what is now GM Korea (Spechler and Spechler, 2010). By 2013, production reached 200 000 units, becoming a major earner of foreign exchange (Nichol, 2013). There is a drive to increase local content, with an engine plant being established. A major part of production is that of the Chevrolet Nexia, a car design that dates back to the Opel Kadett of the 1980s; although very dated, its relatively simple design, and the availability of surplus plant that was trans-shipped from South Korea to manufacture it, lends it to indigenization. The automotive industry in the country can be considered to be relatively successful in that it has proved capable of producing affordable products appropriate to local market conditions (Richet and Bourassa, 2000). Joint ventures ensure a degree of local ownership and control (Demirbag and

Mirza, 2000). However, the MAN scandal points to the omnipresent threats of corruption in doing business in such contexts. Again, the industry remains dependent on a degree of state support and protection; it remains highly vulnerable to competition from low-cost Chinese producers, and legal and illegal second-hand car imports from Europe. Again, the slow move towards electric cars may render the entire local industry obsolete, especially given that local car plants are relatively undercapitalized.

There are also various plants manufacturing agricultural equipment to service the cotton industry. Many of these depend for their viability on contracts with the state or state-aligned firms (firms with close ties to the state and/or government). Again, such firms are capable of producing cost-effective products appropriate to local market conditions and needs. However, they are relatively undercapitalized and ill equipped to cope with major technological changes, and would be vulnerable to further reductions in state sponsorship and protection.

Unlike some of the other countries in the region, Uzbekistan has managed to preserve a fair component of its traditional industrial base and, indeed, to attract significant foreign investment, most notably in the form of joint ventures. These effectively serve not only local needs, but also those of neighbouring states (Nichol, 2013). However, many players face structural crises of competitiveness and lack access to new investment or technologies. This would make a large proportion of industry vulnerable to further liberalization; or indeed, to significant inflows of illegal imports, if the government proved incapable of stemming these.

CORRUPTION AND FDI IN TELECOMS

In many developing countries, telecommunications has become an attractive area for foreign direct investment (FDI). Not only has deregulation opened more opportunities, but modern mobile phones serve poor consumers very well. Not only do they enable communication in the absence or failure of wired telephone networks, but low purchase prices and pay-as-you-go contracts free users from high entrance or fixed monthly expenses. Again, unlike wired networks, mobile phone masts are relatively cheap to maintain. Given this, there has been intense competition from rival telecoms companies to gain access to even quite unstable markets; relatively stable countries such as Uzbekistan, with low levels of absolute poverty, are particularly attractive.

However, allegations of bribery involving then presidential daughter, Gulnara Karimova, have brought into question the involvement of foreign investors in the country's telecoms sector. It also highlights the broader challenges of corruption and presents well-documented examples of wrongdoing. In 2012, it was alleged that TeliaSonera, a Swedish telecoms firm, had paid Takilant, a Gibraltan firm linked to Gulnara Karimova, a sum of $320 million for 3G licences and telecoms frequencies. Later, allegations surfaced as to whether Vimpelcom, a Norwegian–Russian telecoms group, had also entered into questionable dealings with Takilant in return for rights to enter the mobile telephone market (Reuters, 2016). Both Telia and Vimpelcom faced corruption charges in the Netherlands and the US, the latter leading to a substantial bribery settlement (Reuters, 2016). Telia followed suit in 2017, paying an almost $1 billion penalty to the US and Dutch authorities (Putz, 2017). This highlights two issues. The first is that relatively little-known players have been enabled to gain substantial advantages over established players in the global telecoms industry. Secondly, the country remains a highly risky investment environment, due not only to the shifting political sands, but also to the risk of legal action from abroad.

Despite Uzbekistan's reform and policies on FDI, the high political and operational risk level appears to affect FDI flow dramatically. Data from an FDI markets database indicate that there were only 193 greenfield FDI projects between 2003 and 2014 (some are expansion projects from the same multinational firms). The trend also indicates that while up to 2009 there were modest numbers of entries to Uzbekistan, the trend appeared to be declining throughout 2010–2014. While this may partly be attributed to early entrants' experience with the country (Demirbag et al., 1998), there may also be a role played by the scandals of recent years, which may have affected the political risk perception of potential foreign investors.

Within source countries of greenfield FDI projects, Russia and South Korea lead with a significant number of projects between them (more than 34 per cent in total) followed by the US, Germany and the UK. Surprisingly, the Chinese FDI projects in Uzbekistan are fewer than those of European multinational enterprises. Given the Chinese presence in Africa and in many resource-rich countries, this pattern is rather surprising. Other European Union (EU) countries (Table 2.1) are involved in a significant number of greenfield FDI projects. These countries are mostly Eastern European, and have ongoing industrial and commercial links from the Soviet era. The quite high proportion of FDI from South Korea is primarily centred around the investment in the automotive industry led by Daewoo and its successor, GM Korea, and their key suppliers. Predictably, Russia is the major source of FDI, which reflects close ties (Anceschi, 2010); but more surprisingly, China has been (until recently) a more modest source – perhaps a reflection of the close ties between the Uzbek government and the Russian one. This is despite China being one of the two main markets for Uzbek cotton (the other being

Table 2.1   Greenfield foreign direct investment projects in Uzbekistan by year and source countries

FDI projects by year			FDI projects by source countries		
Year	Number of FDI projects	%	Source countries	Number of FDI projects	%
2003	31	16.1	Russia	46	23.8
2004	16	8.3	South Korea	21	10.9
2005	14	7.3	US	16	8.3
2006	18	9.3	Germany	14	7.7
2007	12	6.2	UK	14	7.3
2008	20	10.4	China	13	6.7
2009	21	10.9	Netherlands	9	4.7
2010	13	6.7	Other EU	31	16.1
2011	16	8.3	Other Commonwealth	5	2.6
2012	13	6.7	of Independent		
2013	10	5.2	States (CIS)		
2014	9	4.7	Other Asia	14	7.3
Total	193	100	Rest of World	10	5.2
			Total	193	100

Source: FDI Markets (https://www.fdimarkets.com).

Bangladesh). However, it is worth noting that there has been a history of state re-expropriation in the sector (the same is true for mining), making it a riskier proposition than some other areas of the national economy.

As for industrial breakdown of greenfield FDI projects in Uzbekistan, projects largely concentrate in manufacturing and extraction (mines and minerals), as Uzbekistan is rich in terms of underground resources. The FDI flow pattern and Uzbekistan's industrial structure seem to be in alignment, as the county has a manufacturing base going back to the Soviet era. As for the size of FDI projects in Uzbekistan, these are largely small-scale projects (74 per cent) creating less than 200 jobs per project, while there are some large projects creating more than 1000 jobs (8.3 per cent) (see Table 2.2). Again, it is worth noting that the most important beneficiary of FDI has been the automotive industry.

As for the size of greenfield FDI projects in Uzbekistan, in terms of capital invested per project, Table 2.2 reveals that most of these FDI projects are still small-scale. More than 78 per cent of these projects seem to have attracted less than $100 million. The remaining FDI projects could be described as medium-sized projects in terms of capital investment, with some exceptions of large projects concentrated in the automotive industry

Table 2.2 *Foreign direct investment projects in Uzbekistan by industry and project size (greenfield)*

FDI projects by industry activity			FDI projects by size		
Industrial activity	Number of projects	%	Employment created	Number of FDI projects	%
Business services	19	9.8	≤50	55	28.5
Construction	3	1.6	51–200	83	43.0
Education and training	1	0.5	201–500	33	17.1
Extraction	23	11.9	501–999	6	3.1
Headquarters	1	0.5	≥1000	16	8.3
Information and	10	5.2		193	100
communication		1.0	Capital invested (million USD)	Number of FDI projects	%
technology		0.5			
and Internet		38.3	<10	59	30.6
infrastructure		0.5	10–99	92	47.7
Logistics,	2	8.3	100–199	25	13.0
distribution and		100	200–499	10	5.2
transportation			>500	7	3.6
Maintenance and	1			193	100.0
servicing					
Manufacturing	74				
Research and	1				
development					
Retail	16				
Total	193				

Source: FDI Markets (https://www.fdimarkets.com).

(3.6 per cent). This pattern is in line with many developing countries, as industrial organizations in these countries in general are dominated by small and medium-sized enterprises; however, the above-mentioned risk of expropriation would make large investments particularly unattractive, especially in cotton, mining, and oil and gas.

CONCLUSION

In his darkest play, *Titus Andronicus*, Shakespeare depicts a world where even decent and upright individuals become brutalized and corrupt; in the end, there is nobody left untarnished. Uzbekistan has an unenviable reputation for autocratic rule and corruption (Dadabaev, 2005; Farchy and Weaver, 2012; *The Economist*, 2016); outside investors engaging with the country risk being trapped in a downward spiral of low-key compromises ultimately leading to full-blown corruption. However, the country may have autocratic rule, but it has proved to be capable of supplying jobs, protecting standards of living, and securing at least some growth, in comparison to many other developing-world dictatorships. The system continues to base its legitimacy on a relatively broad basis of delivery, predicated on a basic degree of economic stability and growth. Significantly, it has managed to retain and develop a significant industrial base that serves not only local but also regional needs. This also highlights the extent to which gradualist economic reforms may work better, and indeed be more conducive to outside investors, than neoliberal shock therapy. In turn, the Uzbek experience confirms that many different forms of state mediation of markets may be viable in providing a temporary and uneven, but nonetheless in some measures sustained, growth.

REFERENCES

Akbarzadeh, S. (2005). *Uzbekistan and the United States: Authoritarianism, Islamism and Washington's New Security Agenda*. London: Zed Books.

Ambrosio, T. (2015). Leadership succession in Kazakhstan and Uzbekistan: regime survival after Nazarbayev and Karimov. *Journal of Balkan and Near Eastern Studies*, 17(1), pp. 49–67.

Amnesty International (2015). Uzbekistan: torture, corruption and lies. 13 April. Available at: https://www.amnesty.org.uk/uzbekistan-torture-corruption-and-lies.

Anceschi, L. (2010). Integrating domestic politics and foreign policy making: the cases of Turkmenistan and Uzbekistan. *Central Asian Survey*, 29(2), pp. 143–158.

Averre, D. (2007). Sovereign democracy and Russia's relations with the European Union. *Demokratizatsiya*, 15(2), pp. 173–190.

Bhat, B. (2015). *Cotton Cultivation and Child Labor in Post-Soviet Uzbekistan*. Lanham (Md.): Lexington.

Beckert, J. (2016). Imagined futures: fictional expectations and capitalist dynamics. Cambridge, MA: Harvard University Press.

Bishkek, D. (2013). In the land of cotton. *The Economist*, 16 October. Available at: https://www.economist.com/blogs/banyan/2013/10/forced-labour-uzbekistan.

Boonstra, J. and Laruelle, M. (2014). Uncharted waters: presidential successions in Kazakhstan and Uzbekistan. EUCAM National Series Policy Brief, April.

Collins, K. (2002). Clans, pacts, and politics in Central Asia. *Journal of Democracy*, 13(3), pp. 137–152.

Dadabaev, T. (2005). Shifting patterns of public confidence in post-Soviet Uzbekistan. *Central Asia–Caucasus Analyst*, 6(5), pp. 9–11.

Delcour, L. and Wolczuk, K. (2015). Spoiler or facilitator of democratization? Russia's role in Georgia and Ukraine. *Democratization*, 22(3), pp. 459–478.

Demirbag, M. and Mirza, H. (2000). Factors affecting international joint venture success: an empirical analysis of foreign–local partner relationships and performance in joint ventures in Turkey. *International Business Review*, 9(1), pp. 1–35.

Demirbag, M., Gunes, R. and Mirza, H. (1998). Political risk management: a case study of Turkish companies in Central Asia and Russia. In Mirza, H. (ed.), *Global Competitive Strategies in the New World Economy*, pp. 283–309. Cheltenham, UK and Northampton, MA, USA: Edward Elgar Publishing.

Dimova, R. (2012). The Ohrid Festival and political performativity in the contemporary Republic of Macedonia. *Journal of Balkan and Near Eastern Studies*, 14(2), pp. 229–244.

EBRD (2007). *Uzbekistan Country Factsheet*. London: European Bank for Construction and Development.

The Economist (2016). Uzbekistan replaces one strongman with another. 10 December. Available at: https://www.economist.com/news/asia/21711263-shavkat-mirziyoyev-wins-886-vote-sham-election-uzbekistan-replaces-one-strongman.

EIA (2017). Uzbekistan: Country Report. Available at: https://www.eia.gov/beta/international/analysis.cfm?iso=UZB.

Farchy, J. and Weaver, C. (2012). Uzbek telecoms corruption probe widens to include VimpelCom. *Financial Times*, 12 March. Available at: https://www.ft.com/content/d5692ff8-a9ff-11e3-8497-00144feab7de?mhq5j=e1.

Forkutsa, I., Sommer, R., Shirokova, Y.I., et al. (2009). Modeling irrigated cotton with shallow groundwater in the Aral Sea Basin of Uzbekistan: II. Soil salinity dynamics. *Irrigation Science*, 27(4), pp. 319–330.

Gerber, T.P. and Hout, M. (1998). More shock than therapy: market transition, employment, and income in Russia, 1991–1995. *American Journal of Sociology*, 104(1), pp. 1–50.

Guardian (2017). Daughter of former Uzbek dictator detained over fraud claims. 28 July. Available at: https://www.theguardian.com/world/2017/jul/28/gulnara-karomova-daughter-former-uzbek-dictator-held-fraud-claims.

Human Rights Watch (2016). Uzbekistan: events of 2016. Available at: https://www.hrw.org/world-report/2017/country-chapters/uzbekistan.

Ilkhamov, A. (2016). For most Uzbeks, it does not matter whether the president is alive or dead. *Guardian*, 1 September. Available at: https://www.theguardian.com/world/2016/sep/01/for-most-uzbeks-it-doesnt-matter-whether-the-president-is-alive-or-dead.

Jabbarov, B. (2014). Mining industry of Uzbekistan. Available at: http://www.mondaq.com/x/331792/Mining/Mining+Industry+Of+Uzbekistan.

Klein, N. (2007). *The Shock Doctrine: The Rise of Disaster Capitalism*. London: Macmillan.

Letzien, C. (2014). MAN AG discloses $344 million in penalties and costs for bribe scandal. FPCA Blog. Available at: http://www.fcpablog.com/blog/2014/4/10/man-ag-discloses-344-million-in-penalties-and-costs-for-brib.html.

Lomonosov, M. (2012). National myths in interdependence: the narratives of ancient past among Macedonians and Albanians in the republic of Macedonia after 1991. Masters dissertation, Central European University, Budapest.

Luhn, A. (2015). Uzbek President bans the teaching of political science. *Observer*, 5 September. Available at: https://www.theguardian.com/world/2015/sep/05/uzbekistan-islam-karimov-bans-political-science.

Malashenko, A.V. (2014). Exploring Uzbekistan's potential political transition. Carnegie Moscow Center. Available at: http://carnegieendowment.org/files/CP_Uzbekistan_web_Eng2014.pdf (accessed 15 May 2018).

McGlinchey, E.M. (2009). Searching for Kamalot: political patronage and youth politics in Uzbekistan. *Europe–Asia Studies*, 61(7), pp. 1137–1150.

MacWilliam, S. and Rafferty, M. (2017). From development and grand corruption to governance. *International Journal for Crime, Justice and Social Democracy*, 6(4), pp. 12–28.

Nichol, J. (2013). Uzbekistan: recent developments and US interests. *Current Politics and Economics of Russia, Eastern and Central Europe*, 28(3/4), pp. 405–431.

Northrop, D. (2000). Languages of loyalty: gender, politics, and party supervision in Uzbekistan, 1927–41. *Russian Review*, 59(2), pp. 179–200.

Pannier, B. (2012). Uzbekistan. *Nations In Transit 2011*. Freedom House, pp. 606–623. Available at: https://freedomhouse.org/sites/default/files/inline_images/NIT-2011-Uzbekistan.pdf.

Pomfret, R. (2000a). The Uzbek model of economic development, 1991–91. *Economics of Transition*, 8(3), pp. 733–748.

Pomfret, R. (2000b). Agrarian reform in Uzbekistan: why has the Chinese model failed to deliver?. *Economic Development and Cultural Change*, 48(2), pp. 269–284.

Popov, V. (2013). Economic miracle of post-Soviet space: why Uzbekistan managed to achieve what no other post-Soviet state achieved. Available at: SSRN: https://ssrn.com/abstract=2303867 or http://dx.doi.org/10.2139/ssrn.2303867.

Putz, C. (2017). Telia agrees to pay $1bn in Uzbek corruption scandal settlement. *Diplomat*, 26 September. Available at: http://thediplomat.com/2017/09/telia-agrees-to-pay-1-billion-in-penalties-in-uzbek-corruption-scandal-settlement/.

Raupova, O., Kamahara, H. and Goto, N. (2014). Assessment of physical economy through economy-wide material flow analysis in developing Uzbekistan. *Resources, Conservation and Recycling*, 89, pp. 76–85.

Reuters (2016). Dutch prosecutors seek 300 mln euros in Uzbek corruption case. 6 July. Available at: http://www.reuters.com/article/netherlands-uzbekistan-corruption-idUSL8N19R56P.

Richet, X. and Bourassa, F. (2000). The reemergence of the automotive industry in Eastern Europe. In Hirschausen, C. von and Blitzer, J. (eds), *The Globalization of Industry and Innovation in Eastern Europe: From Post-Socialist Restructuring to International Competitiveness*, pp. 59–94. Cheltenham, UK and Northampton, MA, USA: Edward Elgar Publishing.

Rodríguez, A. (2016). The road ahead: what the death of Karimov means for Central Asia. *Harvard International Review*, 38(1), pp. 39–41.

Ruddock, L. and Lopes, J. (2006). The construction sector and economic development: the 'Bon curve'. *Construction Management and Economics*, 24(7), pp. 717–723.

Sotivoldiyev, N.J.R. (2014). Economic and social partnership between Uzbekistan and Germany: achieved results and opportunities. *Forschungsberichte: Entwicklungen in Usbekistan: Wissenschaftliche Schriftenreihe*, 6, p. 168.

Spechler, D.R. and Spechler, M.C. (2010). The foreign policy of Uzbekistan: sources, objectives and outcomes: 1991–2009. *Central Asian Survey*, 29(2), pp. 159–170.

Spechler, M.C. (2007). Authoritarian politics and economic reform in Uzbekistan: past, present and prospects. *Central Asian Survey*, 26(2), pp. 185–202.

Starr, S.F. (1996). Making Eurasia stable. *Foreign Affairs*, 75(1), pp. 80–92.

Tikhomirov, V.M. (2018). *Russia After Yeltsin*. Abingdon: Routledge.

World Energy Council (2017). Oil in Uzbekistan. Available at: https://www.worldenergy.org/data/resources/country/uzbekistan/oil/.

3. Mongolian management: local practitioners' perspectives in the face of political, economic and socio-cultural changes

Saranzaya Manalsuren, Marina Michalski and Martyna Śliwa

INTRODUCTION

Mongolia, one of the last remaining nomadic countries, with its rich mineral deposits of coal, copper, gold, uranium and rare earths, estimated at US$2.75 trillion, is considered to have high potential investment opportunities. Since the beginning of transition from a socialist to a democratic regime in 1991, Mongolia has opened its borders to the rest of the world and the country's economy has experienced tremendous changes. It became the world's fastest growing economy with 17.5 per cent gross domestic product (GDP) growth in 2011, and yet had the world's worst-performing currency in 2016, when it lost approximately 7.8 per cent of its value within a month (e.g., Kohn, 2016). Volatility in the local economy and politics has led to a slowdown in foreign direct investment since 2011, although interest in working with Mongolians and conducting business in the country has not declined. Since 1990, more than 10 709 foreign companies have invested more than US$590.3 billion, and 11 514 companies from 35 different countries have entered the Mongolian business sector (National Statistical Office, 2016). Local managers have faced increasing challenges when working with expatriates and foreign investors, and in adapting to international standards. For those wishing to do business in Mongolia, an important need has arisen to develop a deeper appreciation of how management is understood among local practitioners.

Mongolia is one of the newest emerging nations in the global economy, but the Western world does not yet know enough about its management practices. That is not to say that there has been a lack of interest in exploring the wider Mongolian context. Existing studies on Mongolia have tended to focus on its history and wider socio-cultural aspects such as rural area development, pastoralism, shamanism, ethnicity, everyday life and kinship in the pre- and post-Soviet period (e.g., Alexander et al., 2007; Humphrey, 2002; Humphrey and Sneath, 1996, 1999). Since 1992, there has also been a growing focus on understanding the Mongolian economic environment. International economic and financial organizations, including the International Monetary Fund and the Asian Development Bank, have prepared a number of reports addressing the local economic conditions; whereas Mongolian and international non-governmental organizations have published reports about the socio-political and financial situation, focusing on transition processes, unemployment, gender, domestic violence, human rights, education and the needs of children (e.g., Baasanjav, 2002; Bayliss and Dillon, 2010; Bruun and Narangoa, 2011; Buxbaum, 2004; Diener, 2011; Diener and Hagen, 2013). However, apart from studies and reports on mining, there are limited appraisals of business and management practices. For instance, Mongolia was not included in Hofstede's (1984, 2001) studies of former Soviet Republics (FSRs) (e.g., Kiblitskaya, 2000; Siemieńska, 1994; Woldu et al., 2006). Altogether, there is a void with regard to Mongolia in the literature on cross-cultural and indigenous management studies.

This chapter contributes towards filling that lacuna in the current knowledge. It presents findings from the first in-depth study addressing management in the Mongolian context. Being primarily empirically focused, it discusses understandings of the concepts of 'manager' and 'management' by practitioners in Mongolia; explores perceptions of managerial roles and practices characterizing Mongolian management; and explains the complex and interconnected influences shaping management in contemporary Mongolia. The chapter concludes with implications for managers and political authorities in the Mongolian context. Before moving on to examining management and management practices, as viewed by Mongolian management practitioners, we first offer a background discussion, drawing attention to key facts and phenomena that are necessary for developing an understanding of the contemporary business environment in Mongolia.

BACKGROUND TO THE CONTEMPORARY BUSINESS ENVIRONMENT IN MONGOLIA

Political and Economic Transitions

Following many centuries of nomadic history, and after almost 70 years of socialism, the first democratic elections in Mongolia took place in July 1990. The new Constitution in 1992 established a representative democracy in Mongolia by guaranteeing freedom of choice in religion, human rights, travel, speech, government and elections. The People's Great Khural (equivalent to the parliament) created the new position of President of Mongolia, elected every four years. Mongolian citizens now also vote for 76 members of the parliament, who play a key role in setting the country's laws and legislation (Constitution of Mongolia, 1992).

This political shift had direct implications for the business environment. After July 1990, the first Deputy Minister Davaadorjiin Ganbold began to encourage the opening of the country's economy to the West. Under the new Constitution of 1996, the government put in place favourable tax and mining regulations. In the 2000s, foreign corporations arrived in great numbers, attracted by rising commodity prices and the extensive geological work already completed during the socialist era. Major projects were introduced, new deposits were discovered, foreign direct investment (FDI) boomed, and the economy grew at an unprecedented rate (Eyler-Driscoll, 2013). With the enormous reserves of coal, copper, gold and other minerals, strong support for democratic values, a well-educated workforce, and no significant regional or ethnic conflict, Mongolia was considered a promising partner for industrialized countries.

Changes in the country's economic institutions were also dramatic. Mongolia embarked on a turbulent period of 'shock therapy' overseen by the International Monetary Fund and the Asian Development Bank (Murrell, 2012). International investment organizations produced reports on the Mongolian economy and suggested implementing the privatization of banks and other sectors. Fifteen new banks were opened in less than two years, and Prime Minister Dashiin Byambasüren instigated a policy of rapid privatization, modelled on the work of the United States economist Jeffrey Sachs in the countries of post-Soviet Eastern Europe.

That speed of structural change, however, had unintended consequences. Mongolian people became exposed to privatization and a free market economy overnight, but had no prior understanding of the principles of capitalism, or skills to engage with the stock exchange. Furthermore, the reduction of government price controls meant that prices rose dramatically, and in 1992 inflation topped 325 per cent. Industries began to suffer, businesses went bankrupt and the level of unemployment rose accordingly.

The country's trajectory of growth and transformation, therefore, has not always been smooth. Although Mongolia transitioned from socialism to democracy in a peaceful way and became actively involved in international relations, in recent years the government has been subject to criticism by local and international companies, as well as by economists. In particular, they denounced local political institutions' failure to ensure consistency in mining and foreign direct investment laws. For instance, thousands of mining licences were revoked following the introduction of the amended Strategic Entities Foreign Direct Investment Law (SEFIL), the Forests and Water Law, and the Nuclear Energy Law. Part of the problem derived from political uncertainty: the parliament of 2012 appointed three Prime Ministers during its four-year tenure, which contributed to disorder in local politics and the economy.

An unstable government, and poor decisions in foreign investment law and mining regulations, were seen negatively and FDI dropped by 64 per cent in 2014 (World Bank, 2013, 2014). Falling global commodity prices and an increase in government spending meant higher inflation and increasing pressure on the repayment of the sovereign bond interest which was due in 2017 (World Bank, 2014). The reputation of an unstable government with a constantly changing parliament has created uncertainty and made potential investors extremely cautious. Gross domestic product (GDP) growth has decreased by 50 per cent and foreign direct investment plummeted by 58 per cent in 2016 due to inadequate foreign investment laws.

The local economy continues to develop in turbulent times. In 2013, the Prime Minister announced that Mongolia would commence oil exploration, and it was predicted to become a global economic growth generator by 2050. In 2014, Mongolian companies were listed on the Stock Exchange of Hong Kong for the first time (Mongolian Economic Forum, 2014). Moreover, the outcome of the general election in June 2016 created conditions for greater political and economic stability. The Mongolian People's Party (MPP), still known as the Socialist Party, won 65 out of 76 seats in the general election and formed a unicameral parliament (State Hural of Mongolia, 2016). Following that, long-awaited projects have been sanctioned, which have brought renewed optimism to foreign investors and the economy in general.

A further factor to highlight is that of Mongolia's evolving position in the wider global arena. While grappling with the challenges of securing internal political and economic stability, the country has also made strides in establishing its role within international institutions. For instance, in February 2000, Mongolia declared itself a nuclear-free state and became a buffer zone between its two superpower neighbours, China and Russia, as well as stating its intention to take a neutral peacekeeping role internationally. Mongolia is an active participant in United Nations conferences and summits and has announced an interest in taking a seat on the Security Council. It has been a member of the Convening Group of the Community of Democracies since January 2012 (United Nations, 2016). More recently, and as a direct result of its open borders policy, Mongolia hosted the 11th Asia–Europe Meeting (ASEM) in July 2016, thus for the first time contributing significantly to the informal dialogue and cooperation forum (MAD Mongolia Newswire, 2016).

The Emerging Business Context

Since 1990, 11 514 companies from 35 different countries have entered the Mongolian business sector (National Statistical Office, 2016), investing $4.7 billion between 1990 and 2010, 73.9 per cent of which was into the mining industry (Ministry of Economy, 2012a, 2012b). In 2001, Ivanhoe Mines, a Canadian mining company, announced the discovery of the world's largest untapped reserves of copper and gold in the South Gobi desert. It has invested $6 billion for the Phase 1 development of the world's largest copper mine, estimated to have deposits worth $24 trillion, and therefore producing 1.3 per cent of Mongolia's GDP (Oyu Tolgoi, 2013). It is but one of 456 mining companies in Mongolia (Ministry of Economy, 2012a). Following this steep growth in the extractive economy, the private sector has expanded significantly.

Further factors shaping the configuration of the private sector in Mongolia have been the hyperinflation and unemployment levels of the early 1990s, which forced many people to leave their jobs and seek alternative ways of earning livelihoods for themselves and their families. Some used handcrafting skills to earn an income, whereas others started travelling to China to bring back goods to trade. As more people began to experiment in sales, selling on the black market stopped being taboo, and a new profession of 'travelling salesperson' emerged. Most private businesses in Mongolia started from individuals' entrepreneurial efforts and from small, family-run enterprises employing relatives. However, despite technical training gained under socialism, management experience and skills were alien to the emerging small, family-owned enterprises. Those who succeeded are industry leaders today, enjoying an increased market share and consumer spending power. The private sector has become the largest contributor to the local economy, comprising 116 900 companies generating 56 per cent of the local GDP and employing 65 per cent of the total workforce (National Statistical Office, 2015).

Currently, one of the fastest-developing sectors is the hospitality industry, and some of the world's largest hotel chains, such as Shangri-La and Best Western, have opened in Mongolia in the last few years. The latest franchise to enter Mongolia is Holiday Inn, which launched a hotel in Ulaanbaatar in 2016 (Max Group, 2016). One result of foreign companies' incursions into the Mongolian market has been the introduction of Western management practices, such as the use of sales targets and incentive-based salaries.

Crossing Boundaries: Social and Educational Developments

Beyond the economic and business dimensions, the transition from socialism to capitalism has also brought profound changes to the wider Mongolian society. The amended Constitution of Mongolia established a representative democracy which guaranteed freedom of movement for citizens (Constitution of Mongolia, paragraph 18, 1992) and opened its borders to the world. As mentioned above, this has allowed international organizations to enter the local economy, and Mongolians to travel to non-socialist countries. Management consultants and trainers have started to sell their services to Mongolian organizations, whereas local managers have begun to travel abroad for tuition.

The number of Mongolians travelling abroad is steadily increasing, and there were an estimated 120 000 Mongolian citizens living overseas by 2015 (National Statistical Office, 2015). The government of Mongolia now runs a state programme which has enabled students to study abroad with a full scholarship (Ministry of Education, 2015), and a considerable number of students also study abroad using private funding. Young Mongolians returning with international experience represent the most significant change in the local workforce and an important societal change in contemporary Mongolia.

The local higher education sector has also flourished. The first providers of higher education opened in 1994 and began offering degree programmes. Mongolia has 125 universities, and 89 of them offer degrees in business and/or management, which produce 15 850 graduates every year (Ministry of Education, 2015). However, business school curricula remain of limited relevance to aspiring Mongolian managers, as they draw on a combination of socialist-era published textbooks and translations of American texts that present case studies of multinational companies (MNCs) operating in Western business environments.

Beyond the physical transfer of people and services, local approaches to networking and customer service have also been affected by technological advancements. The availability of affordable and reliable Internet connections has enabled everyone, including herders from remote areas of northern Mongolia, to access the Internet. Online-based networking, sales and marketing are all new to Mongolian society; however, they have already become widespread tools for local businesses.

Moving Forward

Altogether, over the past 25 years Mongolia has undergone a range of multifaceted transformations that have changed the landscape of its business environment, and have given rise to unprecedented opportunities and challenges for both local businesses and international partners and investors. As the country continues along the trajectory of transition, it is important for both management scholars and practitioners to develop an understanding of management and management practices in the Mongolian context. The remainder of this chapter focuses on issues involved in management in Mongolia by examining narratives of Mongolian management practitioners.

RESEARCH METHODS

The empirical basis of the research is provided by 45 in-depth qualitative interviews with senior management practitioners in Mongolia. This includes 35 interviews conducted between May and August 2014, and ten follow-up interviews with selected participants carried out between July and August 2015. All interviews were conducted by the first author. The sample of participants consisted of 16 chief executive officers (CEOs) and 19 middle to upper-level managers representing 32 different firms. The participants shared their views on what effective management entails, and brought to light the key influencing factors on their daily practices. In addition, four CEOs were shadowed for three days each to gain detailed knowledge of their management methods and how they engage with the internal and external factors that influence their roles. Table 3.1 provides more detail regarding the sample of participants.

The participants were divided into three groups based on their personal and professional background. The main criteria used in the process of categorization were: (1) temporal – in relation to the participant's age and the number of years of managerial experience; (2) qualifications – in relation to the participant's qualification and training background; (3) geographical – in relation to the participant's country of origin; and (4) the participant's personal definition of management. Using these four main criteria, the management practitioners interviewed were divided into three groups, as follows.

'Socialist era managers', the first group of managers, defined themselves as a 'product of socialism' or 'red socialist managers'. They were trained and had management experience prior to 1991, when Mongolia was a socialist country. Members of this group tended to be older than participants categorized under either of the remaining two groups. However, it is difficult to set an exact age criterion for them, as university graduates at the beginning of the 1990s were still taught the same curriculum as before transition. Broadly, this group tended to be aged from the mid-forties

Table 3.1   Sample of participants

Managers in Mongolia: four main criteria		Socialist era (12)	Transitional (era 14)	Non-Mongolian (9)
Temporal	Age	45–60	30–45	30–60
	Start of managing experience	Prior to 1990	After 1990	n/a
	Number of years of work experience (in Mongolia for non-natives)	Between 18 and 35 years (average 21 years)	Between 3 and 19 years (average 9 years)	Between 3 and 12 years (average 7 years)
Education and training	University (Mongolia or abroad)	Former socialist countries 10 Mongolia 2	Overseas 10 Mongolia 3 Other 1	University 5 Other 4
	Degrees (technical or business)	Technical 9 Other 3	Technical 4 Business 10	Business 5 Other 4
	On-the-job training	n/a	n/a	Apprentice 4
	Management training (after university)	Yes 2 No 10	Yes 12 No 2	Yes 9
Current working sector	Public or private	Public 5 Private 7	Public 4 Private 10	Public 0 Private 9
Involvement with social and political activities	Member of political party	Yes 10 No 2	Yes 8 No 6	No 7 n/a 2
	Voluntary posts	Yes 12	Yes 1 No 2	Yes 4 No 5

upwards and trained primarily in former Socialist countries, such as Bulgaria, Czechoslovakia, Poland and Russia. The paramount reason for studying in these countries was to promote brotherhood relations between socialist countries and learn to build socialism based on each other's best practices.

'Transitional era managers' made up the second group of managers, whose training and work experience took place after the socialist period. They defined themselves as 'people of business' and tended to be younger than the first cohort of managers. Many of them were educated abroad and had business and management degrees obtained at a university. This was in contrast with 'socialist era' managers, who held mainly technical-related degrees. Transitional era managers were more likely to attend management-related training and workshops, and generally worked in the private sector.

'Non-native Mongolian managers', the third group of managers, have settled in Mongolia by choice since 2003, and at the time of the interviews were involved in managing local businesses. They were not categorized using age or previous work experience, as the only criterion used in this case was geographical. Non-native Mongolian managers defined themselves as 'people and business developers' and had worked for international or local companies for a minimum of three years. While they did not constitute an ethnically homogeneous group, their shared views are presented as 'non-native Mongolian' without specifying their nationality.

The interviews started with demographic type questions to explore whether participants had any experience of being a manager during socialism or had studied or worked abroad. These initial questions were followed up by asking about the participants' experiences and opinions on the difference between being a manager in the past and the present. Subsequently, practices-related questions were posed to discover the participants' approaches to managing. The interviews were concluded with enquiries about participants' perceptions of future management practices, the workforce and business environment in Mongolia. All general questions were followed by 'presupposition questions', as described by Patton (2002, p. 369). He suggested that their value lies in allowing the participant to say something within their own time and space, without persuasion, which may bring valuable insight to the research.

The nature of the interviews was narrative and drew on references to participants' experiences. It was common for managers to tell stories of how their organizations were managed during socialism, or what they had learnt from their upbringing in the countryside or education abroad. Most interviews with local managers were conducted in Mongolian, although it was surprising that a few younger managers who had studied and worked abroad preferred the interview to be conducted in English. All interviews with non-native Mongolian managers were conducted in English. It was common for certain phrases and expressions in Russian to be used by the older managers, who had been educated in former soviet countries. As the researcher conducting the interviews is a native Mongolian and a fluent English and Russian speaker, switching between languages did not interrupt the flow of the interviews.

The empirical data collection resulted in more than 1000 pages of text which was coded and analysed using, first, an early data analysis approach adapted from Glesne (2011); and second, a narrative analysis approach (e.g., Cassell and Symon, 2011; Czarniawska, 1998; Feldman et al., 2004; Gertsen and Søderberg, 2011; Miles et al., 2013; Riessman and Quinney, 2005), supported by the use of NVivo software.

MONGOLIAN MANAGEMENT: PRACTITIONERS' PERSPECTIVES

The empirical material provides rich evidence of Mongolian senior management practitioners' understandings of the concepts of 'manager' and 'management', and of the activities and roles carried out by managers in the Mongolian context. Narratives of the three cohorts of managers – namely 'socialist era', 'transitional era' and 'non-native' – highlight both similarities and differences in participants' views. This section first introduces participants' understandings of notions such as 'manager' and 'management' and the roles for which, according to the senior management practitioners interviewed, managers are and should be responsible. This is followed by a section discussing the influence of a range of interconnected contextual factors on management in Mongolia. Table 3.2 provides examples of interview quotes illustrating the points made in the analysis and discussion below.

What is Mongolian Management?

Understandings of the notion of 'manager'
With regard to how they understood the notion of 'manager', the participants placed a key emphasis on the roles and responsibilities fulfilled by individuals. These roles and responsibilities were shaped by circumstances within and outside organizational contexts, including social and cultural influences, as well as political and economic conditions and formal training at the start of their career.

Firstly, participants' perspectives were inspired by their personal experiences of upbringing and education within a specific cultural context, as well as the professional influences of their formal training and workplace. References to a chief, head, guardian and parent were common, particularly amongst older contributors (e.g., 1 and 2). The idea of a head or chief evokes the notion of a manager whose position is above others (e.g., Stewart, 1976) or one who oversees an organization (e.g., Mintzberg, 1973, 2009). The participants' understandings of the roles of a manager extended beyond fulfilling functions within an organization. They included a range

Table 3.2 Interview quotes illustrating points made in discussion

Themes	Examples	Interview quotes
Manager as a head, guardian, chief and parent	1 and 2	'Management is the relationship between people and as a manager I create one big family, where everyone is looked after. Parents treat their children equally despite their differences and in return, they (children or staff) remain loyal to you.' (S-4, Private sector, M, 23 years of experience)
		'After completing my university . . . I was appointed to be a Master. On my first day, I was given a mentor, who took me as her own daughter. She is one of the biggest influences in my life, and I kept in touch with her until she passed away a few years ago. I still have contact with her children.' (S-8, Private sector, F, 30 years of experience)
Expected to have high moral standards and be a role model	3 and 4	'We did not use the term of manager or management. The person in charge was known as "darga" – the chief or master. Being a master means to be the exemplar, professionally and morally and respected by everyone.' (S-1, Public sector, M, 28 years of experience)
		'People, who were with me during the socialist time, are trustworthy and have high morality. If any of us need a favour, we help each other without a condition, which you cannot get from today's youth.' (S-1, Public sector, M, 28 years of experience)
Showing respect to elders and ancestors	5 and 6	'We grew up in a society, where everyone knew their roles and responsibilities. Letting just anybody make decisions was not something that happened in the socialist time. It has always been a part of our culture and history, listening and respecting elders or chiefs.' (S-12, Public sector, M, 28 years of experience)
		'I advise and help my co-workers. They are no different to my children and they respect me like their mother.' (S-8, Private sector, F, 30 years of experience)

Becoming a manager by learning-by-doing	7 and 8	'I have an engineering background; I quit my job when my workplace was privatized in 1993 and started my own business from scratch. The last 20 years have been a constant learning curve for me and continue to be so. Running a business is a new expertise in Mongolia. The first few years have been just to survive, pay the bills and salaries. Nobody knew how to run a business, nor was there an institution to teach us. All we had to do was go with the flow and deal with things as they happened and experiment with what works and what does not. Only in the last five years or so, have we started learning about management. I'd like to know more about how others have managed in the local context.'
		(T-10, Private sector, M, 14 years of experience)
		'I learn a lot from my staff, especially in customer relations. They know the local attitudes and preferences, which can be the total opposite of a Western mind-set at times.'
		(N-9, Private sector, F, 6 years of experience)
Non-native managers' daily challenges	9 and 10	'Mongolia is a relatively new market economy . . . There is a lot to learn from international standards and business practices. On the technical side, international financial and auditing standards are obviously new here. Our company has to follow these standards and I need to train my staff from day one.'
		(N-9, Private sector, F, 6 years of experience)
		'My staff are keen to learn new things and I found that Mongolians are fast learners. However, I often struggle to have open discussions with them during and after training. They are very good listeners, but not good at expressing themselves. I do not know whether it is something to do with how they were brought up or that they still see me as their boss rather than as a tutor who is trying to help them.'
		(N-1, Private sector, F, 5 years of experience)
Importance of empowerment, emergent for younger Mongolian managers	11 and 12	'The role of an HR [Human Relations] manager is to provide the system that allows line managers to have the right to choose their staff and take the responsibility to train and manage them. I empowered line managers by giving them the freedom to choose their staff, and in return, they need to deliver. That is my control. Usually after one or two mistakes, they (line managers)

Table 3.2 (continued)

Themes	Examples	Interview quotes
		learn their rights and responsibilities. The important thing is to provide the system, where they can make decisions and perform at the same time.'
		(T-6, Private sector, M, 18 years of experience)
		'A good manager gives employees an opportunity to grow. By empowering my staff, they become more confident. It has also reduced my time needed for micro-managing them.'
		(N-8, Private sector, F, 6 years of experience)
Need for direction, micro-management	13, 14 and 15	'I get the sense that Mongolians want their management to be strong and have a clear direction. They do not want over-involvement and they expect you to know the answers. So, they get on with their job and feel safe that the company is heading in the right direction. They wanted us to behave like bosses, and when we did, the company was so much happier.'
		(N-2, Private sector, F, 5 years of experience)
		'We started up with a very idealistic approach in terms of work environment. We wanted to create a collaborative environment. I learnt that the Western style of communication is probably more indirect and softer. I was criticised for not being strong and blunt. We spent a lot of time listening to staff ideas, but they still wanted us to make the final decisions.'
		(N-2, Private sector, F, 5 years of experience)
		'Although it has been 25 years since the collapse of the planned economy, Mongolia is still very young as far as a market economy is concerned. There are many graduates, but not enough experienced people out there. Therefore, we (non-native managers) are challenged by the lack of negotiation procedure in business deals too.'
		(N-5, Private sector, M, 11 years of experience)
Preference of being directed	16	'I think that Mongols need a fear factor. (sigh) We – Directors do not want to frighten them, but they need it when it comes to accountability and responsibility. Ever since we were pupils at school, we were reprimanded by the teacher and threatened with

being reported to our parents if we did not do our best. So, that mentality of being pushed is reflected in our work ethic when we became employees. Young people today, know their rights, but fail to understand their responsibilities, so we have to pressurise them to make them understand they work for themselves, not for the manager.'

(T-1, Private sector, M, 12 years of experience)

| | 17 and 18 | 'If you follow the formal process, nothing gets done or it will take months. However, if you know the person who is in charge through a personal connection, it gets done within days. It is all about who you know.' |

(T-9, Private sector, M, 12 years of experience)

Importance of building a network with politicians

'It may sound strange, but getting the correct information is difficult here (in Mongolia). If you ask ten people, you will have ten different answers. Even something simple like a monthly report about export or important figures, which you'd expect to see on their website. We need that information for our marketing strategy and I often use my personal network to get an updated report.'

(T-4, Private sector, M, 19 years of experience)

| | 19 and 20 | 'You know, kid, that moment you realise that your entire education and work experience have become worthless . . . (sigh) I was a qualified accountant with nearly 10 years of work experience when my workplace was privatized. After quitting my job, I applied elsewhere and was confident of getting employed immediately. I was wrong and was asked about my knowledge of the international standard of auditing wherever I went. Many of us gave up the profession, and those who managed to stay were given an international auditing handbook with a Mongolian–English dictionary on their first working day.' |

Demand and challenge for introducing international standards

(S-6, Private sector, F, 27 years of experience)

'In 2010, we (the Mongolian Stock Exchange) were the best performing exchange in the world with share prices that increased by 121% within a quarter of the year, and in 2011, we increased our profit by 70%. Obviously, there is still huge interest from investors to work with local

Table 3.2 (continued)

Themes	Examples	Interview quotes
		companies. Many potential investors have high expectations of their local partners and observe existing companies. It means we need to fast-track ourselves into international standards to keep up with the global market. Easy to say, but we are working at it.'
		(T-13, Public sector, M, 16 years of experience)
Practice of poor planning	21 and 22	'You cannot plan in Mongolia for more than four years. Because every four years, the entire business environment and legislation tend to change depending on who (political party) wins the general election. Hence, there is no point of planning for a longer term.'
		(S-8, Private sector, F, 30 years of experience)
		'We tend to make last minute decisions based on current circumstances than foreseen ones. It is frustrating that things get delayed due to external circumstances and others' poor planning practices. It is hard to push things on time here, it really is.'
		(N-2, Private sector, M, 12 years of experience)
Role of central government in planning practice	23	'Sometimes, I think that the local managers' poor planning practice was inherited from the socialist habit of everything being planned by the central government. Planning was not the manager's job, instead, it was instructed by higher authorities. Therefore, I often think it is a new skill to learn by modern managers.'
		(T-12, Private sector, M, 18 years of experience)
Preference of giving and receiving orders by socialist era managers	24	'Negotiation is a very new practice in local business. Personally, I do not think it is possible to negotiate with people from the socialist era because they are reluctant to put all their cards on the table. For younger managers, again it is something we need to learn. I am learning now but good negotiation involves a lot of ground work.'
		(T-11, Private sector, M, 4 years of experience)

25	Preference of open discussion and communication, by younger local and non-native managers	'I could not say that I am really a Mongolian manager, because I am not, as I was educated in Hong Kong and completed my high school in the States. I am honest with my team and our communication is very open. I even share my personal stories and what I am trying to gain from this position. I told them that after three years I will move on to academia and be a media law professor in the future. This kind of information helps them to open up and contribute their opinions.'
		(T-14, Private sector, M, 6 years of experience)
26	Practice of funding 'Home Council' without financial obligation	'I am the Head of Home Council of the province, where my dad came from. Although I was born in the city, I still attend social activities and fund projects. It is my moral duty for my ancestors and father.'
		(T-8, Private sector, M, 26 years of experience)
27	Vista metaphor: spiritual and symbolic relations between humans and landscape for Mongolians	'We grew up in the generation of Marxist philosophy and our office walls and homes were decorated with portraits of political leaders. After the 1990s, portraits of Lenin and Sukhbaatar were replaced by a painting of my birth-place mountain, sculpture of Chinggis Khaan, and *morin huur* (a traditional musical instrument). I have always been proud of my ancestors and believed in the deity of my mountain, even during the socialist time. Of course, democracy then allowed us (Mongols) to show our devotion to our home town and be proud of our ancestors.'
		(S-2, Private sector, M, 35 years of experience)
28	Doing favours for people who share same locality	'It is a common practice to ask a help or do business with people who are from same province as you. I think dealing with people from the same place is easier as you know them well and trust them more. Also, it is often expected to give or receive a favour from your *nutgiin akh* (brother from same county) in Mongolia'.
		(S-8, Private sector, F, 30 years of experience)
29	Importance of building collegial relations	'I worked in India before, and we also used to run staff social gatherings. The difference in Mongolia is, when we have a staff party, nobody brings their family. I do not know whether it is a cultural thing, but at times, it seems people spend more time with their colleagues than their friends and family. Also, companies (foreign) are judged by how many activities they organize for their staff. It is almost seen as a code of conduct here.'
		(N-8, Private sector, F, 6 years of experience)

Table 3.2 (continued)

Themes	Examples	Interview quotes
Inherited habits from socialist legacy	30	'My staff are keen to learn new things and I found that Mongolians are fast learners. However, I often struggle to have open discussions with them during and after training. They are very good listeners, but not good at expressing themselves. I do not know whether it is something to do with how they were brought up or that they still see me as their boss rather than as a tutor who is trying to help them.' (N-1, Private sector, F, 5 years of experience)
Ingrained impact of socialist thinking in contemporary management	31	'The approaches of managers from the public sector are related to their system, not their personality. When I worked for the Ministry, I had to follow the instructions of my Head of Department and the government sector has not altered since the socialist period, and it will take a long time to change.' (S-9, Public sector, M, 21 years of experience)
Convergent influence from current economy in management thinking	32 and 33	'As a business owner you wear many hats to develop business. People progress quickly in our company on merit. We are a very transparent and fluid team who help each other.' (N-2, Private sector, F, 5 years of experience) 'The manager serves people under you. So, I want Mongolians to reach the mid-level (of management) and share some of my responsibilities in the coming years. That is my target for the next two years.' (N-4, Private sector, F, 3 years of experience)
Managing to 'survive', by transitional era managers	34, 35 and 36	'I started my business from a small shop and employed three people. My duties were to keep my business alive and pay salaries on time. The bigger the business grew the more people could be employed.' (T-4, Private sector, M, 19 years of experience) 'We all started from scratch under great economic pressure. Our entire focus was to survive and pay our bills on time. If we made a profit, it was a bonus and it meant staff could have a pay-rise.' (T-6, Private sector, M, 18 years of experience)

		'When we do well (profitable), then I invest more in new products and people. However, we have to stand on our feet by first developing our business.'
		(T-4, Private sector, M, 19 years of experience)
Importance of creating stable business environment	37	'I do remember my grandmother used to say "I was lucky to see two governments in my lifetime". Look at us now. Having 2–3 parliaments within 4 years is common in Mongolia. It is not something we should be proud of. The whole uncertainty of government pushes us (managers) to take an active role in politics to run our businesses because we cannot trust them (politicians).'
		(S-8, Private sector, F, 30 years of experience)
Managing to create an egalitarian value and treating everyone equally, by older managers	38 and 39	'We had the motto of "Each member of a socialist society devotes his skills to building Communism by reaching our work target and looking after each other as one family."'
		(S-3, Public sector, M, 32 years of experience)
		'Management is the relationship between people and as a manager I create one big family, where everyone is looked after. Parents treat their children equally despite their differences and in return, they (children or staff) remain loyal to you.'
		(S-4, Private sector, M, 23 years of experience)
Western business values, by younger managers	40	'I helped many people to reach their dreams, now I want to help myself to reach mine, which is why I started my company. There are a lot of problems and challenges for any new venture in Mongolia. Things like new company registration, or submitting accounts are a simple and straightforward process in the US [United States], but in Mongolia, it can take several months. Then again, there are lots of opportunities to grow and prosper here, so I try to focus on the bigger picture.'
		(T-12, Private sector, F, 8 years of experience)
Influence of younger workforce, who have overseas qualifications and experiences	41 and 42	'Management is building a successful venture with a great product and the right people. I came here to start my own consultancy. So, starting my business is important, but without the right people, it will not happen.'
		(N-2, Private sector, F, 5 years of experience)
		'I am privileged to be appointed to one of the most prestigious posts in the country at such a young age. This chance will happen only in Mongolia. On my first day, I had a meeting with my senior managers, and asked them to prepare project ideas within

75

Table 3.2 (continued)

Themes	Examples	Interview quotes
		a week. After a week, nobody submitted a thing. I am talking about senior staff, not clerks, you know. It was a culture shock for me. Then, I realised that they did not know how to. So, I had to hire skilled people or at least people, who could be trained.'
		(T-5, Private sector, M, 11 years of experience)
Interference of economic authorities in daily managing practices	43	'The government gets too involved in business in Mongolia, and sometimes I think they are trying to introduce a monopoly like during socialism, which is frightening. One example, they just exempted their (state-owned) airline from tax last week. How can other private airlines compete? It is not economic market policy. The reason is that they have personal and economic interests in certain companies and it is in their interest to kill the competition in the market.'
		(T-3, Private sector, M, 18 years of experience)
Negative effects of frequent changes in key laws and legislations in daily managing	44	'I was the Chief Financial Officer for Z for 15 months, which was without a doubt the most frustrating time in my entire career, because of the dysfunctional nature of management, completely dysfunctional. My feeling is that pretty much most of the state-owned enterprises in Mongolia are run by mostly political appointees and very corrupt. They are supposed to be run by people who have strong business knowledge . . . It is all about keeping their political master happy, irrespective of whether the business fails or succeeds.'
		(N-5, Private sector, M, 11 years of experience)
Non-native practitioners' views on developing networks in Mongolia	45	'Mongolia is a much easier-going environment. It is extremely difficult to link with end-users in China. They have too many middlemen and establishing *guanxi* takes a lot of time and effort. It is almost impossible for someone who is travelling for business for a short time. Just after coming here (Mongolia), I was introduced to one of the top business people in Mongolia through one of my friend's contacts. Then that business person linked me to others. Here, people, especially young business people are much friendlier than the Chinese and share their information and network.'
		(N-6, Private sector, M, 3 years of experience)

Note: S = Socialist era; T = Transitional era; N = Non-Mongolian; M = male; F = female.

76

of responsibilities involved in 'looking after' or 'guarding' subordinates outside of the work context by advising them and developing a 'family tie' relationship with colleagues, rooted in notions of the role of guidance by the elders in traditional upbringing. The narratives also indicated a strong influence of social expectations and norms upon the local definitions of a manager, such as having higher qualifications than the subordinates, acting as a role model for them through displaying high moral standards, having outstanding performance in all tasks, and taking on responsibility for developing the business and the employees (e.g., 3 and 4). In addition, all Mongolian managers saw service to their local county as obligatory within the current social customs.

The country's 21 provincial municipalities and their several districts each have a Home Council, or *Nutgiin Zovlol*, a voluntary-run association with the purpose of promoting and developing the local society. Each *Nutgiin Zovlol* relies on support from businesses and individuals who share the same locality. Many accounts indicated that supporting that association, as well as showing respect to their ancestors, are considered to be among managers' duties (e.g., 5 and 6).

The narratives also indicate that becoming a manager is understood in the Mongolian context as 'an ongoing process', as both professional and personal development (e.g., Watson and Harris, 1999; Mintzberg, 1973, 2009; Watson, 2013). Becoming a manager, moreover, was associated with learning new skills or improving one's own expertise through learning-by-doing (e.g., 7 and 8).

Understandings of the notion of 'management'
The participants elaborated on their understandings of the concept of 'management' through discussing a variety of their own practices and experiences of management. All three groups recognized that the socio-economic and political changes continually shape how they understand and approach management. For example, socialist era managers' narratives highlighted their experience of working towards 'building Communism' during the socialist period; whereas transitional era managers stressed the need to generate income when the country entered the free market economy in the 1990s. Consequently, while older practitioners' understanding of management highlighted the importance of 'looking after people', transitional era practitioners referred to management as reactive rather than proactive by repeated references to the concept of 'survival'. In the case of non-native Mongolian managers, their understandings of management highlighted their daily practice of staff and business development, as well as the wider socio-economic issues, such as the need for a qualified workforce and stability of the legal framework in the local

business environment (e.g., 9 and 10). Following from the above, local practitioners' understandings of the notion of management to an extent reflect the traditional management literature that focuses on roles and responsibilities (e.g., Fayol, 1916, 1930; Mintzberg, 1973, 2009), while at the same time also showing affinity with more recent views of management as a practice and process (Mintzberg, 2009; Watson, 2011, 2013; Watson and Harris, 1999).

Mongolian managers' views of managerial roles

All three groups of participants made references to four key roles of managers, understood as: leading; networking; personal development and learning; and decision-making and negotiation. Interestingly, one of the typically considered managerial roles of planning (e.g., Mintzberg, 1973, 2009; Stewart, 1976) was hardly mentioned. Instead, the roles of being a parent, applying fear and pressure, looking after people from the same county and learning by experience emerged as sub-roles discussed by the Mongolian practitioners interviewed.

The first main managerial role highlighted by participants was that of leading, which is one of the most frequently addressed in classical management literature (e.g., Fayol, 1916, 1930; Mintzberg, 1973, 2009). However, the understandings of what this role involves differed between the three cohorts of managers. While the narratives of Mongolian practitioners tended to emphasize a more paternalistic approach characterized by a strong hierarchy, non-Mongolian managers and some younger local managers highlighted the importance of empowerment (e.g., 11 and 12). Furthermore, four sub-roles of parenting, controlling, applying fear or pressure, and empowering employees emerged in participants' perspectives on the role of leading.

In particular, 'parenting' or 'being a parent' was a common phrase amongst Mongolian managers. It referred to creating a situation in the organization whereby the subordinates would feel more content and supported at work as a result of being directed and guided, be it through 'mother-like nurturing' or 'father-like directiveness'. The local paternalistic approach had mixed connotations, linking an obligation to look after descendants or co-workers to practising an autocratic, top-down management approach. A similar understanding of leading as a role which requires the fostering of individuals has been noted in indigenous management literature, for example in relation to African contexts (e.g., Jackson et al., 2008).

All three cohorts of managers acknowledged that they exerted some form of control as part of their leadership approach. Here, socialist era managers emphasized that systematic control over financial and human resources makes effective and successful leadership possible, and leads to the achievement of results. They shared a view that the entire economy worked much better when tighter controls were in place before the transition in 1991. In contrast, non-native Mongolian managers said that they were impelled to control their local colleagues regardless of their personal preference, due to a lack of self-direction and poor performance by the local workforce (e.g., 13, 14 and 15).

The third sub-role that emerged from the narratives consisted of exerting pressure upon subordinates and invoking fear in them as tools to increase productivity, punctuality and/or accountability. While many of the older practitioners justified their use of pressure and fear as a matter of managers' right to be 'respected' and 'listened to', younger Mongolian managers saw pressurizing colleagues as a way of promoting self-accountability and responsibility among their staff. Similarly, non-native Mongolian managers admitted to utilizing pressure to improve punctuality, and suggested that the role of pressurizing arose from their employees' preference for being directed (e.g., 16). At the same time, opposing the idea of leading by control or fear, some non-native and younger Mongolian managers' accounts indicated the importance of empowerment and staff initiatives in their approach to management and leadership.

In addition to the above, networking was identified as one of the main managerial roles in the narratives. It was suggested that practitioners engage in networking in looking after *nutgiin hun* (people from the same county), and use it to access information and achieve results faster. In the indigenous management literature, networking is identified as a set of context-specific practices, rooted in local social and cultural traditions. As described by the managers interviewed, the approach to networking in the Mongolian context is similar to the Chinese concept of *guanxi* (e.g., Tsui, 2004; Yang, 2012), though not identical. Its application is derived from a sense of ancestral lineage and moral duty of the individual – for example, a business manager – to the local community. Social networks in Mongolia stem from four types of relationships: kinship, classmates and co-alumni, co-workers, and *neg nutgiinhan* (people from the same homeland) (Dalaibuyan, 2012). Both younger and older Mongolian managers discussed their networking role as linked with a moral responsibility towards their close circles – such as those originating from the same province, commonly referred to as 'brothers from the same county' – rather than merely in relation to business-related purposes. The narratives suggested that in the local management environment, gaining favourable access in business largely depends on 'who you know'. Accounts of all three cohorts of managers indicated that developing extensive industry networks as well as links with politicians is one of the primary tasks of local management practitioners (e.g., 17 and 18). To manage effectively in Mongolia, and to navigate smoothly through the bureaucratic landscape of local rules and business formalities, it is necessary to develop and cultivate mutual networks of favour exchanges. In this sense, business networking in Mongolia fulfils a role similar to that of *blat* in the context of (post)socialist Russia: a way of taking advantage of informal networks to facilitate and speed up business deals (Ledeneva, 1998, 2009).

Improving one's own skills and supporting staff professional development as a key managerial role was also discussed by the senior managers interviewed. Many listed the rapid economic transition and changes in the business environment as the reasons why they had to improve their computer literacy, test new management methods or become entrepreneurial in business development. Particularly, older managers saw being the head of an organization as being able to guide everyone in the right direction, and meeting the expectation of having all the answers. Hence, they explained that their approach towards learning and development focused on improving their own skills, and they saw it as the biggest challenge in their career. Similarly, transitional era and non-native Mongolian managers repeated the idea that local employees expected the manager to be able to provide answers to all questions and solutions to all problems within the organization. In the view of these two categories of participants, it was important for managers not only to learn and develop new skills themselves, but also to focus on staff development, especially to meet new business demands such as customer orientation and competence in applying internationally recognized accounting and auditing standards (e.g., 19 and 20).

The final managerial role that emerged in the narratives was that of communicating in decision-making and negotiating. Decision-making is considered one of the main roles of managers (e.g., Anderson et al., 2015; Mintzberg, 1973, 2009), and scholars argue that approaches to communicating involved in decision-making vary in different cultures (e.g., Ang et al., 2007; Nishi et al., 2016). The empirical findings suggested that local managers' perspectives on decision-making were influenced mainly by the socio-economic and political context. Accounts of all three cohorts highlighted the impact of political uncertainty on poor planning practices and the need for last-minute decisions. They suggested that long-term planning barely exists in local businesses due to the frequent amendments in key legislation and local parliamentary appointments (e.g., 21 and 22). A few also explained that planning has never been a strength of Mongolian managers, as planning issues used to be dealt with by central government (e.g., 23; see also Yang, 2012).

Furthermore, the empirical findings indicated that negotiating is an emergent role within Mongolian practitioners' understanding of communication.

Participants pointed out that the decision and communication process requires constant negotiation with political and industry partners; an activity that proved particularly challenging for socialist era managers, because under socialism decision-making involved giving and receiving orders rather than engaging in a discussion (e.g., 24). In contrast, transitional era and non-native Mongolian managers tended to express a greater openness towards negotiation and decision-making processes, although they acknowledged that engendering honesty and openness in communication – for example with staff – was a difficult task to accomplish (e.g., 25). Negotiating, then, while an important skill and role of the manager, emerged as a new and challenging competence for Mongolian management practitioners.

Influences on Management within the Mongolian Context

Contextual influencing factors are a well-studied area within cross-cultural management, international business and institutional theories-based approaches to management (e.g., Al Ariss and Sidani, 2016; Jamali and Neville, 2011; Kwon et al., 2016; Ralston et al., 2008 [1997]; Ralston et al., 2015). Existing studies discuss the impact of a range of factors on local management, including culture (e.g., Hofstede, 1984, 2001; House et al., 2004; Schein, 1985, 2010), political and legal institutions (e.g., Holmes et al., 2013; North, 1991; Scott, 2013), and economic ideologies (Deeg and Jackson, 2008; Friel, 2011). Research has tended to address the cultural and institutional aspects separately by focusing on the cultural consequences (e.g., Hofstede, 1984, 2001; House et al., 2004; Schein, 1985, 2010), the macro-level institutional influences (e.g., Holmes et al., 2013; North, 1991; Scott, 2013), or micro-level business-related impacts (e.g., Deeg and Jackson, 2008; Friel, 2011; Morgan, 2007).

Our empirical findings point to a comprehensive set of contextual factors that influence management in Mongolia: from the traditional nomadic culture, to past and present economic ideologies, to societal trends and local politics. The perceived salience of various contextual influences on Mongolian management – and how it is understood – emerged as being related to three temporal phases: before, during and after socialism.

Traditional nomadic culture

In participants' views, management during the pre-socialist period was heavily influenced by nomadic values and ancestral lineage, though such values remain. In particular, the accounts bore numerous references to the 'vista' metaphor of homeland, 'my mountain' or 'birthplace'. Consistent with Wickham-Smith's (2013) explanation, nomadic culture and society can be described as a symbolic relationship between the landscape and the Mongolian people. This relationship was manifested in most native managers' active participation in promoting their home town by funding a Home Council or *Nutgiin Zovlol* (a voluntary association that relies on support from native people) (e.g., 26). Both older and younger Mongolian managers suggested that contributing to the development of their homeland is their moral duty, and intrinsic to the symbolic and spiritual connection between their mountain and themselves (e.g., 27). Furthermore, participants used references to the 'golden thread': a notion representing Mongolians' belief in being connected to their ancestors, history and origins, especially the thirteenth-century ruler Chinggis Khaan and his family tree, which is known as the 'golden lineage' in local history. Participants explained their understanding of favouring *nutgiin hun* in the recruitment process or conducting business with them as their moral duty to the ancestors. Simultaneously, many accounts indicated that senior Mongolian managers perceive their managerial role as a 'guardian' or 'parent' to the younger generation from the same county. Some accounts suggested that being looked after by *nutgiin akh* ('brother from the same county') is an expected social norm among people who share localities. Perceiving a moral obligation towards *nutgiin hun* was common among local practitioners' narratives. Some accounts suggested that their approach was linked to the nomadic concept of sharing trust with people from their neighbourhood. The nomadic society neighbourhood known as *hot ail* (a group of families, who are not necessarily relatives) shared resources and bonded during the seasonal moves. Favouring people from the same county, funding projects for one's home province, or creating an extensive network among people from the same town, was considered acceptable behaviour in the local business context (e.g., 28).

The socialist legacy

Following the influence of culture, the second recurring theme in practitioners' narratives was the influence of the socialist legacy. For example, the effects of a centrally planned economy and inherited habits in relation to planning and communication are still ingrained in Mongolia, according to local practitioners.

The notions of 'employer' and 'employees' first emerged when Mongolia became a socialist country in 1924. During socialism, groups of nomadic families formed collective farms, called *negdel*, supported by a cooperative transport and agricultural system (Humphrey and Sneath, 1999). In urban areas, communist principles and collective ethics were observed in workplace organizations (Dalaibuyan, 2012), and *hamt olon*, a workplace collective, played a key role in social life. The narratives of all three groups of managers in Mongolia suggested that maintaining a good collegial relationship remained one of their key roles (e.g., 29).

Moreover, some practitioners' approaches to leading were reflected by the values of a socialist work code of conduct. During socialism, *darga* (*pl. darguud*) ('masters of the urban landscape') became the power term to describe leaders in collective farms (*negdel*), organizations and institutions (*alban baiguullaga*) (Zimmermann, 2012, p. 84). Some accounts suggested that the expectation of being directed and having decisions made for them by a *darga*-style leader, coupled with a habit of poor self-accountability, remained strong among Mongolian employees (e.g., 30). The *darga* approach to leadership can still be found in Mongolian organizations also because those who used to be junior managers during the socialist era are today's top executives in the private sector or government.

Younger Mongolian and non-native participants emphasized the deeply rooted influence of the socialist legacy in local management despite the growing effect of FDI, the increasing number of foreign firms and graduates with overseas qualifications (e.g., 31). Some narratives touched upon the educational system of Mongolia as part of the remaining socialist legacy in local management. Transitional era managers, who studied for business degrees locally, criticized the irrelevance of the curriculum to their current practice; whereas non-native Mongolian managers observed the incongruity between qualifications and skills in their younger employees.

Western management knowledge and 'market forces' ideology

Empirical findings also indicated strong links between Mongolian management practice and the current market economic conditions. Specifically, the narratives suggested that Western management techniques are becoming more popular due to the demands of working with foreign investors, entering an international market and managing a younger workforce with overseas experience (e.g., 32 and 33).

The accounts of transitional era managers suggested that their approach to management differed from socialist era managers in terms of work ethics, human relations and leadership roles. Younger practitioners' perception of business development and monetary rewards coincided with Linz and Chu's (2013) findings about how younger workforces in transitional economies were driven by individual gain, achievement and results-orientated performance. Many accounts of transitional era managers linked the dramatic economic and social changes to their focus on business development. The participants, many of whom are today's successful business owners and senior managers, started their careers either selling on the black market or establishing family-run small and medium-sized enterprises (SMEs). Consequently, transitional era managers defined their managerial approach and business strategies through an emphasis on survival (e.g., 34, 35 and 36). That contrasted with the older practitioners' view of management as looking after people or promoting a collegial culture.

As with other major transitional economies (e.g., Drahokoupil and Myant, 2015), Mongolia has experienced the expansion of MNCs and the inflow of foreign direct investment. Correspondingly, the narratives indicated that local managers faced both challenges and opportunities due to the local economic growth and the cash flow from FDI. Participants stressed the importance of a stable business environment for attracting more investment (e.g., 37).

Moreover, they acknowledged that one of the main challenges brought about by the current economic situation is that managers are expected to be more innovative and skilful to manage successfully in the competitive environment. In line with this, both younger Mongolian and non-native Mongolian managers highlighted the importance of a reward structure and shared their experiences of linking monetary reward to personal achievement and technical competency. Younger participants saw monetary reward as one of the key motivating factors for their employees, and underlined the importance of individual performance and introducing different approaches to promote competitiveness and individual accountability.

Such views clashed with those of older participants, who considered adapting to the new conventions of competitive behaviour and individual reward orientation as a struggle. They stressed that their understanding of managing and being managed revolved around the egalitarian value of treating everyone equally and promoting morality (e.g., 38 and 39). Conversely, there were many overlaps between younger Mongolian managers' accounts and those of the non-native Mongolian managers: for instance, with respect to leadership, decision-making and staff development. Both groups shared common views on empowerment, motivation, staff training and development, financial reward, as well as on encouraging staff initiative and participation in decision-making. This demonstrates that at least some Mongolian managers have internalized the Western capitalist ideologies and values surrounding the economy and business, as well as management techniques (e.g., 40; see also Brewster et al., 2015; Budhwar et al., 2016; Katz and Darbishire, 2000; Yip et al., 1992).

Importantly, the influence of Western management philosophy was seen as being sustained not only by the presence of MNCs in the country, but also by the changing profile of the Mongolian labour force. The influx of a foreign workforce, and a growing number of graduates who have studied abroad, were highlighted as among the most significant influences on Mongolian management within the past decade. Although the narratives indicated the different challenges of working with a younger workforce, all three groups of Mongolian senior managers acknowledged that employees with overseas experience benefit their organization by meeting the demand for local knowledge and skills, and by having the ability to perform at an international level (e.g., 41 and 42). At the same time, most practitioners expressed the opinion that working with overseas-educated colleagues who tended to be more open in their communication style often meant that they had to amend their own approach. Altogether, the narratives pointed to the development of hybrid approaches and management practices which combined socio-cultural and institutional effects (e.g., Al Ariss and Sidani, 2016; Ralston et al., 2008 [1997]; Ralston et al., 2015). A tendency towards reliance on informal networks, and 'last-minute' planning and decision-making, were results of their nomadic heritage and reliance on the socialist 'centre', whereas the newly arrived capitalist ideals and norms have introduced notions of inter- and intra-organizational competitiveness, as well as working to international accounting and auditing standards.

Evolving financial and political institutions

Beyond the impact of individual and organizational-level values and ideology, the role of evolving institutions in the country came across as particularly powerful influences on how management is understood, how it is put into practice, and what the roles performed by managers should entail. The role of the government and regulatory institutions in establishing a stable business environment is not a new idea in the management and international business literature (e.g., Holmes et al., 2013; Scott, 2013). Institutional theory scholars have also argued that formal institutions established by the government play a key role in promoting stability in the society and economy through laws and legislation (e.g., North, 1991; Scott, 2013). The empirical material has provided evidence of that very same idea with respect to the Mongolian context. All three groups of participants stressed the importance of local government for forming a supportive legal environment for domestic and foreign businesses and investors. Furthermore, some narratives indicated that their daily approach to management was influenced by local economic authorities with respect to their handling of the country's monetary policy and financial regulations (e.g., 43; see also Deeg and Jackson, 2008; Hall and Soskice, 2001; Witt and Redding, 2009).

In addition, the impacts of newly developed financial and economic systems were seen as necessarily mediated by still unstable political processes and institutions. Many practitioners shared their disappointment with the performance of the Mongolian government since 2011, highlighting the negative consequences of frequent amendments in key laws and legislation, which tended to change after each general parliamentary election (e.g., 44). Simultaneously, practitioners drew attention to the fact that poor planning practices in organizations are, at least in part, a consequence of the need to operate under conditions of local political and economic uncertainty. Further, the managers – especially those based in private sector organizations – highlighted the over-involvement of local authorities in pricing strategies, which discouraged competition and the organic growth of businesses in the local environment.

All of the managers interviewed suggested that they are required to take precautionary action due to the pressure of local political institutions. Consequently, most native Mongolian practitioners admitted they were a member of one of the main political parties in Mongolia, took an active interest in local politics, and networked with influential individuals in order to have an impact on the development of new business- and industry-related legislation. While non-native Mongolian managers were not members of political parties in Mongolia, their accounts suggested that securing the presence of influential 'names' in their networking circle was common (e.g., 45). In addition, political involvement was also pursued by Mongolian management practitioners out of a more personal motivation: to take advantage of extensive networking with industry executives and politicians, and to benefit from the increased social status associated with political involvement. It was evident from the narratives that there was a two-way influence between the political and legal institutions, and business practices in Mongolia.

CONCLUSIONS

Understanding Mongolian Management

An awareness of history is essential for building an understanding of Mongolia as a country and Mongolians as people. The discussion presented in this chapter has drawn attention to the importance of understanding a range of influences – such as local history, nomadic cultural heritage, and current socio-economic and political changes – for building a picture of contemporary Mongolian management and management practices. The understandings and practices of management by senior practitioners within the Mongolian context emerge from a unique combination of factors and influences (see Figure 3.1).

At the same time, this chapter has shown that the practices of managing, planning, leading and organizing have existed throughout history with different purposes and names. Before socialism, the understanding and practice of management was focused on livelihood, and was inspired by

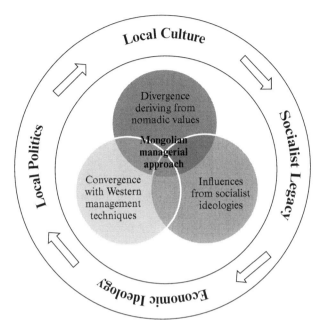

Figure 3.1   The Mongolian approach to management

a traditional paternalistic approach and charismatic leadership. Socialism brought central planning, a collegial culture and regulated working hours, and created autocratic leadership amongst practitioners. The transition from a planned to a free economy in the 1990s brought rapid change: the terms 'management' and 'managers' arrived for the first time in Mongolia, along with privatization, socio-political reforms, and freedom of speech and movement. All these changes have had an impact on management in the Mongolian context. The study underpinning this chapter provides an important contribution to research into management within transitional contexts, due to Mongolia's ongoing economic growth and its emerging role within the global political arena.

Implications for Managers

The empirical material has highlighted the existence of tensions to which managers at different levels and of different profiles are exposed on a daily basis. On the one hand, younger Mongolian managers have highlighted the benefits of familiarizing themselves with Western management techniques and experimenting with new methods. On the other hand, the inherited socialist era approaches to working still actively influence management and business practice in Mongolia. Furthermore, as Mongolian managers are constantly being challenged to keep abreast of cultural and institutional changes, there is an inclination among local practitioners to lean towards managing in a reactive manner.

The analysis presented in this chapter allows drawing a number of implications for managers and other organizational stakeholders, whether native or non-native Mongolian. The empirical material has provided a plethora of examples evidencing the challenges of managing in Mongolia, not least due to the underlying dynamics of local political, economic and socio-cultural changes that contribute to its complex nature. While the environmental uncertainties are inherently difficult to address, Mongolian practitioners would benefit from systematic approaches to problem-solving and analysis. The ad hoc, last-minute decisions that are common in Mongolian organizations at present bring the danger of overlooking significant trends and phenomena affecting mid- to long-term business activities. Adopting more structured ways of appraising the current situation would enable managers to shift to less reactive and chaotic approaches to practising management and making decisions.

Further, the study has demonstrated that there are significant differences in approaches to communication between older and younger managers, as well as managers who studied overseas and those who had graduated from local universities. The differences between socialist and transitional era managers are particularly complex. Socialist era managers tend to adopt a 'top to bottom' approach to communication, and exhibit a preference for hierarchical decision-making. By contrast, younger managers are more likely to adopt a two-way communication style and to encourage employees' participation in decision-making. In order to develop successful collaboration between potential and existing business partners in Mongolia as well as foreign firms, it is essential to establish effective communication between different generations of Mongolian managers.

The empirical findings suggest that non-native Mongolian managers' knowledge about the local management practices is, in general, limited due to the lack of studies addressing the Mongolian management context. Considering the significant influence of both past and present contextual factors on management in Mongolia, it is therefore important for non-native managers to familiarize themselves with locally meaningful knowledge, including the nomadic culture and traditions, and the way in which these influence ways of working and managing in contemporary Mongolia. Understanding locally meaningful constructs will help non-native managers to develop a better understanding and rapport with their local colleagues and business partners.

Non-native practitioners should also be aware of the continuing influence of the legacy of socialism on management in Mongolia. The socialist approach to managing and organizing still manifests itself in, for example, the bureaucratic processes associated with registering and conducting business, and in top-down autocratic approaches to leading within organizations, especially where leadership roles are fulfilled by managers who started their careers during the socialist era. Understanding the present impacts of socialism on management will enable non-native managers to navigate more effectively through the local institutional and business landscape.

In addition, the empirical material has shown a disparity between the expectations of native and non-native Mongolian managers in relation to work performance, competence and self-initiative. In particular, non-native participants expressed their frustration over the lack of professional competence locally. It is important for both native and non-native Mongolian managers to be conscious of the multifaceted challenges faced by all stakeholders within the turbulent Mongolian economy, and to address the development of skills constructively and collaboratively, towards the implementation of international accounting and auditing standards, as well as advanced technologies in the Mongolian context.

Implications for Political Authorities

There is a need for political institutions in Mongolia to focus on stabilizing the local business environment by ensuring consistency in the local parliament and legal frameworks. It is also important for the local government to work towards improving the dialogue and communication with businesses and industry leaders to provide more support to SMEs and the private sector. Within the last ten years the private sector has become the largest employer and contributor to the local economy (National Statistical Office, 2016). However, as the empirical material has indicated, there is very limited support and cooperation from local government for Mongolian organizations. By engaging in closer relations with industry leaders, government ministers will gain a better understanding about the needs and demands of the business environment. Overall, the mutual understanding and collaboration between government and businesses will help formal institutions create a more supportive business environment, as well as contribute to the local economy.

REFERENCES

Al Ariss, A. and Y. Sidani (2016), 'Divergence, convergence, or crossvergence in international human resource management', *Human Resource Management Review*, 26 (4), 283–284.

Alexander, C., V. Buchli and C. Humphrey (2007), *Urban Life in Post-Soviet Asia*, London: UCL.

Anderson, D.R., D.J. Sweeney, T.A. Williams, J.D. Camm and J.J. Cochran (2015), *An Introduction to Management Science: Quantitative Approaches to Decision Making*, Boston, MA: Cengage Learning.

Ang, S., L. Van Dyne, C. Koh, K.Y. Ng, K.J. Templer, C. Tay and N.A. Chandrasekar (2007), 'Cultural intelligence: its measurement and effects on cultural judgment and decision making, cultural adaptation and task performance', *Management and Organization Review*, 3 (3), 335–371.

Baasanjav, U. (2002), 'The digital divide in the Gobi Desert: spatiality, the national identity collapse and a language gap', *Online Journal of Space Communication*, 5. Available at: http://satjournal. tcom.ohiou.edu/pdf/issue05/undrahbuyan.pdf (accessed 2 September 2014).

Bayliss, P. and P. Dillon (2010), 'Cosmologies and lifestyles: a cultural ecological framework and its implications for education systems', *Anthropological Journal of European Cultures*, 19, 7–21.

Brewster, C., W. Mayrhofer and F.L. Cooke (2015), 'Convergence, divergence and diffusion of HRM in emerging markets', in Frank Horwitz and Pawan Budhwar (eds), *Handbook of Human Resource Management in Emerging Markets*, Cheltenham, UK and Northampton, MA, USA: Edward Elgar Publishing, pp. 451–469.

Bruun, O. and L. Narangoa (2011), *Mongols from Country to City: Floating Boundaries, Pastoralism and City Life in the Mongol Lands*, The University of Michigan: NIAS Press.

Budhwar, P.S., A. Varma and C. Patel (2016), 'Convergence–divergence of HRM in the Asia-Pacific: context-specific analysis and future research agenda', *Human Resource Management Review*, 26 (4), 311–326.

Buxbaum, E. (2004), 'Finding the door in the mirage: the politics of cultural change in Mongolia', SIT Digital Collections, *ISP Collection*. Available at: http://digitalcollections.sit.edu/isp_collection/494/ (accessed 19 April 2017).

Cassell, C. and G. Symon (2011), 'Assessing "good" qualitative research in the work psychology field: a narrative analysis', *Journal of Occupational and Organizational Psychology*, 84 (4), 633–650.

Constitution of Mongolia (1992), *The Constitution of Mongolia*, Ulaanbaatar: Parliament of Mongolia

Czarniawska, B. (1998), *A Narrative Approach to Organization Studies*, Thousand Oaks, CA: SAGE Publications.

Dalaibuyan, B. (2012), 'Formal and informal networks in post-socialist Mongolia: access, uses, and inequalities', in Julien Dierkes (ed.), *Change in Democratic Mongolia: Social Relations, Health, Mobile Pastoralism, and Mining*, Leiden: Brill Press, pp. 31–54.

Deeg, R.E. and G. Jackson (2008), 'How many varieties of capitalism? From institutional diversity to the politics of change', *Review of International Political Economy*, 15 (4), 679–708.

Diener, A.C. (2011), 'Will new mobilities beget new (im) mobilities? Prospects for change resulting from Mongolia's Trans-State Highway', in Stanley D. Brunn (ed.), *Engineering Earth*, Netherlands: Springer, pp. 627–641.

Diener, A.C. and J. Hagen (2013), 'From socialist to post-socialist cities: narrating the nation through urban space', *Nationalities Papers – The Journal of Nationalism and Ethnicity*, 41 (4), 487–514.

Drahokoupil, J. and M. Myant (2015), 'Putting comparative capitalisms research in its place: varieties of capitalism in transition economies', in Matthias Ebenau, Ian Bruff and Christian May (eds), *New Directions in Comparative Capitalisms Research*, Basingstoke, UK and New York, USA: Palgrave Macmillan, pp. 155–171.

Eyler-Driscoll, S. (2013), *Pits and the Pendulum Mining Leaders Mongolia*, 1st edn, Ulaanbaatar: Freestone Publishing.

Fayol, H. (1916), 'General principles of management', *Classics of Organization Theory*, 2, 15.

Fayol, H. (1930), *Industrial and General Administration*, London: Sir Isaac Pitman & Sons.

Feldman, M.S., K. Sköldberg, R.N. Brown and D. Horner (2004), 'Making sense of stories: a rhetorical approach to narrative analysis', *Journal of Public Administration Research and Theory*, 14 (2), 147–170.

Friel, D. (2011), 'Forging a comparative institutional advantage in Argentina: implications for theory and praxis', *Human Relations*, 64 (4), 553–572.

Gertsen, M.C. and A.-M. Søderberg (2011), 'Intercultural collaboration stories: on narrative inquiry and analysis as tools for research in international business', *Journal of International Business Studies*, 42 (6), 787–804.

Glesne, C. (2011), *Becoming Qualitative Researchers: An Introduction*, Boston, MA: Pearson.

Hall, P.A. and D. Soskice (2001), *Varieties of Capitalism: The Institutional Foundations of Comparative Advantage*, Oxford: Oxford University Press.

Hofstede, G. (1984), 'Hofstede's culture dimensions: an independent validation using Rokeach's value survey', *Journal of Cross-Cultural Psychology*, 15 (4), 417–433.

Hofstede, G. (2001), *Culture's Consequences: Comparing Values, Behaviors, Institutions, and Organizations Across Nations*, Thousand Oaks, CA, USA and London, UK: SAGE Publications.

Holmes, R.M., T. Miller, M.A. Hitt and M.P. Salmador (2013), 'The interrelationships among informal institutions, formal institutions, and inward foreign direct investment', *Journal of Management*, 39 (2), 531–566.

House, R.J., P.J. Hanges, M. Javidan, P.W. Dorfman and V. Gupta (2004), *Culture, Leadership, and Organizations: The GLOBE Study of 62 Societies*, Thousand Oaks, CA: SAGE Publications.

Humphrey, C. (2002), *The Unmaking of Soviet Life: Everyday Economies After Socialism*, Ithaca, NY, USA and London, UK: Cornell University Press.

Humphrey, C. and D. Sneath (1996), *Pastoralism and Institutional Change in Inner Asia: Comparative Perspectives from the MECCIA Research Project*, Overseas Development Institute, Pastoral Development Network, Vol 39 (b).

Humphrey, C. and D. Sneath (1999), *The End of Nomadism? Society, State, and the Environment in Inner Asia*, Durham, NC: Duke University Press.

Jackson, T., K. Amaeshi and S. Yavuz (2008), 'Untangling African indigenous management: multiple influences on the success of SMEs in Kenya', *Journal of World Business*, 43 (4), 400–416.

Jamali, D. and B. Neville (2011), 'Convergence versus divergence of CSR in developing countries: an embedded multi-layered institutional lens', *Journal of Business Ethics*, 102 (4), 599–621.

Katz, H.C. and O.R. Darbishire (2000), *Converging Divergences: Worldwide Changes in Employment Systems*, Ithaca, NY: Cornell University Press.

Kiblitskaya, M. (2000), 'Once we were kings: male experiences of loss of status at work in post-communist Russia', in Sarah Ashwin (ed.), *Gender, State and Society in Soviet and Post-Soviet Russia*, Abingdon: Routledge, pp. 90–104.

Kohn, M. (2016), 'The world's worst currency is in a record slide. Available at: https://www.bloomberg.com/news/articles/2016-08-16/world-s-worst-currency-in-record-slide-as-mongolia-sees-crisis (accessed 3 September 2016).

Kwon, B., E. Farndale and J.G. Park (2016), 'Employee voice and work engagement: macro, meso, and micro-level drivers of convergence?', *Human Resource Management Review*, 26 (4), 327–337.

Ledeneva, A.V. (1998), *Russia's Economy of Favours: Blat, Networking, and Informal Exchanges*, New York: Cambridge University Press.

Ledeneva, A.V. (2009), 'From Russia with blat: can informal networks help modernize Russia?', *Social Research*, 76 (1), 257–288.

Linz, S. J. and Y.-W. Chu (2013), 'Weber, Marx, and work values: evidence from transition economies', *Economic Systems*, 37 (3), 431–448.

MAD Mongolia Newswire (2016), 'ASEM's significance to Mongolia'. Available at: http://mad-intelligence.com/asems-significance-to-mongolia/ (accessed 25 March 2016).

Max Group (2016), Holiday Inn Ulaanbaatar. Available at: http://www.maxgroup.mn/eng/pages/ (accessed 4 January 2015).

Miles, M.B., A.M. Huberman and J. Saldaña (2013), *Qualitative Data Analysis: A Methods Sourcebook*, Thousand Oaks, CA: SAGE Publications.

Ministry of Economy (2012a), 'Registered FDI company by countries', *Economy*, 30 June, Ulaanbaatar: Ministry of Economic Development.

Ministry of Economy (2012b), 'Registered FDI company by sector', *Economy*, 30 June, Ulaanbaatar: Ministry of Economic Development.

Ministry of Education (2015), 'Statistic information about graduates for the academic year of 2015–2016', *Committee*, Ulaanbaatar: Ministry of Education, Culture and Science of Mongolia.

Mintzberg, H. (1973), *The Nature of Managerial Work*, New York, USA and London, UK: Harper & Row.

Mintzberg, H. (2009), *Managing*, San Francisco, CA: Berrett-Koehler Publishers.

Mongolian Economic Forum (2014). 'The economic strategy of Mongolia'. Available at: http://meforum.mn/4 (accessed November 18 2014).

Morgan, K. (2007), 'The learning region: institutions, innovation and regional renewal', *Regional Studies*, 41, S147–S159.

Murrell, C.N.a.P. (2012), 'Prosperity in depth: Mongolia, the paradox of riches', Global Transitions Prosperity Studies. Available at: http://www.li.com/docs/default-document-library/prosperity-in-depth-the-paradox-of-riches.pdf (accessed 8 August 2013).

National Statistical Office (2015), *Yearly Report on Population of Mongolia and Well-being*, Ulaanbaatar: National Statistical Office, Mongolia.

National Statistical Office (2016), Information of Local Economy (First Quarter 2016). Ulaanbaatar: National Statistical Office of Mongolia. Available at http://www.nso.mn/content/1424#.WGN_ztKLSpo (Accessed 5 October 2016).

Nishi, A., N.A. Christakis and D.G. Rand (2016), 'Cooperation, decision time, and culture: online experiments with American and Indian participants', *PLoS ONE*, 12 (2): e0171252. Available at: https://doi.org/10.1371/journal.pone.0171252 (accessed 19 April 2017).

North, D.C. (1991), 'Institutions, ideology, and economic performance', *Cato Journal*, 11, 477–488.

Oyu Tolgoi, L. (2013), Official statement of Oyu Tolgoi LLC in relation to information, data and facts related to Oyu Tolgoi discussed during open session of the State Great Khural dated 1 February, 2013. Ulaanbaatar: Rio Tinto.

Patton, M.Q. (2002), 'Qualitative interviewing', in Michael Quinn Patton, *Qualitative Research and Evaluation Methods*, 3rd edn, Thousand Oaks, CA: SAGE Publications, pp. 344–347.

Ralston, D.A., C.P. Egri, C.M. Karam, et al. (2015), 'The triple-bottom-line of corporate responsibility: assessing the attitudes of present and future business professionals across the BRICs', *Asia Pacific Journal of Management*, 32 (1), 145–179.

Ralston, D.A., D.H. Holt, R.H. Terpstra and Y. Kai-Cheng (2008 [1997]), 'The impact of national culture and economic ideology on managerial work values: a study of the United States, Russia, Japan, and China', *Journal of International Business Studies*, 39 (1), 8–26.

Riessman, C.K. and L. Quinney (2005), 'Narrative in social work: a critical review', *Qualitative Social Work*, 4 (4), 391–412.

Schein, E.H. (1985), 'Defining organizational culture', *Classics of Organization Theory*, 3, 490–502.

Schein, E.H. (2010), *Organizational Culture and Leadership*, 4th edn, San Francisco, CA: John Wiley & Sons.

Scott, W.R. (2013), *Institutions and Organizations: Ideas, Interests, and Identities*, Stanford University: SAGE Publications.

Siemieńska, R. (1994), 'Women in the period of systemic changes in Poland', *Journal of Women's History*, 5 (3), 70–90.

State Hural of Mongolia (2016), 'The results of the 2016 election of the State Great Hural (Parliament) of Mongolia', in *Affairs*, State Hural (Parliament).

Stewart, R. (1976), *Contrast in Management: A Study of Different Types of Managers' Jobs, their Demands and Choices*, Maidenhead: McGraw-Hill.

Tsui, A. (2004), 'Contributing to global management knowledge: a case for high quality indigenous research', *Asia Pacific Journal of Management*, 21 (4), 491–513.

United Nations (2016), *Mongolia and the United Nations*. Available at: https://www.un.int/mongolia/mongolia/mongolia-and-united-nations-0 (accessed 5 March 2016).

Watson, T.J. (2011), 'Ethnography, reality, and truth: the vital need for studies of "how things work" in organizations and management', *Journal of Management Studies*, 48, 202–217.

Watson, T.J. (2013), 'Entrepreneurial action and the Euro-American social science tradition: pragmatism, realism and looking beyond "the entrepreneur"', *Entrepreneurship and Regional Development*, 25 (1/2), 16–33.

Watson, T. and P. Harris (1999), *The Emergent Manager*, Thousand Oaks, CA, USA and London, UK: SAGE.

Wickham-Smith, S. (2013), *The Interrelationship of Humans and the Mongol Landscape in G. Mend-Ooyo's Altan Ovoo*, Lewiston, NY: Edwin Mellen Press.

Witt, M.A. and G. Redding (2009), 'Culture, meaning, and institutions: executive rationale in Germany and Japan', *Journal of International Business Studies*, 40 (5), 859–885.

Woldu, H.G., P.S. Budhwar and C. Parkes (2006), 'A cross-national comparison of cultural value orientations of Indian, Polish, Russian and American employees', *International Journal of Human Resource Management*, 17 (6), 1076–1094.

World Bank (2013), 'Mongolia economic update'. Available at: http://www. worldbank.org/content/dam/Worldbank/document/EAP/Mongolia/MQU_ April_2013_en.pdf (accessed 26 February 2015).

World Bank (2014), 'Mongolia economic update – June 2014'. Available at: http:// www.worldbank.org/en/news/feature/2014/07/03/mongolia-economic-update-july-2014. (accessed 19 April 2017).

Yang, B. (2012), 'Confucianism, socialism, and capitalism: a comparison of cultural ideologies and implied managerial philosophies and practices in the P.R. China', *Human Resource Management Review*, 22 (3), 165–178.

Yip, G.S., P.M. Loewe and M.Y. Yoshino (1992), 'How to take your company to the global market', in Franklin R. Root and Kanokart Visudtibhan (eds), *International Strategic Management: Challenges and Opportunities*, Abingdon, UK and New York, USA: Frank Cass & Company, pp. 99–119.

Zimmermann, A.E. (2012), 'Local leaders between obligation and corruption: state workplaces, the discourse of "moral decay", and "eating money" in the Mongolian province', in Julien Dierkes (ed.), *Change in Democratic Mongolia: Social Relations, Health, Mobile Pastoralism, and Mining*, Leiden: Brill Press, pp. 83–109.

4. Political risk, political instability and the transitional periphery in the age of global uncertainty

Ali Resul Usul

INTRODUCTION

The world's politics and economy have already become so complicated, interdependent and interconnected that social scientists in general have been in desperate need to develop more sophisticated methods of a strong interdisciplinary nature to understand and explain social, political or economic affairs in the current world scene. The discussions on political risk, which is 'officially' in the domain of the discipline of international business studies, and its strong relationship with the disciplines of political science, international relations and conflict studies, serve as a perfect example of the need for more sophistication in this regard, requiring a real synergy among the disciplines and sub-disciplines just mentioned.

As a political scientist, when I started my research on political risk and related concepts I realized, first, that the academic literature on political risk is epistemologically and methodologically so diverse as to render the field as 'pre-theory'; and second, that the literature naturally borrows heavily from the relevant literature in political science and international politics, and sometimes conflict studies. In other words, the very nature of political risk forces studies in this field to have a more interdisciplinary character. Nonetheless, it would not be easy to argue that the studies of political risk are well-developed in the conceptual and methodological senses, thus more academic studies are absolutely necessary to make the field more comprehensive, predictive, analytic and conceptually stronger.

A few studies strive to combine the concepts and methodologies of politics and international relations, business studies and economics, to understand the interrelationship between the political world and the economic and business world. One of the main difficulties in this regard is that it is naturally not an easy task to combine or synthesize different disciplines. In addition, contrary to other types of risk in the business world, it seems that political risk, as a fuzzy concept, has been relatively neglected. There are also not enough academic studies on the application of political risk to the area of the 'transitional periphery' that this chapter focuses on. In this chapter, the concept of political risk is re-evaluated in a multidisciplinary manner that connects political risk with political stability/instability. Then, the chapter proceeds to discuss theoretical and conceptual findings within the context of some countries from the transitional periphery.

Political Risk as an Ambiguous Concept

Bremmer and Keat (2010), in their book, *The Fat Tail: The Power of Political Knowledge in an Uncertain World*, which can be considered as an attempt to integrate the findings of politics and international relations with business studies, underline three basic reasons for the neglect of political risk, among other types of risks: first, it is too complex to be easily explained; second, 'risk managers' encounter enormous difficulties in putting political risks into quantitative forms; and third, no regulatory or legal requirements are necessary for managing political risk, contrary to financial or operational risk.

Indeed, political risk is not as quantifiable or 'mappable' in the same way as other financial risks (Bremmer and Keat, 2010, p. 23). Similarly, the American Institute of Certified Public Accountants (AICPA) demonstrated that 84 per cent of American firms did not formally integrate social and political risks into their investment decisions, because of the reasons mentioned above (Bekefi and Epstein, 2008, p. 33).

Researchers studying the nature of political risk, in addition to methodological problems, do not even agree on the definition of the concept. Sottilotta, in her recent book, admits that 'conceptual confusion' continues to affect the literature on political risk in international business and political science despite several decades of scholarly endeavours (Sottilotta, 2017, p. 18). According to Jarvis, 'defining political risk proves an elusive task if approached as a deductive-typological exercise, most obviously because its genealogy is discursive, its epistemology situated between disciplines . . . and because the generative agents of political risk are heterogeneous' (Jarvis, 2008, p. 1). Baas (2010, p. 137) also highlights this point: 'there is neither a generally accepted definition of political risk nor any widely accepted methodologies to evaluate it'. Even some researchers have serious doubt about the term and its usefulness. Kobrin (1979, p. 480), for instance, finds the term conceptually and operationally problematic.

Minimalist and Maximalist Definition of Political Risk

When analysing the literature on political risk, a minimalist and maximalist definitions come to the fore in almost all discussions of the definition of a political concept. Researchers who stick to the minimalist definition generally would like to restrict the conceptual territory to the realm of business, and not extend the borders to include local, national and international politics. On the other hand, the maximalist school, drawing heavily from the academic methodology and concepts of political science and international politics, attempts to develop more sophisticated and comprehensive quantitative and qualitative methods to, first, understand and explain the phenomena; and second, sometimes to forecast the domestic, regional or international developments that can potentially generate a risky environment for companies operating in the international arena.

Kobrin, perhaps the best example of strict minimalism, was against the stretching of the concept to the political and social conditions within the environmental context. For Kobrin, stretching the concept to cover other social, economic and political variables adds little to the understanding of political risk. Thus, the true definition of political risk, according to him, refers to 'governmental or sovereign interference with business operations' in negative ways (Kobrin, 1982, p. 32). For Kobrin, if there is any conceptual stretching of the concept to include political instability, the result could be misleading because 'political instability may not result in managerial contingencies and contingencies certainly arise in the absence of instability', and therefore political risk should not be identified with political instability (Kobrin, 1982, p. 36). He asked the question, 'when does political instability result in increased investment risk?', and answered that, 'the most important means by which instability or conflict affects the firm is not direct threats such as plant bombings, kidnapping, or even the deterioration of the social and economic infrastructure, but rather potential changes in government policy' (Kobrin, 1978, p. 115).

However, the extended or maximalist version of political risk may include many other variables in addition to what Kobrin stated. Howell's definition of political risk, as a good example of maximalism, refers to ten categories of political risk: 'inconvertibility' or transfer risk; expropriation or nationalization; civil strife; war; terrorism; sea piracy; 'contact repudiation' (breach of contract); 'negative government actions'; 'losses from process deterioration' (which refers to corruption, bribery and an inefficient judicial system); and losses from event intervention (refers to 'a loss that results from some event that is political in its nature or source, while not being a result of a known government decision' (Howell, 2014, p. 307).

Taking into account all discussions on political risk, perhaps it would be better to differentiate three kinds of political risk in accordance with the basic approaches to the notion. One type involves classical and conventional understanding of the concept, which includes confiscations, contact repudiation, currency inconvertibility, discriminatory taxation, embargo, 'creeping expropriation' and nationalization. This is the classical, convention political risk group, which refers to the negative conditions originated from the governmental actions on particular firms. Second, political risks that are associated with the political, social and economic conditions of the country where foreign companies invest may include civil strife, variables of political instability, or efficiency of the state apparatus. The third type refers to the geopolitical risks, such as war risk. In other words, 'any changes in the political environment that may adversely affect the value of the firm's business activities' could be classified within the category of political risk (Griffen and Pustay, 1998, p. 209). As Czinkota et al. (2000, p. 107) put it, political risk categorically includes other events caused by factors outside the control of governments. Bouchet, Clark and Groslamber even differentiate political risk from 'governmental policy risk' (such as expropriation) and political risk involving potential and actual changes in the system (civil strife, revolution or war, for example; or changes in political regimes) that 'may be disruptive to the business environment' (cited in Howell, 2014, p. 307).

The definition of political risk is connected to the fact of how the political risk is assessed; in other words, to political risk assessment, which refers to 'measurement, a probability measure (into the future) that acts as warning of level of threat' (Howell, 2014, p. 310). According to Howell, political risk assessment involves two stages or phases: the measurement of the current level, and expert judgement of a regression projection into the future. Even he differentiates political risk assessment from political risk analysis; the second refers to origins and reasons of the risks or threats. Political risk assessment currently not only deals with the identification and assessment of political risk for companies abroad, but also the discipline has started to concentrate on tools and methods to manage or mitigate political risk (Hough et al., 2008).

Thus, governmental or non-governmental agencies (such as the PRS Group, headquartered in New York) dealing with the political risk assessment (insurance companies as well) render the minimalist or 'government decision-making' approaches the backbone of their system; and other governmental assessment organizations (Export Development Canada, EDC, for example) and non-governmental assessment organizations – Business Environment Risk Intelligence (BERI), the International Country Risk Guide (ICRG) and the Economist Intelligence Unit (EIU), for example –

take into consideration not only the issues related to governmental decision-making problems, but also the 'underlying attributes' (the nature of political regimes, fractionalization and other variables associated with political instability) which, in Howell's words, are connected to the concept of political risk.

The PRS Group utilizes the Coplin–O'Leary Country Risk Rating System, which is the methodology designed by Professors Coplin and O'Leary. They define 11 types of governmental intervention that may adversely affect the business environment. However, the methodology does not normally investigate the underlying causal factors. In addition to the PRS Group, the 'Euromoney model' focuses in general on the risk of bad debt for goods and services that companies provide (Howell, 2014, p. 309).

Other political risk assessment models basically incorporate 'underlying attribute configuration' into their political risk assessments. The ICRG (within the PRS Group), BERI and EIU are examples of the commercial institutions of political risk assessment that employ an extended under-standing of political risk in their assessments. For example, contrary to the PRS Group, the ICRG (though they are within the same PRS Group) political risk assessment components include government stability, socio-economic conditions, investment profile, internal conflict, external conflict, corruption, military in politics, religious tensions, law and order, ethnic tensions, democratic accountability and bureaucracy quality, though what data its staff employ, and 'how it transforms that data into index ratings', is not transparent (Yackee, 2014, p. 484).

Howell classifies 14 'key political risk assessments' into 33 'attribute variables' and 11 'decision variables'. Thirteen models of the political risk assessments incorporate the attributions, and these are classified into three categories. First, external factors involve, for example, influence of major powers, negative regional influences, international war and international economic alliances. Second, the nature of government and politics includes, for example, the nature of politics, stability, authoritari-anism, legitimacy, political parties, political opposition forces, staleness, military involved, religion in politics, corruption, regulatory investment environment, judicial legal system and political intrusion on economic management. And third, 'societal character' includes, for example, ethnic tension, socio-economic condition, domestic violence, attitudes toward foreigners, domestic economic problems and culture. The level of democracy and the fractionalization in a country, for example, are among the variables that the assessments models, such as BERI, ICRG and EIU, incorporate.

Political Risk Assessment and Political Stability/Instability

One of the most interesting dimensions of the studies of political risk assessments is that the bulk of those assessments depend largely upon the discussions on political stability/instability and its components. The question of to what extent a political regime in a state is stable and will continue to be stable has become the central point in the studies of the political risk assessment institutions, in addition to the conventional risks, such as 'creeping expropriation' and nationalization, or restrictions on money transfer. For example, in addition to the private political risk assessment organizations mentioned above, the Canadian governmental organization EDC's 'Overall Risk Score' includes a 'Political-Polity Stability Filter Score' and 'Country Level Factors' in its risk analysis.

One basic question to which all these institutions attempt to find an answer is how it is possible to measure the notion and variables of political stability/instability, and to predict any negative condition that can be considered before any possible serious losses. What it is possible to observe in this regard is that though, from time to time, the business literature appraises the tools and methods of political science for the purposes of more comprehensive and robust assessments, new studies are needed to create a real synergy between different disciplines for more effective and vigorous analysis and prediction.

When the notion of political risk and political risk assessment or analysis stretches its conceptual borders to include the question of political stability/instability (civil strife, and so on), a popular but still mysterious area of investigation appears: how is it possible to understand the nature of stable polities in the world, and thus how is it possible to predict any deterioration in the stability in the states that might be necessary not only for statecraft but also for business people and companies, in particular those that invest in 'unstable' parts of the world?

As already stated, the extended definition of political risk is associated with discussions of political stability/instability. In other words, global or foreign companies need to know the level of political stability in the countries where they invest. There exist many different indexes to measure – directly or indirectly – the extent of political stability/instability in states, which are prepared by the centres in universities (Carlton University and George Mason University, for example), prestigious global think tanks (the Brookings Institution), foundations (the Bertelsmann Stiftung Foundation and the Fund for Peace), international governmental organizations (the World Bank for example), and business consulting companies (Eurasia Group and EUI).

Though the notion of political stability/instability has always been at the centre of discussions in politics, academic studies on the nature of

Table 4.1   Key political risk assessment organizations and political stability/instability indexes

Key political risk assessment organizations	Key political stability/instability assessment indexes

The PRS Group
   International Country Risk Guide
 	
   Political Risk Services
	Political Stability Index, EIU
	Worldwide Governance Indicators, World Bank
	State Fragility Index, Center for Systemic Peace; Center of Global Policy, George Mason University

Business Environment Risk Intelligence (BERI)
   Political Risk Index
   Operational Risk Index
	Country Indicators for Foreign Policy (CIFP), Carleton University
	Failed State Index, Fund for Peace
	Peace and Conflict Instability Ledger (Risk of Future Instability), Center for International Development and Conflict Management, University of Maryland

Economist Intelligence Unit Moody's Investor Services Control Risks Group Economists' Method – 1986 S.J. Rundt & Associates Standard & Poor's Rating Group Eurasia Group Chase – 1988 IHS Energy Group Euromoney	Index of State Weakness in the Developing World, the Brookings Institution Global Political Risk Index, Eurasia Group Corruption Perception Index Bertelmann Transformational Index

Source: Adapted from Howell (2014: 308–315).

political stability are surprisingly underdeveloped. Leon Hurwitz once differentiated five different forms of political stability: (1) the absence of violence; (2) governmental longevity and duration; (3) the existence of a legitimate constitutional regime; (4) the absence of structural change; and (5) a multifaceted societal attribute (Hurwitz, 1973, p. 449). Although Hurwitz's definition of political stability is quite ambiguous and undeveloped, as discussed by Margolis (2010), it seems that the current popular understanding of political stability explicitly or implicitly draws significant inspiration from Hurwitz's study. Thus, the popular understanding of political stability often refers to the attributions of 'absence of violence', 'absence of structural change' (by, for example, a revolution), 'absence of control' (the state's inability to control its territory), and 'state functionality' (the degree to which a state can fulfil its responsibilities) to prove stable character of a polity (Margolis, 2010, p. 326). Margolis and some other researchers think that Hurwitz's definition is more Eurocentric and place much importance on the strong state tradition in the Western world. Similar criticisms are also reflected in the literature on 'state failure' discussed below.

The changing dynamics of the perception of regional and international threats in the aftermath of the end of the Cold War, and in particular the post-9/11 period, started to change the discussion of political stability to a discussion of 'state failure', which began to be considered the fundamental new security consideration in the new world (dis)order. In fact, the first academic usage of the term of 'failed state' goes back to 1993, when the relevant article appeared in *Foreign Policy*, penned by Helman and Ratner. It was defined as 'a disturbing new phenomenon' in world politics: 'From Haiti in the Western Hemisphere to the remnants of Yugoslavia in Europe, from Somalia, Sudan and Liberia in Africa to Cambodia in Southeast Asia, a disturbing new phenomenon is emerging: the failed nation-state, utterly incapable of sustaining itself a member of the international community' (Helman and Ratner, 1993, p. 3). In the authors' mind, the basic characteristics of the failed state covered the attributes of serious political instability, civil strife and grave human rights violations. However, the focus in this and similar works has always been on the nature of the 'state-ness'. The nation-states were under great pressure in the developing parts of the world, which created a real danger to the architecture of global security. This apocalyptic view of the political future of the world was academically backed by Zartman's study titled *Collapsed States*. For Zartman, the collapsed state is a new phenomenon in the post-Cold war period and refers to 'a situation where the structure, authority, law and political order have fallen apart' (Zartman, 1995, p. 1). He underlined the collapse of the central authority, with power shifting downwards to local power networks and other non-national criminal organizations and transnational terrorists. These new 'facts' of world politics in 1990s were further marked in the United States (US) National Security Strategy in 1998 which underscored the increasingly growing threats of terrorism, international crime, drug trafficking, illicit arms trafficking, uncontrolled refugee migrations and environmental damage (Taylor, 2013, p. 14).

The State Failure Task Force and Political Instability Task Force

When discussion moved to the problems of 'state failure', or 'failing' or 'failed' states, or fragile states, Al Gore, US Vice-President, gave an order in 1994 to the Central Intelligence Agency (CIA) to study deeply the reality of 'state failure'. Following the Clinton–Al Gore administration, US President George W. Bush continued this approach in the aftermath of 9/11 and revealed the 'new' American security doctrine: 'The events of September 11, 2001, taught us that weak states . . . can pose as great a danger to our national interests as strong states' (Rice, 2003; *New York Times*, 2002).

One of the concrete results was the emergence of the State Failure Task Force (SFTF) funded by the CIA at the request of Vice-President Al Gore, with the collaboration of a group of academics, in particular the Center for Global Policy at George Mason University. Since state failure had become a fundamental threat to the global (hence, US) security architecture, developing a new robust methodology to understand and 'identify key factors and critical thresholds signalling a high risk of crisis in countries some two years in advance' constituted the basic mission of the Task Force in 1995. The original data set was prepared by the Center for International Development and Conflict Management at the University of Maryland, where Ted Gurr was the director.

Two more reports were prepared by the SFTF in 1998 and 2000, in addition to the first one in 1995. The 1995 report included four variables in terms of state failure: (1) revolutionary wars; (2) ethnic wars; (3) genocides and politicides; and (4) adverse or disruptive regime transition (Taylor, 2013, p. 36). The academic team employed various quantitative methods to test many variables, including multivariate logistic regression models, neural networks and genetic algorithmic analysis. The report used 40 data sets with more than 2 million data points, and examined 617 potential independent variables; 75 independent variables were selected by experts and T-tests and chi-square tests on the 75 variables were realized, and 31 were considered statistically significant: 11 demographic/social, 10 economic/environmental, and 10 political variables.

In addition to the political regime variables, eventually two independent variables appeared to be the best indicators and predictors of state failure: high infant mortality and low trade openness. The level of democracy exerted an impact on the relative effect of these two variables: accordingly, low trade openness was more strongly associated with the risk of state failure in less democratic states, while high infant mortality was more strongly associated with the more democratic states (Taylor, 2013, p. 37). The factors associated with failure were deemed to be indicators of but not the direct causes of the failure; they were indicators for more complex combinations that affect the risks of state failure (Taylor, 2013, p. 37).

The 1995 SFTF report concluded that general living standards (represented by infant mortality) exerted a strong impact on political stability.

Therefore, any improvement in the general quality of life would result in a relative decline in terms of risk of failure. In new democracies or transitionary democracies with high infant mortality, the risk of failure would increase the risk relatively more than in consolidated democracies and autocracies. The infant mortality relationship with the risk of failure in authoritarian regimes remained low; and the relationship between trade openness and the risk of failure was understood to reflect the need to ensure the rule of law and economic well-being. The 1995 report ignored the question of 'trigger' events, such as assassinations, in the onset of civil strife, for example. The next report of the SFTF still employed logistic regression, neural network analysis and genetic algorithm analysis, and reached the same conclusions as the previous one, with some minor modifications (Esty et al., 1999).

After the SFTF was transformed into the Political Instability Task Force (the PITF) model, with a more predictive power, it was based on four factors: the level of development as measured by the infant mortality rate; extreme cases of economic and political discrimination against minorities; bad neighbourhood (if a country has at least four neighbours that suffered violent conflicts); and political regime type (democracy, autocracy or hybrid regimes). The model arguably explains and predicts 80 per cent of outbreaks of instability; however, the model cannot forecast the timing and duration of an outbreak.

The third report shifted the basic framework of the SFTF's research agenda from state failure to political instability, and the report still indicated infant mortality as the best predictor of state failure. Nonetheless, infant mortality should be considered not as a causal factor but as an indicator of a wider set of influences, which means that reducing infant mortality per se would not automatically reduce the risk of state failure. As indicated before, hybrid regimes, like semi-democracies were seven times more prone to infant mortality when compared to established political regimes, because of the fractious and polarized nature of polities in transition without efficient institutional frameworks to mitigate domestic conflicts. Apart from 'trade openness', the report revealed that economic variables were hardly associated with the failure.

CAST and the Failed States Index

The US State Department and the US Army in general uses the FfP CAST project. The CAST methodology includes 12 indicators chosen from the political, economic and societal realms; and five from core state institutions, which are called 'Core Five': efficient security and police departments; efficient and functional state bureaucracy; an independent judiciary and the rule of law; a professional and accountable military under the authority of elected civilian governments; and robust executive governmental leadership. Thus, Core Five concentrates on three qualities: legitimacy, representativeness and professionalism (Taylor, 2013, p.213). The social indicators, on the other hand, include three basic components: 'demographic pressure', referring to refugee flows; existence of vengeance-seeking group grievance; and chronic human flight. The economic indicators are uneven economic development; and severe and sudden economic decline. And the political ones include 'criminalization' and/or de-legitimization of the state; progressive deterioration of public services and the rule of law; gross human rights violations; the existence of security forces as a 'state within the state'; rising factionalized elites; and intervention by external forces. There are 12 indicators and 41 sub-indicators, and the system employs the Bayesian logic, scanning around 130 000 open sources and calculating the number of relevant hits of keywords. The CAST method takes a snapshot in time, which is compared to other snapshots in a time series to understand whether the situation in a state is improving or getting worse. Therefore, the CAST model aims for 'more precise forecasting with a goal of calculating the probability of change' (Baker, 2006, p.vi). One of the elements of the CAST model is to identify 'STINGS', which refers to: surprises, triggers (an assassination, for example), idiosyncrasies, national temperaments (cultural characteristics), and spoilers (excluded parties, for example).

The Worldwide Governance Indicators

The Worldwide Governance Indicators (WGIs) project collects collective or individual governance indicators for more than 200 countries and territories for six dimensions of governance: voice and accountability; political stability and absence of violence; government effectiveness; regulatory quality; rule of law; and control of corruption. 'Voice and accountability' aims to collect data on the level of freedom of expression, freedom of association and media freedom, as well as the extent to which a state's people can participate in electing the government. It employs various democracies and human rights indexes, such the indexes of Freedom of Association, EIU's Democracy Index and Press Freedom Index. The 'political stability' dimension attempts to measure perceptions of the likelihood of political instability and/or politically motivated violence, including terrorism. 'Government effectiveness' covers perceptions of the quality of public services, the quality of the civil service, and the degree of its independence from political pressure. 'Regulatory quality' is about the ability of the government to formulate and implement sound policies and regulations that permit and promote private sector development. The 'rule of law' dimension embraces perceptions of the extent to which governmental agencies are controlled and restricted by the rules. 'Control of corruption' includes both petty and grand forms of corruption perceptions.[1] Despite some methodological criticisms, the WGIs are considered one of the most methodologically transparent and sophisticated indices, 'setting the gold standard[;] and they are used as a proxy for failure and to develop policy' (Taylor, 2013, p. 52).[2]

Political Stability Index, the Likelihood of Political Unrest by EUI

The EUI Political Instability Index in 2009 and 2010 basically employed the PITF model mentioned above. The index has two basic dimensions: (1) underlying vulnerability; and (2) economic stress, covering 15 economic, social and political indicators in total, which are defined as 'underlying vulnerability'; inequality (measured by Gini coefficient); state history (measured according to date of independence); corruption; ethnic fragmentation; trust in institutions; status of minorities (according to Minorities at Risk Project); history of political instability (as recorded by the PITF); proclivity to labour unrest; level of social provision; a country's neighbourhood; political regime type; regime type and factionalism. 'Economic distress' is believed to be a necessary condition for a serious outbreak of instability. There were many cases of instability identified by the PITF since 1980; countries suffered a decline in gross domestic product per head in at least one of the two years prior to the occurrence of political instability. According to the model, economic distress is associated with three indicators: growth in incomes (growth in real GDP per head in 2009), unemployment rate, and level of income per head.

Predicting or forecasting political risk with political instability could sometimes be crucial for companies that invest in foreign territories. Forecasting is always problematic from the social science perspective. The huge amount of data collected by the State Failure Task Force can also be considered as a comprehensive attempt to forecast possible state failure in advance. Jack A. Goldstone and colleagues (Goldstone had been part of the SFTF project until 2012) later continued to study the forecasting of political instability (Goldstone et al., 2010). The team determined 141 separate instability episodes (civil wars, state collapse, revolutions, adverse regime change, and so on) between 1955 and 2003 and found 44 adverse regime changes, 12 revolutions, 13 ethnic wars, and 71 combinations of different types of instability.[3]

The model, largely similar to the PITF model, depends on four independent variables: regime type, infant mortality, conflict-ridden neighbourhood, and state-led discrimination. The authors define factionalism as a pattern of sharply polarized and uncompromising rivalry between blocs that compete for their 'parochial interest' in a country. Politics in these countries basically follows the winner-take-all logic, with confrontational mind-sets between polarized groups.

The authors argue that their model can explain and predict 80 per cent of civil war outbreaks; and the most striking result they have found is that partial democratic regimes with high factionalism have a large potential to produce serious political instability (Goldstone et al., 2010, p. 197). In addition to regime type, some other variables appeared as important factors for possible instability: infant mortality and 'bad neighbourhood' (four or more neighbours experiencing violent conflict) emerged as significant elements in the explanation and prediction of an outbreak of political instability. The authors found that the likelihood of instability in countries at the 75th percentile in global infant mortality levels is seven times higher than in states at the 25th percentile. In a similar vein, the likelihood of a country with bad neighbourhoods to be affected by political instability in future is much more than a country without bad neighbourhoods. Governmental discrimination against minorities and the nature of political institutions in a country also play important roles in this regard. A resilient polity therefore needs high incomes, low discrimination, few conflicts in the neighbourhood, and a non-contested or unified political regime. Goldstone concludes:

> While infant mortality, discrimination, and bad neighbourhood effects are significant, our categorical measure of political institutions was by far the most powerful factor for distinguishing stable country-years from those that soon experienced instability onsets. Indeed, once regime characteristics are taken into account, most other economic, political, social, or cultural features of the countries in our sample had no significant impact on the relative incidence of near-term instability. In our view, this finding should encourage scholars in this field to redirect their attention from the economic to the institutional foundations of political instability. (Goldstone et al., 2010, p. 204)

The discussions on the political risk, political instability and political regime types mentioned above are popular topics in both political science and business studies. Relatively early analysis on the relationship between political risk and political stability came from Green. He mentioned seven types of political regime: instrumental adaptive, instrumental non-adaptive, quasi-instrumental, modernizing autocracies, military dictatorships, mobilization systems and newly independent states. Green thought that it was possible to imagine a spectrum starting from the 'instrumental adaptive' system (modernized Western state) and ending with newly independent states (post-colonial states such as India), and he argued that political risk in the instrumental adaptive states would be at a minimum, while it is at a maximum in new states (Green, 1974). Green's argument is about the increasing possibility of risk in younger political systems, which are supposed to be less adaptive than older political systems; which can be compared to the recent discussion on the increasingly risky conditions in the hybrid regimes (Jensen, 2008; Jensen and Young, 2008; Sottilotta, 2017; Baas, 2010).

In addition to what has been discussed above, according to Sottilotta (2017), there is an inverse relationship between level of democracy and the risk of expropriation of foreign investments. According to Jensen, the existence of 'veto players' and robust democratic institutions plays a large role in curbing political risk (Jensen, 2008, p. 1049) Thus, if few constraints on the executive exist, as is the case in Russia, Bolivia and Venezuela, the possibility of political risk would be relatively higher. In a similar vein, Jensen and Young (2008, p. 539) suggest that a high level of democracy is theoretically associated with less conflict, due to the ability of the political opposition to channel grievances into a formal political process; and foreign investors in general perceived democratic regimes in a positive way in terms of political risk. The authors found, contrary to the PITF, no significant non-linear impact of ethnic fractionalization on political risk. The researchers revealed that there is a 'parabolic relation-ship' between ethnic diversity and civil strife (Jensen and Young, 2008). Diversity alone does not generate a negative outcome, unless that diversity creates a situation of political and economic rivalry polarization. However, Jensen and Young found that the level of wealth exerts a large impact over the risk of violence. If a country moves from the mean level of wealth to the maximum level of wealth, the risk of being in one of the lowest-level categories of violence will increase by 46 per cent; and if a state moves from the lowest level of wealth to the mean level of wealth, it will increase the chance of being in one of the three least risky categories by 47 per cent (Jensen and Young, 2008, p. 541). Thus, it is possible to anticipate that a higher level of gross domestic product (GDP) per capita is associated with lower levels of risk. In addition, almost all studies on the relationship between political regimes and political instability reveal the fact that the 'hybrid regimes' – semi-democracies and political regimes in transition to democracy – are much more instability- or conflict-prone when compar-ing them to both established democracies and autocracies (Knutsen and Nygard, 2015).

'Geopolitical Risk' in the Age of Global Uncertainty

What this chapter suggests so far is that more interdisciplinary approaches need to develop more robust and comprehensive analysis, not only of the complex nature of political risk and political stability/instability phenomena. Indeed, the concepts, tools and methods of politics and business studies need to create a sort of synergy in the academic sense. However, one more fact is that all these developments in terms of politics, economy and business do not happen in a vacuum. All the risk issues discussed so far need to be analysed in an international or global context. The term 'geopolitical risk' is often employed when referring to regional and international political risk, albeit in a quite vague manner.

Geopolitical risk, which can be considered as a type of political risk, refers to the group of risks 'posed to economic actors and governments by the relative rise and decline of great powers and the impact of conventional wars on states and corporations' (Bremmer and Keat, 2010, p. 38). Bremmer and Keat's definition of geopolitical risk is accurate, but inadequate. In other words, if geopolitical risk is still considered as a consequence emanating from the inter-state system, Daesh and similar non-governmental or quasi-state phenomena in world politics could not be comprehended well. Therefore, the literature (though there is not enough separate literature on 'geopolitical risk') needs to broaden its outlook, adding non-state actors into its analysis, and enriching the relevant conceptual and methodological tools, such as the 'networked world' (Slaughter, 2017).

'Geopolitical risk' is one of the five categories cited in the *Global Risks Report* published by the World Economic Forum, and it seems that the Forum has already broadened its employment of the term. The *Global Risks Report 2017*, prepared by the World Economic Forum, suggests that terrorist attack, interstate conflict and 'failure of national governance' are the top global geopolitical risks, 'in terms of likelihood'. On the other hand, in terms of impact, top geopolitical risks include weapons of mass destruction, terrorist attack and interstate conflict. The Forum suggests that 'large-scale involuntary migration' is among the top ten global risks in the social sphere, along with possible food crisis. In terms of geopolitics, 'deteriorating commitment to global cooperation' is cited as a 'worrying' development (World Economic Forum, 2017, p. 15). Five basic factors that exacerbate geopolitical risks are listed in the report as follows. The first is that unilateral approaches have replaced international cooperation; the second, that the high interconnectedness of global politics produces 'cascading risks' at national levels and in domestic politics. The civil strife in Syria, and refugee flows, are examples of this reality. Third, 'a declining sense of trust and mutual good faith in international relations' can make domestic political tension worse, accusing outside forces of interfering in domestic issues. Fourth, innovation in technology, such as robot warriors or artificial intelligence in military sectors, has the potential to exacerbate the risk of conflict. Fifth and last, international security institutions' reactions to all these new technological and other risks are quite slow and inadequate.

The World Economic Forum's *Global Risks Report* discusses social and political challenges as well, and underlines the crisis of Western democracy and the rise of anti-establishment parties in the West. When reading other important reports from the business world on the global, international or geopolitical risk, similar points of concern often appear. For example, the *Global Political Risk 2016* report, published by Citi GPS, underlines similar points as existing and emerging political risks at a global level. According to the report, the world in the last few years has become a more dangerous place, where 'old geopolitics risks' and new 'socio-economic risks' have started to converge. The report reveals that while 'old' geopolitical risks' (for example, armed conflict) are increasing, 'new socio-economic risks', which the report defines as 'Vox Populi', have emerged, such as: unconventional election results; the increasing power of 'fringe politics'; 'flash mob' mass protests; declining trust in old institutions and politics and elites; and referenda crises.[4] Similar conclusions can be seen in other reports from other significant institutions (e.g., National Intelligence Council, 2017). The basic point that almost all reports on the global political risks share is the fact that weak global governance and structural shifts in global power allocations have dramatically increased global political and economic uncertainty.

Damage to the fabric of the global order can be observed with respect to four interrelated developments. First, and perhaps most alarming, is the proliferation and diversification of the regional and global destabilizing units; that is, states or non-state actors that the global security architecture has already been struggling to deal with. The second development is related to the slow but sure erosion of the liberal democratic values even in the old, consolidated democracies, especially in Europe. The third is the rise of authoritarian regimes as centres of attraction in the international system. Finally, the erosion in the institutional capacity and legitimacy of the United Nations (UN) undermines the foundation of the global order (Usul, 2017).

Russian invasion and annexation of Crimea, as well as its destabilizing actions in the eastern part of Ukraine, can be considered a big sign of the post-American – even perhaps post-Western – world (Charap and Colton, 2017). However, it is not possible to argue currently that a new world order is under construction. The growing influence of China in the international economy is evident in almost all economic and financial measures. China now has the third-largest International Monetary Fund (IMF) quota and voting share after the United States and Japan. One should keep in mind, however, that despite China's ongoing contribution to the consolidation of the existing system, it also seems to construct its authentic economic and financial ecosystem through some new international initiatives such as the Asian Infrastructure Investment Bank and the One Belt One Road initiative. If China decides to (and is able to) come up with an alternative economic order, it may increase China's attractiveness, and could even hasten the current disintegration of the global order.

The world leaders seem to have already abandoned their hopes and trust that the global and regional security problems could be solved within the current structure of the UN system. Therefore, new semi-global or pseudo-global institutions, such as the G20, which was originally created to deal with global financial issues, have increasingly been used as platforms to discuss global and regional security issues and other problems. Thus, if 'hegemony' refers to a global leadership in terms of value construction, agenda setting, building global institutions, financial and economic governance of the world and providing global security, we can easily talk about the deep crisis of hegemony in current world politics and the economy.

POLITICAL RISK IN THE GLOBAL UNCERTAINTY AND THE TRANSITIONAL PERIPHERY

There are parallels between the emergence of the political risk concept and the 'third world countries', 'developing world', or 'less developed states'; the concepts can vary according to where the authors stand theoretically. It would not be wrong to argue that how we consider these terms varies in accordance with the character of their history. In other words, the concern of Western companies about political risk started in the 1960s when the 'third world' started to emerge with the global wave of de-colonization and as the number of independent states had risen steadily. However, the new third world was a risky if not dangerous business environment for international companies. Among the serious risks in this new world was the possible ideological inclination of the political leaders of newly established states towards a socialist state model, which was popular among third world countries at the time, and the possible political instability that could generate a risky environment for the investment. The trend of socialism in the 'less developed world' could lead to the most serious risk in a political sense: expropriation (Zink, 1973). However, when it comes to the twenty-first century, political developments have made it clear that the political risk is now not only a matter for 'developing' countries but also for 'developed' ones (Jarvis and Griffiths, 2007, p. 15). The political developments in some European countries – for example, the political and economic consequences of Brexit in the United Kingdom and the European Union, and the Catalonia crisis in Spain – illustrate the fact that political risk is a phenomenon not only in the developing world but also in 'developed' Western states.

However, it is still possible to argue that foreign investors hesitate to invest in developing countries, particularly in the states that are considered to be within 'the transitional periphery'. According to Wood and Demirbag, the 'transitional periphery' refers basically to remote post-Soviet economies of the Caucasus, Central Asia and other peripheral outposts of the former Soviet Union (Wood and Demirbag, 2015; Demirbag et al., 2015). When analysing the Central Asian region, which can be considered an area that possesses the character of the transitional periphery, five independent states demonstrate some common and different characteristics in terms of political risk assessments.

With respect to the categories of political risk other than political violence, civil strife and critical political instability, the literature on political risk discussed above suggests the relatively institutionalized polity with some constraints over the political executive, which can be considered as another definition of the principle of the rule of law. Kazakhstan comes to the fore as a more secure country in terms of political risk, as indicated by the indicators of the rule of law, regulatory quality and government effectiveness. Kyrgyzstan follows Kazakhstan in respect of the rule of law and regulatory quality; however, Uzbekistan's performance on government effectiveness is better than Kyrgyzstan's. Turkmenistan falls behind the other four Central Asian states in terms of worldwide governance indicators that are associated with political risk other than political violence in home countries.

When it comes to another general category of political risk – that is, state fragility, political violence, political instability, revolution or rebellions – Kazakhstan again has a relatively better record than the other four states, when taking into account the Political Stability Indicator of the World Bank, the Organisation for Economic Co-operation and Development's (OECD) Country Risk Classification and the State Fragility Index. The Political Stability Indicator for Kazakhstan was 43.81 in 2015, and 47.62 in 2016 (100 points is the best), despite falling GDP growth from 7.4 per cent per annum in 2011 to 1.0 per cent in 2016. Turkmenistan follows Kazakhstan in terms of political stability, with scores of 42.86

in 2105, and 34.76 in 2016; a significant downgrading in the score. In a similar way, the State Fragility Index gave a score of 9 to Kazakhstan and Turkmenistan (24 is the worst and 0 is the best in the index) in 2015 and 2016, while Kyrgyzstan received 12, and Uzbekistan 12 in 2015 and 11 in 2016. The OECD's Country Risk Classification, similarly, put Kazakhstan and Turkmenistan (and Uzbekistan) in category 6, and Kyrgyzstan and Tajikistan in category 7, which means a worse score. The Fragile State index, on the other hand, again scored Kazakhstan as the most stable country in Central Asia, with a score of 65.9, thus ranking Kazakhstan as the 113th state in the world in terms of state fragility. Tajikistan is the worst in this regard; and the general situation in all Central Asian states, according to the index, is slightly worsening when comparing the scores in the 2016 fragility report. The Freedom Index generally shows both political freedom and democracy in countries, political freedom and level of democracy. See Tables 4.2–4.6.

The nascent business literature on Central Asia suggests that the weak and fluid institutional character of the transitional peripheral countries renders the business environment more unpredictable, which potentially increases the perception of political risk in these nations. One piece of academic research in this regard demonstrates that the greater institutional fluidity in the nations belonging to the 'transitional periphery' leads to a 'more unpredictable business environment', which means bigger risks for multinational firms (Demirbag et al., 2015, p.964). The authors recommend that 'any adverse consequences of bribery and corruption on reinvestment choices' could be mitigated by proper institutional settings (ibid., p.965). In addition to the weak and fluid character of the national institutions in the Central Asian states, 'clan politics' (Collins, 2003, 2006) or 'capitalism based on clans', informal patronage networks, is another key characteristic of the region which contributes heavily to the absence of viable institutionalization (Demirbag et al., 2015, p.956; Nölke and

Table 4.2   GDP growth in the Central Asian states (% per annum)

	2011	2012	2013	2014	2015	2016
Kazakhstan	7.4	4.8	6.0	4.2	1.2	1.0
Kyrgyz Republic	6.0	−0.1	10.9	4.0	3.9	3.8
Turkmenistan	14.7	11.1	10.2	10.3	6.5	6.2
Uzbekistan	8.3	8.2	8.0	7.8	8.0	7.8
Tajikistan	7.4	7.5	7.4	6.7	6.0	6.9

Source: World Development Indicators.

Table 4.3 Worldwide governance indicators

	Voice and accountability	Political stability	Government effectiveness	Regulatory quality	Rule of law	Control of corruption
Kazakhstan	13.30	47.62	51.44	51.92	34.62	20.67
Kyrgyzstan	32.51	22.86	17.79	40.38	12.98	12.02
Tajikistan	4.93	19.52	14.42	12.02	10.58	12.50
Turkmenistan	0.49	34.76	11.54	1.92	5.89	4.33
Uzbekistan	2.46	34.29	30.77	4.3	11.06	10.10

Source: Worldwide Governance Indicators.

Table 4.4 OECD's Country Risk Classification

| | Country Risk Classification, OECD ||
	2015	2016
Kazakhstan	6	6
Kyrgyzstan	7	7
Tajikistan	7	7
Turkmenistan	6	6
Uzbekistan	6	6

Source: OECD's Country Risk Classification.

Table 4.5 Fragile State Index

Country	2017 ranking (178 states)
Kazakhstan	113
Kyrgyzstan	65
Tajikistan	61
Turkmenistan	86
Uzbekistan	63

Source: http://fundforpeace.org/.

Table 4.6 Freedom Index

Country	Political Rights 2016	Civil Rights 2016	
Kazakhstan	7	5	Not Free
Kyrgyzstan	5	5	Partly Free
Tajikistan	7	6	Not Free
Turkmenistan	7	7	Not Free
Uzbekistan	7	7	Not Free

Source: Freedom House.

Vliegenthart, 2009, p. 696). Thus, it can be concluded that the institutional fluidity and informal patronage networks based on clan politics contributed to a less predictable business environment; however, predictability is crucial for the reinvestment decisions of multinational corporations in transition economies.

CONCLUDING REMARKS: A POLITICAL RISK ASSESSMENT AGENDA IN THE AGE OF UNCERTAINTY

Irregular and unpredictable characteristics of world politics and the world economy have been on the rise in the twenty-first century. It is possible now to see Russia annex part of another sovereign country; a terrorist organization establishes its 'state' in the middle of Syria and Iraq. It is now perceived as 'ordinary politics' in Europe that a leader without a political party could win a presidential election, as is the case in France. While the political and security architecture of the globe has been in the process of falling apart, paradoxically, the world has become more interconnected and interdependent. The refugee flow crisis in Syria, for example, has the potential to change the roots of European politics. In this political and economic global environment, the literature of political risk assessment needs to enrich its theoretical, conceptual and methodological performance. One possible way to achieve this is through more synergic and multidisciplinary studies embracing business studies, politics and international relations.

The age of uncertainty that the world is passing through has put the developing countries, in particular countries from 'the transitionary periphery', in quite a difficult position. The conventional international norms and institutions, such as democracy, liberalism and the authority of the United Nations, have been corroding for some time now, and this fact is visible not only in the less developed part of the world, but also in 'developed' Western countries. However, states such as the Central Asian countries suffer more when it comes to the rise of political risk parameters, as this chapter has revealed.

The institutional weakness and fluidity of the countries from the transitional periphery increase the potential of the political risk there. As discussed above, the literature reveals the fact that the fragile and feeble political and economic institutions in the Central Asia countries in general escalate the unpredictability in these states, rendering a substantial total magnitude of uncertainty and unpredictability. Traditional informal patronage networks, clan politics, or 'capitalism based on clans', constitutes one of the reasons for or consequences of the fragility of institutions in these nations. Thus, it is possible to claim a sort of double unpredictability and uncertainty when it comes to the states from the transitional periphery, including the Central Asian nations.

NOTES

1. http://info.worldbank.org/governance/wgi/#doc.
2. See also Kaufmann et al. (2010).
3. The growing literature on state failure, state fragility, fragile states, failed or failing states, weak states, collapsed or collapsing states, also draws criticisms. See, for example, Hampel (2015) and Grimm et al. (2014).
4. Global Political Risk, The New Convergence Between Geopolitical and Vox populist Risks, and Why it Matters, Citi GPS, January 2016.

REFERENCES

Baas, D. (2010), 'Approaches and challenges to political risk assessment: the view from Export Development Canada', *Risk Management*, 12 (2), pp. 135–162.

Baker, P.H. (2006), *The Conflict Assessment Tool (CAST). An Analytical Model for Early Warning and Risk Assessment of Weak and Failing States*, Washington, DC: Fund for Peace.

Bekefi, T. and M. Epstein (2008), 'Measuring and managing social and political risk', *Strategic Finance*, 89 (9), pp. 33–41.

Bremmer, I. and p. Keat (2010), *The Fat Tail: The Power of Political Knowledge in an Uncertain World*, Oxford: Oxford University Press.

Charap, S. and T. Colton (2017), *Everyone Loses: The Ukraine Crisis and the Russian Contest for Post-Soviet Eurasia*, Abingdon: Routledge.

Collins, K. (2003), 'The political role of clans in Central Asia', *Comparative Politics*, 35 (2), pp. 171–190.

Collins, K. (2006), *Clan Politics and Regime Transition in Central Asia*, New York: Cambridge University Press.

Czinkota, M.R., I.A. Ronkainen and M. Moffet (2000), *International Business*, Fort Worth, TX: Dryden Press.

Demirbag, M., M. McGuinnness, G. Wood and N. Bayyurt (2015), 'Context, law and reinvestment decisions: why the transitional periphery differs from other post-state socialist economies', *International Business Review*, 24 (6), pp. 955–965.

Esty, D.C., J.A. Goldstone, T.R. Gurr, B. Haff, et al. (1999), State Failure Task Force Report: Phase II findings. *Environmental Change and Security Project Report*, Issue 5, Summer.

Global Political Risk, The New Convergence Between Geopolitical and Vox Populist Risks, and Why It Matters (2016), Citi GPS, January. Available at: https://ir.citi.com/FkRWxk1%2Fy86lIAtbvyY8ML8YyODMoMdqRVsL%2FtTbK9xVC9ZIjTo%2F1QkAgqQzd6uzE3rF6wmrpD0%3D.

Goldstone, J., R.H. Bates, D.L. Epstein, et al. (2010), 'A global model for forecasting political instability', *American Journal of Political Science*, 54 (1), pp. 190–208.

Green, R.T. (1974), 'Political structures as a predictor of radical political change', *Columbia Journal of World Business*, 9 (1), pp. 28–36.

Griffen, R.W. and M.W. Pustay (1998), *International Business: A Managerial Perspective*, Reading: Addison-Wesley.

Grimm, S., N. Lemey-Hebert and O. Nay (2014), '"Fragile states": introducing a political concept', *Third World Quarterly*, 35 (2), pp. 197–209.

Hampel, K.A. (2015), 'The dark(er) side of "state failure": state formation and socio-political variation', *Third World Quarterly*, 36 (9), pp. 1629–1648.

Helman, G. and S. Ratner (1993), 'Saving failed states', *Foreign Policy*, 89, pp. 3–20.

Hough, M., A. Du Plessis and P.G. Kruys (2008), *Threat and Risk Analysis in the Context of Strategic Forecasting*, Pretoria: Institute for Strategic Studies, University of Pretoria.

Howell, L.D. (2014), 'Evaluating political risk forecasting models: what works?', *Thunderbird International Business Review*, 56 (4), pp. 304–316.

Hurwitz, L. (1973), 'Contemporary approaches to political stability', *Comparative Politics*, 5 (3), pp. 449–563.

Jarvis, D.S.L. (2008), 'Conceptualizing, analyzing and measuring political risk: the evolution of theory and method', Lee Kuan Yew School of Public Policy Research Paper No. LKYSPP08-004. Available at SSRN: http://ssrn.com/abstract=1162541.

Jarvis, D. and M. Griffiths (2007), 'Learning to fly: the evolution of political risk analysis', *Global Society*, 21 (1), pp. 5–21.

Jensen, N.M. (2008), 'Political regimes and political risk: democratic institutions and expropriation risk for multinational investors', *Journal of Politics*, 70 (4), pp. 1040–1052.

Jensen, N.M. and D.J. Young (2008), 'A violent future? Political risk insurance markets and violence forecasts', *Journal of Conflict Resolution*, 52 (4), pp. 527–547.

Kaufmann, D., A. Kravy and M. Maustruzzi (2010), 'The Worldwide Governance Indicators methodology and analytical issues', Policy Research Working Paper 5430, Washington, DC: World Bank.

Knutsen, C.H and H.M. Nygard (2015), 'Institutional characteristics and regime survival: why are semi-democracies less durable than autocracies and democracies?', *American Journal of Political Science*, 59 (3), 656–670.

Kobrin, S.J. (1978), 'When does political instability result in increasing investment risk?', *Columbia Journal of World Business*, Fall, pp. 113–122.

Kobrin, S.J. (1979), 'Political risk: a review and reconsideration', *Journal of International Business Studies*, 10 (1), pp. 67–80.

Kobrin, S.J. (1982), *Managing Political Risk Assessment: Strategic Response to Environmental Change*, Berkeley, CA: University of California Press.

Margolis, J.E. (2010), 'Understanding political stability and instability', *Civil Wars*, 12 (3), pp. 326–345.

National Intelligence Council (2017), *Global Trends: Paradox of Progress*. Available at: https://www.dni.gov/files/documents/nic/GT-Full-Report.pdf.

New York Times (2002), 'Bush's national security strategy', 20 September. Available at: https://www.nytimes.com/2002/09/20/politics/full-text-bushs-national-security-strategy.html.

Nölke, A. and A. Vliegenthart (2009) 'Enlarging the varieties of capitalism: the emergence of dependent market economies in East and Central Europe', *World Politics*, 61 (4), pp. 670–702.

Rice, S.E. (2003), 'New national security strategy: focus on failed states', Brookings Institution Policy Brief 116, February.

Slaughter, A. (2017), *The Chessboard and the Web: Strategies of Connection in a Networked World*, New Haven, CT: Yale University Press.

Sottilotta, C.E. (2017), *Rethinking Political Risk: Concepts, Theories, Challenges*, New York: Routledge.

Taylor, A. (2013), *State Failure*, Basingstoke: Palgrave.

Usul, A.R. (2017), 'American elections and the global (dis)order', *All Azimuth*, 6 (1), pp. 103–108.

Wood, G. and M. Demirbag (2015), 'Business and society on the transitional periphery: comparative perspectives', *International Business Review*, 24, pp. 917–920.

World Economic Forum (2017), *Global Risks Report*. Available at: http://www3. weforum.org/docs/GRR17_Report_web.pdf.

Yackee, J.W. (2014), 'Political risk and international investment law', *Duke Journal of Comparative and International Law*, 24, pp. 477–500.

Zartman, W. (1995), 'Introduction: posing the problem of state collapse', in W. Zartman (ed.), *Collapsed States: The Disintegration and Restoration of Legitimate Authority*, London: Lynne Rienner, pp. 1–11.

Zink, Dolph Warren (1973), *The Political Risks for Multinational Enterprise in Developing Countries, with a Case Study of Peru*, New York: Preager.

PART II

Transitional periphery: Caucasia

5. International business view of economic and institutional transformation in the transitional periphery: Armenia and Georgia

Aleksandr V. Gevorkyan

INTRODUCTION

From the international business perspective, there are five forces of socio-economic change active today in the post-socialist Eastern European (EE) and former Soviet Union (FSU) transitional periphery. Feeding off (and transforming) existent macroeconomic and geopolitical foundations, those forces are: (1) domestic labor and social developments; (2) foreign direct investment (FDI) flows; (3) international trade structure and patterns; (4) broader institutional and business climate changes; and, finally, (5) the role of diaspora networks. Motivated by emerging topics in international business (IB), this chapter attempts to further develop the "five forces" model in connection with post-socialist transformation of the Republic of Armenia and the Republic of Georgia ("the duo").

Derived in an earlier work (Gevorkyan, 2015), the "five forces" model (FFM) allows the categorizing of key economic and social change factors based on their dynamic exogenous and endogenous origins. Such categorization is helpful as IB scholars and firm managers are mystified by the dilemma of whether "to wait or to act" on the promise of post-socialist transformation. The problem is most acute in the smaller transitional economies, where geopolitics sets the operational background.

On the applied level, institutional legacy systems are visible and remain decisive. It is important to appreciate the complexity involved as institutional legacy layers gradually yield to the pressures of the new local context-adapted formations. Often, the evolved symbiosis of the old and the new institutional frameworks cannot be easily catalogued under the confines of the established approaches. Not surprisingly, then, knowledge of local content dynamics, and partnerships with local or diaspora-led counterparts, serves equally as a critical requirement and a competitive advantage for new market entrants. Relevant to the present discussion, problems of shadow economies, hierarchical and segmented market structures, often emerge at the forefront of institutional transformation debates.

This chapter's analysis suggests that today both Armenia and Georgia have evolved as economies with somewhat renewed potential. The critical takeaway from the two experiences for institutional economics is the concept of gradualism. For international business the lesson is in the dynamic evolution of macro structures and business categories. The challenge, then, is to take action towards developing multifaceted methodological instruments of analysis critical for institutional economists and international business managers alike. Country specifics are primary in either academic or business strategy evaluation.

Leaving a discussion of geopolitical complexities outside of this contribution, the discussion first turns to what may be seen as endogenous aspects of Armenia's and Georgia's macroeconomics and labor market evolution. The chapter then briefly reviews the structure and patterns of external capital flows and trade for the two countries. More substantially, the following section delves deeper into the institutional aspects of the post-socialist transformation. Complementing the problems of institutional change, the chapter then brings the concept of "diaspora" to the forefront, as one of the most distinctive forces in the duo's socio-economic dynamic. The chapter concludes with a summary and analysis.

MACROECONOMICS AND LABOR MARKETS TRANSFORMATION

Following the 1990s economic collapse and massive social crisis, both Armenia and Georgia saw some macroeconomic improvement in the early 2000s. Measured in constant purchasing power parity (PPP) terms, both economies expanded at a compound annual growth rate (CAGR) exceeding the average for the entire EEFSU group and a collective sample of lower- and middle-income transition economies. In fact, pre-crisis, Armenia's economy expanded at an estimated 10.5 percent a year, while Georgia's grew at roughly 7 percent (Table 5.1), both significantly exceeding either of the two benchmarks.

The World Bank designated Armenia a "Caucasian Tiger" (World Bank, 2006) following the country's stellar mid-transition growth. In both countries, agriculture and raw materials exports contributed positively to the domestic economy. Construction, diaspora involvement, labor migrants'

*Table 5.1   CAGR annual GDP purchasing power parity (2011) growth
          rates*

	CAGR 2000–15, %	CAGR 2000–08, %	CAGR 2010–15, %
Armenia	6.3%	10.5%	3.6%
Georgia	5.4%	6.7%	4.0%
EEFSU Average	3.6%	5.5%	1.5%
Lower & Middle Income Average (EEFSU)	3.8%	6.1%	1.4%

Note: Hereinafter, the "lower and middle income average" designation follows World Bank's latest classification by income (e.g., World Bank, 2017c) for the EEFSU countries. The EEFSU sample includes all 29 post-socialist transition economies in the EEFSU region.

Source: Author's own calculations based on World Bank (2017c).

remittances, tourism and rising domestic consumer culture were other contributing factors (e.g., Gevorkyan, 2015; Manookian and Tolosa, 2011).

Yet, not all seems to be going so well. Comparing the duo's performance to the full EEFSU sample reveals a sharp contrast in relative gains since the 1990s. Of the few conclusions from Table 5.1 and Figure 5.1, three seem to be primary: (1) the wide (and widening) gap between the duo and sample averages; (2) the scarring losses of the shock therapy reforms, followed by slow recovery; only to be (3) again offset by the 2008–2009 global crisis.

The differences in living standards (proxied in Figure 5.1 by the PPP per capita income) are visible in the starting points of both countries vis-à-vis the two derived sample benchmarks and against each other. In the latter case, Armenia's and Georgia's differences in economic structures as well as the administrative center's redistributive policies preferences, exacerbated the pre-transition gaps. However, by 2002–2003 Armenia regained its pre-transition income per capita. Georgia remained behind until 2013, despite the country's relatively stronger starting point.

In the case of Georgia, stronger than average recovery efforts may have been required as output declined from initially higher pre-transition levels before sufficient capital was rebuilt. Popov (2007) shows that in such cases macroeconomic distortions across transition samples have been more severe and extensive. More broadly, for an informed reader, the trajectory of the macroeconomic declined in Armenia (1993 output growth losses of up to 42 percent) and in Georgia (up to 45 percent), and subsequent slow recovery may be reminiscent of the sharp decline and slow recovery patterns of the 2008 Great Recession.

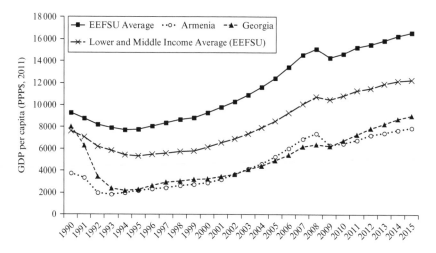

Note: Country income gaps vis-à-vis the average are confirmed in normalized visualizations, hence for presentation purposes an unweighted chart suffices here.

Source: Author's own calculations based on World Bank (2017c).

Figure 5.1   GDP per capita (PPP\$, 2011) for the EEFSU sample average vs. Armenia and Georgia

In the latter case, Armenia suffered a decline of 14 percent in real gross domestic product (GDP) in the global crisis, while Georgia lost 3.8 percent in its output. In per capita terms Armenia needed five years to recover its 2008 income peak, in contrast to Georgia's relatively steady progression. While technical structural aspects are at play here (see below), this story is not complete without a brief primer on social (under)development in the Caucasus duo.

The problem of social underdevelopment in the post-socialist economies following liberalization reforms is quite well researched (e.g., Blanchard, 1997; Mikhalev, 2003; Milanovic, 1993, 1999; Popov, 2007; and studies cited therein). A recent informative addition comes by way of the 2016 Transition Report (EBRD, 2016). The report brings the problem to the forefront through analysis of equality of opportunities in the labor market and macroeconomy across the EEFSU region.

The overall positive assessment in EBRD (2016) is overshadowed by several conclusions with dual interpretations. For example, the report finds "happiness convergence" as residents of the post-socialist world express similar satisfaction with life to residents in other (developed) countries. However, the caveat, as the report promptly acknowledges, is not just that living standards in the EEFSU have been improving, but that the quality of life may have declined, due to the bleak macroeconomic recovery, across the advanced economies. It is likely that both observations hold some truth, which should not be ignored in the IB context.

Further, EBRD (2016) emphasizes relatively low levels of broad income and wealth inequality across the region prior to transition. Yet, following the reforms, income and wealth inequality severely worsened, while poverty and unemployment rates increased dramatically. The transitional periphery saw the worst impact, and the Caucasus duo were no exception. Table 5.2 captures the prevailing concerns. Improvements across the vital areas of unemployment, income distribution and poverty have been slow, unsteady and scattered. Deeper social problems are epitomized in the Transition Report's observation of a reduction in average height (1 cm) among people born at the beginning of the transition compared to the older population cohorts.

While some in the younger generation on average appear to be more satisfied in life, substantially large population shares remain economically vulnerable, lagging behind overall economic development. Confirmation comes via the latest data on inequality-adjusted human development indexes for Armenia and Georgia, these being significantly below the higher-income post-socialist group (0.67 average versus 0.71, respectively, as of 2015), albeit Georgia only recently has caught up to Armenia's levels (UNDP, 2016). Vulnerable employment (typically, unpaid domestic work or unpaid part-time) averaged 42.4 percent of total employment for Armenia in 2013, and 59.8 percent for Georgia in the same year. While in Georgia the share has not moved much since the early 2000 averages, for Armenia the indicator has gone up in the post-global crisis years.

As Gevorkyan and Gevorkyan (2012) argue, such stubborn high levels of social underdevelopment have acted as push factors for out-migration in Armenia and Georgia, and the region in general. While official data point to improvement in net migration (Table 5.2), the relatively well-educated and capable labor force remains the key export for the Caucasus duo.

Following waves of migration, unprecedented remittances inflows have been quite significant, substantially contributing to poverty alleviation and feeding into the strengthening of household consumption indicators (e.g., Gevorkyan and Canuto, 2015; Karapetyan and Harutyunyan, 2013; Gerber and Torosyan, 2013). Dependent largely on Russia's business cycle (the origin of more than two-thirds of remittances to both economies), for the 2000–2015 period those inflows averaged 16 percent and almost 9 percent of GDP for Armenia and Georgia, respectively. The numbers are higher in the 2010–2015 period (17.6 percent and 11.1 percent,

Table 5.2 *Select social and labor market indicators*

	Unemployment (ILO, % of total labor force)			GINI coefficient			Poverty (% of population)		Net migration (% of total population)	
	1995	2000	2014	1995	2000	2014	2000	2014	1992	2012
ARM	24.00	18.90	17.10	44.42	35.36	31.48	48.30	30.00	−14.4%	−0.33%
GEO	14.40	10.80	13.40	37.13	40.48	40.09	20.10	14.80	−11.2%	−7.75%
EEFSU Average	12.62	13.42	11.63	33.90	32.79	30.64	26.79	16.87	−0.9%	−0.04%
Lower & Middle Income Average (EEFSU)	13.51	13.65	12.31	35.71	33.56	30.57	32.35	16.71	1.0%	0.04%

Note: The most recent years available were used in calculating sample averages for Gini and poverty ratio indicators. Net migration is a share of total population in the given year, and should not be conflated with outward migration rates.

Source: Author's own calculations based on World Bank (2017c).

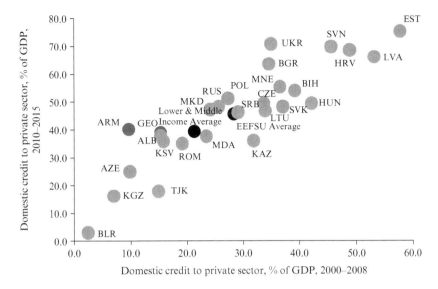

Source: Author's own calculations based on World Bank (2017c).

Figure 5.2   Changes in domestic credit to private sector (% of GDP)

respectively), possibly indicating increased structural stress on lower-income households that largely rely on labor migrants' support.

The increase in household consumption (averaging 81 percent and 74 percent of GDP for Armenia and Georgia, respectively, during the 2000–2015 period) has broader macroeconomic and institutional ramifications in the IB context. Strong domestic consumer markets reinforce positive aggregate demand feedback into GDP growth. Rising consumer markets also suggest the emergence of the middle-income groups, which in the Caucasus duo would be more accurately clarified as a "middle income-like behavior", given the role of remittances and tourism spending in the economy and, critically, rising credit availability.

On the issue of increased credit availability, Figure 5.2 helps to appreciate the magnitude of the credit growth in the EEFSU and the Caucasus duo. It is apparent that structurally weaker Armenia and Georgia have seen their private credit shares expand from pre-crisis single digits to almost 40 percent of GDP in each case, in the post-Great Recession period. Much of this rise in credit can be explained by the global liquidity expansion and suppressed borrowing costs.

Two extreme scenarios are probable. First, if left unchecked, private credit expansion may lead to significant overleveraging in the private sector. Lacking financial literacy, inadequate collateral or sophisticated credit history checks, in the environment of social underdevelopment, lower income households are at risk of building up unsustainable debt (e.g., EBRD, 2016). Second, with reliance on funds from foreign counterparts, once global financial markets conditions reverse and liquidity dries out, domestic banks will be facing difficult times in rebalancing their credit intermediation roles and paying back on foreign short-term debt, which may put strain on the structurally weaker economies.

Finally, growth in speculative consumer markets may lead to crowding out of domestic investment activity, worsening concerns over the duo's competitiveness and local economy development. On the conceptual level, credit growth has far-reaching institutional and structural impacts. Still, if sustained, this tendency may add to domestic and international business development in the region.

FDI AND TRADE: THE RELEVANCE OF THE TWO FORCES FOR INSTITUTIONAL TRANSITION

Much of the detailed country-specific sector-based analysis of FDI and trade is covered in Gevorkyan (2015). Instead, to make room for a more intense subsequent discussion on institutional and diaspora development, this section offers a high-level overview of FDI and trade trends in Armenia and Georgia.

Foreign direct investment and international trade are two distinct transformative forces in the context of the present discussion. And in the post-socialist experience, it is essential to appreciate the significance of obtaining some degree of control over external relations for a newly independent country. The effect is dual for structurally weaker Armenia and Georgia.

Consider, first, that being part of the socialist economy guaranteed a sustained inflow of capital investment and highly cross-system integrated established trade patterns. However, those guaranteed patterns also came with clear administrative plan instructions on sector development and other quotas, limiting to some extent the ability for an individual country to develop. Following the break-up of the socialist market system, established financial and trade patterns collapsed within months as macroeconomic, social and political crises heightened. Yet, in turn, that opened up an opportunity for individual countries to now compete for and attract international FDI (and trade) as per each economy's needs. Have all countries fared equally under the free market approach?

Since the mid-1990s, FDI net inflows relative to GDP for both Armenia and Georgia have stayed in single digits. In the pre-crisis years (2000–2008) the duo approached the full transition average, seeing net inflows of 6 percent and 9.3 percent of GDP for Armenia and Georgia, respectively (the EEFSU average is estimated at 7.1 percent of GDP for the same period). In the years since the crisis (2010–2015), FDI net inflows declined to averages of approximately 4.2 percent and 8 percent, respectively.

Furthermore, in the FSU, Armenia's and Georgia's shares have stayed roughly the same, receiving respectively 0.8 percent and 2.0 percent of the total FDI inflows to the CIS economies across the 2000–2015 period. Results are consistent when adjusting for pre- and post-Great Recession periods. Considering that average post-global crisis FDI inflows to the CIS group amounted to US$58 billion (all data from UNCTAD, 2017), one can quickly visualize the structural problems the duo is facing. In particular, this is of concern for Armenia, significantly lagging behind its peer.

One could also generalize about FDI by comparing the inflows in terms of shares of gross capital formation in each country. Figure 5.3 helps to paint the picture. The increase in the FDI to capital ratio in Armenia in the late 1990s and early 2000s was mostly driven by increased infrastructure and

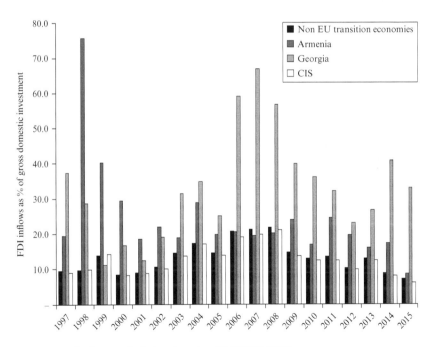

Source: Author's own calculations based on UNCTAD (2017).

Figure 5.3   FDI net inflows as percentage of gross capital formation

construction spending, largely financed by the diaspora entities. In turn, the increase in Georgia's ratio towards the mid-2000s would appear to be more structural, exceeding Armenia in the overall number of greenfield FDI projects since 2003 by close to 50 percent (yet, still accounting for barely 3.6 percent of the overall number of announced greenfield FDI deals in the CIS).

Investment in the telecommunications and mining sectors has been on the rise in Armenia, while energy and manufacturing projects have received larger shares in Georgia. Yet, despite Georgia's position as a regional logistics corridor and a tourism destination (Invest in Georgia, 2013; ADA, 2011), its track record in sustaining FDI inflows in the real estate, hotels and hospitality sector has been rather weak.

Complicating matters further, there appears to be a high concentration of FDI origins in the case of Armenia. Gevorkyan (2015) finds that Russia and France are the main sources for inflows to Armenia. Coincidentally, both are the countries with Armenia's largest established and institutionally integrated diaspora communities (e.g., Gevorkyan, 2013, 2016). Not surprisingly, GIZ (2011, 2012) estimates that up to 65 percent of total FDI over the past decade is due to diaspora-driven investments in Armenia. By contrast, Georgia maintains a diversified pool, with the bulk of FDI coming from Germany and the United Kingdom. Yet, Georgia benefits from the regional integration with the economies of Azerbaijan and Turkey, which is virtually inexistent in the case of Armenia due to objective political reasons.

The above-mentioned coordinated financial backing of the socialist system helped both Armenia and Georgia develop foundations for full employment across the manufacturing, agriculture and services sectors. Following the reforms, the duo have joined the group of developing countries trying to make it on their own overcoming by now familiar narratives of the collapses in productive capacity of the period (e.g., Åslund, 2001, 2002; Blanchard, 1997; Gevorkyan, 2011; Popov, 2007). It would be timely to recall the often-considered dual nature of FDI (e.g., Wang et al., 2013): contributing to an economy's growth, but also resulting in negative externalities by way of reduction in low-skilled employment. Moreover, as advanced technology replaces previously labor-intensive production, smaller economies lack the capacity to absorb the shocks or institute labor market safety nets. For example, consider Armenia's information technology (IT) sector, employing predominantly younger and modern skilled workers.

The FDI trends are connected with the problems of external exposure in Armenia and Georgia. The original four dimensions of risk analyzed in Gevorkyan (2015) remain relevant: (1) a persistent trade balance deficit; (2) limited composition of exports versus imports; (3) a lack of trade partner diversification; and (4) high dollarization, as reliance on consumer imports persists in the current macroeconomic context.

Following the worsening in the wake of the global crisis, the trade deficit has somewhat improved for Armenia (8.6 percent of GDP in the 2010–2015 period), but remained high for Georgia (10.5 percent), according to the latest World Bank data (World Bank, 2017c). Contributing to the trade balance deficit in both cases were severe drops in agricultural exports from Armenia (2.8 percent to 0.43 percent of GDP before and after the crisis, respectively) and Georgia (from 2.4 percent to 0.9 percent of GDP). Armenia's manufacturing exports collapsed, from a pre-crisis high of 53.5 percent to the post-crisis 22.5 percent of total merchandise exports, with commodity exports (minerals, metals and food products) dominating total exports. Georgia, on the other hand, recorded a post-crisis pick-up in manufacturing exports, from 39.5 percent before and 47.9 percent of GDP following the crisis. Georgia significantly outperforms Armenia in transportation services, supporting its claim as a cargo hub. At the same time, Armenia has outperformed Georgia in IT and communications services exports in more recent periods.

In trade, Georgia appears to be more regionally integrated (Gevorkyan, 2015). A recent International Monetary Fund report (IMF, 2013) confirms Georgia's relatively higher involvement in the Caucasus and Central Asia regional trade (10 percent of the country's total trade in 2010; compared with Armenia, where it is below 5 percent of its total trade). Armenia is largely dependent on Russia – its main agricultural and jewelry exports destination – for at least one-fifth of its trade. These patterns have held up since the early 2000s and are sustained due to two reasons: (1) varying degrees of political instability for both countries; and (2) dominance of the diaspora factor in Armenia's economy.

The exports exposure risk index (EEI), estimated as the ratio of merchandise exports to GDP by trading partner (Gevorkyan, 2015), partially explains Armenia's longer post-crisis recovery. Results suggest that Georgia's greater regional involvement (with shorter trade routes and lower logistical costs) holds over the longer term as well. Yet, for Armenia, severe deterioration in the destination markets would send negative shocks to domestic exporters in the medium term. As a counterbalance, growth in new sectors (specifically, IT and tourism) is yet to gain larger shares. However, to the extent that Armenia's current trade pattern and new sector growth is substantially diaspora-driven, the economy enjoys an implicit competitive advantage over Georgia in terms of its access to the larger Russian consumer market.

Finally, the exchange rate remains the most complex and technical risk factor in international market access for Armenia and Georgia in particular, and the FSU in general (for example, survey evidence in Kuriakose, 2013; Gevorkyan, 2017). Foreign exchange inflows via remittances, diaspora transfers, FDI and reliance on short-term denominated loans in the banking sector collectively spur the phenomenon of dollarization in both economies.

According to the Central Bank of Armenia (2014) and the National Bank of Georgia (2013), foreign currency loans ranged from highs of 80 percent of the total in the early 2000s, to approximately 60–64 percent of total loans more recently. This observation is consistent with earlier research on both economies (on Armenia, Zoryan, 2005; and on Georgia, Aslanidi, 2008) and connects with earlier mentioned concerns over misalignment of financial flows and productive capacity, artificially sustaining credit and consumer markets growth in both economies. In the next section I attempt to connect the diverse pieces of the institutional framework puzzle based on the above discussion.

WHY INSTITUTIONS MATTER IN THE CASES OF ARMENIA AND GEORGIA

The lesson from the above discussion of broad macroeconomic categories is not that Armenia and Georgia are caught in an underdevelopment trap. It is quite the opposite. It is a lesson of gradual progress and transformation. In that sense the understanding of the institutional basis is critical, as above-mentioned trends are contributing elements to it. At a certain high level of abstraction, the Caucasus duo has followed the EEFSU experience of institutional transformation.

Now, with hindsight, it appears that the most unexpected element for the early reforms was the evolutionary (transformative) nature of institutional development (Gevorkyan, 2018). North's definition of institutions as "the rules of the game in a society" (North, 2004, p. 3) captures the essence of the problem at hand. What rules have emerged out of transition? A partial answer, justly so, would lead to a "varieties of capitalism"-like arrangement (e.g., Lane, 2007; Hall and Thelen, 2009; Myant, 2016). Based on a range of structural and institutional indicators, there have been substantial improvements in the market-based institutions across the diverse EEFSU palette. Yet, another part of the answer would also suggest that the 1990s experience in the EEFSU showed that abrupt top-down changes to economic and social models resulted in wide-scale degradation and inadequate competitive environment, fostering shadow economy and market failures.

Clearly, a common political past serves as a necessary aggregation criterion in the post-socialist experience. There is no lack of research on the problem of institutional change and economic development (e.g., Acemoglu and Robinson, 2012; Rodrik, 2004). In the post-socialist context the sequencing of reforms appeared to be an important factor (Fischer and Gelb, 1991; Fischer et al., 1996; Hare, 2001, 2013, for example, offer a comprehensive overview of literature on the subject). In a defense of the macroeconomic policy of transition, Fischer and Sahay (2004) emphasize the role of evolving institutions for future researchers.

Yet, the problem of the 1990s transition policies was their standardization, fixated on rigid interpretation of the transition process. Strictly speaking that approach entailed a hypothetical movement from a centrally planned system to a market-based one. In his excellent summary of collected studies, Dale (2011) annotates the subsequent trajectories of the resulting off-market outcomes. Jackson and Deeg (2008) issue a justifiable warning over simplistic interpretation of institutional dynamics. They point to the need to account for "country-specific configurations" instead of resorting to analysis in "bundles" of the "types" of economic systems driven by overgeneralized home and host country effects. In turn, Vonnegut (2010) analytically models the fallacy of the one-size-fits all approach in understanding the transition process.

Perhaps one of the most substantial contributions to the institutional debate in transition is the work of Gaidar (2012). Yegor Gaidar was widely considered to be the architect of the economic transformation in Russia in the early 1990s. Adaptations of that model would reverberate to varying degrees across the transitional periphery. In his assessment, Gaidar emphasized his realization of the need for a gradual nature of new institutions' evolution. He argued that new institutions lacked foundational traditions and required a long time to evolve; a clear contradiction to the standardization of the 1990s. However, Gaidar's argument is consistent with North's (1991) definition of institutions, given above, and his view of society at a given time as the outcome of an evolving web of accumulating institutional tendencies. This necessarily implies gradual institutional emergence and adaptation to the new social norms and business practices, as the dynamic self-regenerating process of economic development takes over.

Extending the logic further, one enters into the "varieties of capitalism" discussions of more recent years. For example, Myant (2016) attempts to rationalize through established frameworks (e.g., Hall and Soskice, 2001) in the case of transition economies. Yet, the author is compelled to look for a unique characterization in the transition economies, and further nuanced individual country experience. As examples of much broader ongoing work, Lane's (2007) and Myant's attempts to assess and emphasize country-specific factors, something that was omitted at the most crucial time of launching reforms, help to develop a more informed understanding of the unending social evolution in the EEFSU region and the transitional periphery in particular. Complementing the debate, Puffer et al. (2015; and related work) discuss varieties of communism, suggesting the influence of a more complex mix of individual and nuanced social motivations rather than an all-encompassing institutional change. The former approach helps to explain the diversity of post-socialist economic models.

Institutional changes are notoriously difficult to capture. Of particular concern are problems of corporate governance, perceptions of corruption, favoritism, the shadow economy and other aspects of an uneven marketplace. And just as there is a plethora of conceptual studies on institutional development, there is equally a substantial body of empirical observations and survey analysis of the process.

The European Bank for Reconstruction and Development report (EBRD, 2016) relies on a measurement scale ranging from 1 (no change from centrally planned economy) to 4+ (industrialized market economy standards) in its assessment of institutional indicators in transition economies. Both Armenia and Georgia appear to be making progress, moving up from a score of 1 in 1989 to 4+ in 2014 for price liberalization, trade and foreign exchange, and small-scale privatization reforms (Armenia, with a score of 3.7, lags behind Georgia's 4.0 in large-scale privatization, but has a score of 2.3 in competition policy compared with Georgia's 2.0). Moreover, despite scant data, the EBRD (2016) also reports high private sector shares in the economy (as a percentage of GDP): approximately 75 percent as of 2010 for both economies.

Similarly, the World Bank's Doing Business 2017 survey (following 2017 updated methodology) shows improvement in the business climate in the Caucasus duo. According to the latest data, Georgia maintains a global rank of 16 on the ease of doing business, while Armenia is ranked as 38 (the lower the better). For both countries, the new ranking represents improvements in business conditions. Figure 5.4 summarizes the key results, reflecting a relatively healthier business climate compared to prior years.

Furthermore, a recent analysis, also sponsored by the World Bank, found a strong propensity for entrepreneurial activity in both Armenia and Georgia (Kuriakose, 2013). According to that research, Armenia has the highest level of entrepreneurial activity in the South Caucasus, surpassing its competitors by such measures as founder characteristics, founders' motivation, innovative activity, and others. An overwhelming majority of respondents in Armenia reported that their business resulted in the introduction of new products or services, or substantial improvement of existing ones, with at least 80 percent of offerings being new to Armenia and 3 percent new to the world. In Georgia, by contrast, no products or services were reported that were new to the world.

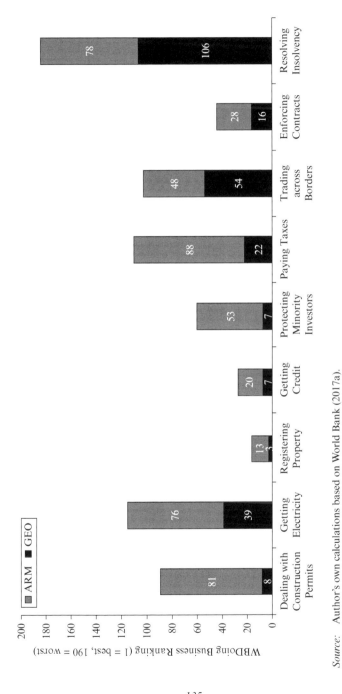

Source: Author's own calculations based on World Bank (2017a).

Figure 5.4 Summary of Armenia's and Georgia's World Bank Doing Business survey 2017 results

135

The entrepreneurship survey touched on the problems of market environment and perceived obstacles to business. Armenian respondents noted low levels of competition (due to the relatively more innovative nature of Armenian business). Georgian respondents, engaged in the production of existing products with only small modifications, indicated higher competition levels.

Changing tax rules and government favoritism were reported as the top problems in Armenia. In Georgia, the frequently changing tax rates were also an issue, complemented by higher overall tax rates. In both countries, difficulty in recruiting highly skilled personnel and market uncertainty were cited as additional obstacles to entrepreneurship, partly due to out-migration. In Armenia, the problems are compounded by difficulties with procuring adequate financing.

This leads to another critical point: the role of shadow economies in the transitional periphery. Consider the data in Table 5.3, derived from yet another survey attempting to pierce through the institutional transformations, the World Bank's series of Enterprise Surveys (World Bank, 2017b). These data are helpful in highlighting some of the firms' nuanced sentiments (as opposed to more macro trends of the Doing Business report). The differences between Armenia and Georgia, apparent from Table 5.3, seem to further complicate any potential desire to declare a winner: country specifics matter.

Certainly, survey data must be taken with a grain of salt. Not every firm or business manager participates in a survey, nor are surveys free from statistical errors. Still, one could use the above results as directional. On a global scale, Schneider et al. (2010) offer a prescient summary of shadow economy operations. The authors find the weighted average size of the shadow economy in the EEFSU region between 1999 and 2007 to be approximately 36.5 percent of the overall economy (though declining). The key contributing factors were the heavy taxation burden and low quality of public goods, that is, lapses in corporate governance. These results seem to indirectly corroborate the observations from the surveys discussed above.

Furthermore, Schneider et al. (2010) also provide rankings of the EEFSU economies based on the size of the shadow economy. The smallest three were the Slovak and Czech Republics and Hungary as of the period under study (18.1, 18.4 and 24.4 percent of the total, respectively). Armenia's share was estimated at 44 percent and Georgia's at 65.8 percent of the total (one of the lowest in the 151 country sample).

Shadow economies in EEFSU are primarily the outcome of the contradictions that emerged during the early years of transition. The complexity of shadow economies is such that in many cases, across the transitional

Table 5.3 Summary of firm experiences with informality (Armenia and Georgia)

Indicator	Armenia	Georgia	Europe & Central Asia	All Countries
Percent of firms competing against unregistered or informal firms	12.8	54.1	39.9	53.4
Percent of firms formally registered when they started operations in the country	99.9	97.2	97.9	89
Number of years firm operated without formal registration	0.1	0.5	0.4	0.7
Percent of firms identifying practices of competitors in the informal sector as a major constraint	9.5	13.7	20.7	27.4
Percent of firms identifying corruption as a major constraint	13.5	2.9	23.5	32.9

Notes: Data as of 2013. * as per World Bank categories.

Source: World Bank (2017b).

periphery in particular, such a structure plays a critical "backbone" role for the functioning of society. A recent colloquium in Henig and Makovicky (2017) channels the discourse into more subtle analysis of "economies of favor" that persist in the post-socialist environment as characteristic features, to the broader formal and informal economies operation.

Some data presented above point to a gradual (comparatively speaking) improvement across all indicators of the informal economy. In fact, consistent with Hare (2001) and Popov (2007), as legacy conditions persist, their relevance declines with time as new factors emerge. North et al. (2009) find that on average institutional transformations required approximately 50 years to allow for technological change, cultural transitions and political stability. In turn, Roth and Kostova (2003) find that changes in corporate governance – one of the pillars of the emerging corporate culture in the FSU – depend on the institutional environment, with attention to cultural characteristics and local context, in transition economies.

Hence, some degree of shadow economy is to be expected in the transitional periphery. The weaker the economic structure, the stronger is the informal economy. In his applied analysis of Armenia's shadow economy, Mikaelian (2016) offers an empirical justification of this view. He finds that during the worst early transition years, society welcomed informal relations as a means of survival. The official state was too weak to combat the expanding informality. At the same time, while the old political guard were removed from power as the economies of Armenia and Georgia were realigned to new rules, a new business elite group emerged. The ill-fated privatization, as well as the military conflicts and lost competitiveness, collectively contributed to the emergence of consolidated groups, dominating key economic sectors in the Caucasus duo today.

As a result, fitting the two economies within IB literature frameworks, it may be suggested that Armenia and Georgia resemble the hierarchical market economies (HMEs) attributed to Latin American economies (e.g., Schneider, 2009). At the same time, on a microeconomic level they seem similar to segmented business systems (SBSs) attributed to African countries (e.g., Wood and Frynas, 2006). Here, Georgia emerges as less of an HME, given its latest high rankings on market institutions in conjunction with external investors' low risk perceptions (GIZ, 2012), compared to Armenia.

Legacy state involvement remains, as do some elements of the legacy hierarchical labor markets. In fact, to some extent, as argued in Rehm (2017), such involvement may be necessary to maintain some degree of economic and social stability in modern economies. At the same time, the markets remain segmented (consistent with a detailed review in the post-socialist context by Martin, 2008) between larger entities and smaller domestic business elites. The pattern is consistent across the post-socialist FSU and Eastern Europe, as documented in Dale (2011).

In a hierarchical and segmented small-country environment such as in the Caucasus duo, the key, when introducing new business, is to follow through with needed capital investment while leveraging well-trained and motivated local staff. Entering either Armenia or Georgia (or both) on their own, foreign investors, likely adapting with some difficulty to local business culture, may see lower returns and become discouraged with underdeveloped consumer markets. And while both Armenia and Georgia are open to international business, knowledge of local business culture and connection with a capable domestic or diaspora partner (either public or private) is helpful before opening up shop.

To that end, both countries have taken quite active steps with state-sponsored international trade expos, investment forums, and other engage-ments with the international business community. Often such efforts are co-sponsored or managed via diaspora members with connections to the global business groups. And at this point, the Caucasus duo assume yet another unique feature, unlike some in the EEFSU group. Through its engagement with the historical homeland, the diaspora is becoming a comprehensive force of economic, social and institutional change. I review some of the specific factors below.

WHY THE DIASPORA MATTERS IN ARMENIA AND GEORGIA

The national diasporas of Armenia and Georgia are quite diverse, multi-fac-tional, and spread across a range of countries. Historically, Russia has been the main host country in both cases, with the United States, France, Canada and Iran following next for Armenia; and Greece, Italy, Spain and Turkey for Georgia (for an extensive analysis of diaspora numbers, see Gevorkyan, 2011; for the latest diaspora assessments see GIZ, 2011, 2012; Gevorkyan, 2016 offers a detailed account on trends in the Armenian diaspora).

Since the liberalization reforms in the early 1990s, the diaspora has been theorized to be a positive contributor to post-socialist economic and social transformation. In fact, poverty rates in transition economies might be (and to some extent have been) reduced through active involvement of the diaspora community through local humanitarian efforts, economic revival, politics or social activities. This model may be viable in particular for the resource-constrained, net importer, transition economies. However, diasporas are not monolithic entities that act uniformly; an insight often omitted in the academic literature.

Nielsen and Riddle (2010) posit that the diaspora's socio-economic experiences may be particularly welcome contributions towards peace and stability in countries that have emerged from a period of military conflict. One finds confirmation for such views in the real-life interactions in the Caucasus duo. On a policy scale, Agunias and Newland (2012) offer general assessments of diaspora potential in home country development. The overall view is almost always positive, with a substantial focus on the role of remittances as one of the major factors. In the FSU, diaspora investors are portrayed as "first movers" (e.g., McGregor, 2014; Gevorkyan and Gevorkyan, 2012; Freinkman, 2001). Diaspora-driven investment may play a role in stimulating initial investment flows from the host economies, and ensuring project sustainability (e.g., Gevorkyan, 2011; Wang et al., 2013), as is the case given Armenia's precarious geopolitical circumstances (e.g.,GIZ, 2011).

The diaspora is also an important harbinger of an institutional change and home country civil society emergence in Armenia and Georgia. Ironically, Bang and Mitra (2011) find a positive correlation between a developing country's higher institutional capacity and stronger incentives for higher-skilled workers to emigrate than lower-skilled ones, even in the presence of political stability. Spread across the world, expatriates of the Caucasus duo are heavily involved in the social and political affairs of the home countries. Finally, the diaspora may reinforce the home country's innovative capacity via scientific, technological and cultural exchanges. In this effort, the diaspora is seen as a profound source of growth for smaller developing economies, as case study after case study attempts to illustrate (e.g., Gevorkyan, 2016; Agunias and Newland, 2012).

The critical factor often omitted in the diaspora debate is the distinction between the "old" and "new" diaspora entities, as both have varying affiliations to their ancestral lands (e.g., Gevorkyan, 2015, 2011). The "new" diaspora is comprised of recently relocated expatriates (possibly a temporary move) from the home to the host economy, with strong family and cultural ties in their country of origin. In contrast, the "old" diaspora is characterized by its well-established (and often culturally assimilated) and socially integrated host countries' citizens. The "old" diaspora, perhaps due to its more established status in the society, may be potentially more altruistically inclined to assist the ancestral home and participate in larger projects (for example, as in the case of Armenia with the institutionally embedded "old" diaspora heralding the entry of large multinational corporations into the otherwise unknown economy (GIZ, 2011).

Gevorkyan (2016) raises the problem of "dispersion" in a case study of Armenia. The term is contrasted to the diaspora, the latter implying a perceived unity in action. Yet, the experience in Armenia and Georgia suggests that the opposite is true. Although the "old" and "new" diaspora Armenians and Georgians may still offer a vision that mirrors that of their historical home on major strategic issues, their actions, ideas and beliefs on other issues indicate much more plurality. The dispersion effect is present in diaspora communities, lacking political or superficial background unity, and between the expatriate community and home countries. The effect is exemplified in diverse home country involvement efforts and a lack of systematic institutional engagement aimed at comprehensive home economy development, aside from a few stand-alone projects.

However, it may be argued that it is the dispersion, in terms of the variety, of expertise and experiences that may be most beneficial to the ongoing economic and social transformation in Armenia and Georgia. In fact, assuming open access to the country for diaspora members (which is the case in the duo), voluntary engagement with local activities would suggest a more natural symbiosis between the home society and the introduction of new, market-based, norms and institutions by way of diaspora involvement. It is a viable view that both Armenia and Georgia have achieved comparatively stronger performance, across the institutional indicators discussed above, in part due to the countries' engagement with diaspora. The engagement is not equal for the two countries, and is more vital and intense in the case of Armenia. Separately, Gevorkyan (2018) derives a diaspora engagement index (see Figure 5.5) that posits Armenia as one of the leaders in the EEFSU group in terms of its diaspora engagement.

Yet, despite a range of proactive measures and an even greater variety of opportunities for direct engagement between diaspora and home, there is evidence that cultural perceptions matter. For example, the GIZ (2011) survey suggests that low investment flows into Armenia might be due to diaspora investors' negative perceptions of the country's actual economic potential and progress. A broad spectrum of institutional underdevelopment is often blamed. This finding is reconfirmed in a recent survey of the Armenian diaspora (Gevorkyan, n.d.). At the same time, as the dispersion effect persists in both Armenia and Georgia, the "new" and "old" diaspora business networks and entrepreneurial talent have been instrumental in creating some opportunities back home. The problem is whether the "giving-back" momentum can be sustained in the face of more complex dynamic modalities of redefined fundamental uncertainty, linking economic stability, competitiveness and rational risk–return strategy to a totality of financial economy and real social costs.

Therefore, leaning against a dispersion effect may actually be a strategy for successful economic, social and institutional transformation. The

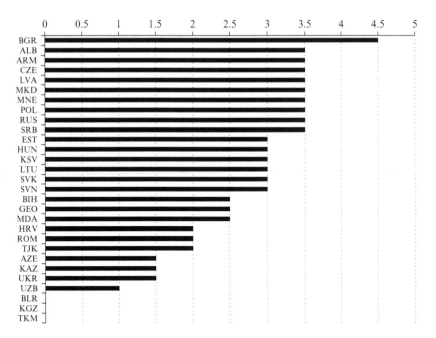

Note: The index is based on the country's diaspora policy priority (e.g., economic development, identity, etc.), existence of diaspora institutions (e.g., Ministry of Diaspora), combined per capita shares of FDI and remittances and extent of "new" and "old" diaspora engagement with home country.

Sources: Author's estimates based on World Bank (2017c), Heleniak (2011) and Gevorkyan (2011).

Figure 5.5   Index of effectiveness of a diaspora in its country of origin

first-movers are especially critical for these economies, where external pressures are strong while domestic market mechanisms are weak and fiscal effort may be insufficient due to objective budget constraints pulled by the ongoing post-socialist transformation. As the cumulative impact of diaspora actions increases, there is a spillover to the domestic institutional base, as portrayed above. Consequently, both Armenia and Georgia are trying to find a balance between their legacy structures and becoming more open to change. Here, purely institutional, business and macro-economic factors combine in one all-encompassing process of social and economic transformation.

SUMMARY AND CONCLUSIONS

This chapter has attempted to shed some light on the economic and social transformation processes ongoing in the republics of Armenia and Georgia. Structured along a discussion of the key five forces of change – the macroeconomic (labor market) dynamics; FDI; international trade; institutional trends; and the diaspora factor – the analysis in this chapter leads to three critical conclusions. Implications for international business and foreign firms' managers are straightforward.

First, any broad macroeconomic and social transition assessments of the Caucasus duo must be done in comparative, country-specific terms. In the context, this chapter shows relative improvements and resilience in the domestic and external markets of Armenia and Georgia. Both economies are open to international cooperation and have overcome most recent setbacks following the Great Recession. This is not to say that there are no risks: the uncertainty factor (macroeconomic and geopolitical) always remains. This chapter alludes to the most tangible in macro terms (for example, credit growth, external exposure and financial flows concentration).

Second, on the institutional scale, both countries have covered much ground in relatively short periods of time. Still, objective assessments and surveys, some of them discussed in this chapter, may raise alarm around problems of corporate governance, business climate and the shadow economy. Yet, when contrasted to the early or mid-transition periods, the institutional progress in both countries is impressive. In turn, that should serve as another justification for additional research effort and international business participation in the region. Much of the progress, in particular in Armenia, has been achieved largely due to country–diaspora and diaspora–country engagements, overcoming the dispersion effect.

Third, the analysis above, across the five dimensions of the proposed conceptual model, also suggests that the key lesson in the transitional periphery, if the Caucasus duo examples are any guide, is summed up in one word: gradualism. Gradual macroeconomic, social, political and institutional transformation has been the characteristic of the post-socialist development in the smaller FSU economies. The experience is not exactly the same in the more European Union integrated EE economies. There, proximity to an advanced market and a shared institutional base helped to speed up the transformation into and adoption of complex market structures. The Caucasus duo offer researchers and IB managers alike an example of longer-term focus emerging from less advantageous starting conditions.

It is critical for IB researchers and managers to appreciate the diversity of characteristics and experiences, even in the cases of Armenia and

Georgia, despite their shared legacy. The two countries are in fact structurally and institutionally different economies. Hence, international firms' managers may need to gain a stronger appreciation for the local context prior to market entry. Foreign managers would be wise to seek capable local partnership (public or private entity), informed of domestic policy nuances, given each economy's small scale and risk factors. Diaspora business may be a viable alternative.

Overall, for scholars in institutional economics and international business, experiences of Armenia and Georgia emphasize, time and again, the need for a country-specific approach in comparative studies. The institutional varieties view, and the struggle many researchers have had in cataloging it, has a place in the present analysis. In that context, this chapter's "five forces" model of economic and social change is an attempt to synthesize the relevant evolving aspects at play in the transitional periphery.

REFERENCES

Acemoglu, D. and J. Robinson (2012). *Why Nations Fail: The Origins of Power, Prosperity, and Poverty.* New York: Crown Business.

Agunias, D.R. and K. Newland (2012). *Developing a Road Map for Engaging Diasporas in Development.* Washington, DC: Migration Policy Institute.

Armenian Development Agency (ADA) (2011). Mining Industry Report, http://www.ada.am, accessed 20 December 2013.

Aslanidi, O. (2008). Dollarization in transition economies: new evidence from Georgia. CERGE-EI, Working Paper Series 366.

Åslund, A. (2001). Ten years after the Soviet breakup: the advantages of radical reforms. *Journal of Democracy*, 12(4), 42–48.

Åslund, A. (2002). *Building Capitalism: The Transformation of the Former Soviet Bloc.* Cambridge: Cambridge University Press.

Bang, J.T. and A. Mitra (2011). Brain drain and institutions of governance: educational attainment of immigrants to the US 1988–1998. *Economic Systems*, 35, 335–354.

Blanchard, O. (1997). *The Economics of Post-Communist Transition.* Oxford: Oxford University Press.

Central Bank of Armenia (CBA) (2014). Databank, https://www.cba.am.

Dale, G. (2011), *First the Transition, then the Crash.* London: Pluto Press.

European Bank for Reconstruction and Development (EBRD) (2016). *Transition Report 2016–2017. Transition for All: Equal Opportunities in an Unequal World.* London: EBRD.

Fischer, S. and A. Gelb (1991). The process of socialist economic transformation. *Journal of Economic Perspectives*, 5(4), 91–105.

Fischer, S. and R. Sahay (2004). Transition economies: the role of institutions and initial conditions. *Festschrift in Honor of Guillermo A. Calvo* (conference paper, 15–16 April 2004). Washington, DC: International Monetary Fund.

Fischer, S., R. Sahay and C. Vegh (1996). Stabilization and growth in transition economies: early experience. *Journal of Economic Perspectives*, 10(2), 45–66.

Freinkman, L. (2001). Role of the diasporas in transition economies: lessons from Armenia. Paper presented at the 11th annual meeting of the ASCE, http:// papers.ssrn.com/sol3/papers.cfm?abstract_id=2401447, accessed 1 May 2014.

Gaidar, Y. (2012). *Russia: A Long View*. Cambridge, MA: MIT Press.

Gerber, T.P. and K. Torosyan (2013). Remittances in the Republic of Georgia: correlates, economic impact, and social capital formation. *Demography*, 50(4), 1279–1301.

German Agency for International Cooperation (GIZ) (2011). *Current Situation of the Diaspora Connected FDIs in Armenia*. Yerevan: GIZ Private Sector Development Program South Caucasus.

German Agency for International Cooperation (GIZ) (2012). *The Georgian Diaspora Study*. Tbilisi: GIZ Private Sector Development Program South Caucasus.

Gevorkyan, A.V. (2011). *Innovative Fiscal Policy and Economic Development in Transition Economies*. Oxford: Routledge.

Gevorkyan, A.V. (2013). Armenian diaspora. In I. Ness and P. Bellwood (eds), *The Encyclopedia of Global Human Migration*, Oxford: J. Wiley & Sons/Blackwell, https://doi.org/10.1002/9781444351071.wbeghm038.

Gevorkyan, A.V. (2015). The legends of the Caucasus: economic transformation of Armenia and Georgia. *International Business Review*, 24(6), 1009–1024.

Gevorkyan, A.V. (2016). Development through diversity: engaging Armenia's New and Old Diaspora. *Migration Information Source,* http://www.migrationpolicy. org/article/development-through-diversity-engaging-armenias-new-and-old-diaspora.

Gevorkyan, A.V. (2017). The foreign exchange regime in a small open economy: Armenia and beyond. *Journal of Economic Studies*, 44(5), 781–800.

Gevorkyan, A.V. (2018). *Transition Economies: Transformation, Development, and Society in Eastern Europe and the Former Soviet Union*. Oxford: Routledge.

Gevorkyan, A.V. (n.d.). Results from the online Armenian Diaspora Questionnaire. Unpublished.

Gevorkyan, A.V. and O. Canuto (2015). Toward a migration development bank for transition economies. *Huffington Post*, 2 June, http://tinyurl.com/pq7okdb.

Gevorkyan, A.V. and A. Gevorkyan (2012). Factoring turbulence out: diaspora regulatory mechanism and Migration Development Bank. *International Migration*, 50(1), 96–112.

Hall, P.A. and D. Soskice (eds) (2001). *Varieties of Capitalism: The Institutional Foundations of Comparative Advantage*. Oxford: Oxford University Press.

Hall, P.A. and K. Thelen (2009). Institutional change in varieties of capitalism. *Socio-Economic Review*, 7, 7–34.

Hare, P. (2001). Institutional change and economic performance in the transition economies. Paper prepared for the UNECE Spring Seminar, Geneva.

Hare, P. (2013). Institutions and transition: lessons and surprises. *Society and Economy*, 35(1), 1–24.

Heleniak, T. (2011). Harnessing the diaspora for development in Europe and Central Asia. MIRPAL Discussion Series. Washington, DC: World Bank.

Henig, D. and N. Makovicky (eds) (2017). *Economies of Favour after Socialism*. Oxford: Oxford University Press.

International Monetary Fund (IMF) (2013). Caucasus and Central Asia: need to increase resilience and accelerate reforms to become emerging markets. *Regional Economic Outlook*, Washington, DC: IMF, pp. 63–73.

Invest in Georgia (2013). Invest in Georgia: key sectors reports. Georgian National Investment Agency, http://www.investingeorgia.org, accessed 25 December 2013.

Jackson, G. and R. Deeg (2008). Comparing capitalisms: understanding institutional diversity and its implications for international business. *Journal of International Business Studies*, 39(4), 540–561.

Karapetyan, L. and L. Harutyunyan (2013). The development and the side effects of remittances in the CIS countries: the case of Armenia. CARIM-East Research Report 2013/24, http://www.carim-east.eu/media/CARIM-East-RR-2013-24.pdf.

Kuriakose, S. (2013). *Fostering Entrepreneurship in Armenia and Fostering Entrepreneurship in Georgia*. Washington, DC: World Bank.

Lane, D. (2007). Post-state socialism: a diversity of capitalisms?. In D. Lane and M. Myant (eds), *Varieties of Capitalism in Post-Communist Countries*. New York: Palgrave Macmillan, pp. 13–39.

Manookian, A. and G. Tolosa (2011). Armenia's housing boom–bust cycle. Report by the IMF Resident Representative Office in Armenia, http://www.imf.org/external/country/arm/rr/2011/112811.pdf, accessed 10 December 2013.

Martin, R. (2008). Post-socialist segmented capitalism: the case of Hungary. Developing business theory. *Human Relations*, 61(1), 131–159.

McGregor, J.A. (2014). Sentimentality or speculation? Diaspora investment, crisis economies and urban transformation. *Geoforum*, 56, 172–181.

Mikaelian, H. (2016). *Shadow Economy in Armenia*. Yerevan: Caucasus Institute. (In Russian.)

Mikhalev, V. (2003). *Inequality and Social Structure During the Transition*. New York: Palgrave Macmillan.

Milanovic, B. (1993). Social costs of the transition to capitalism: Poland, 1990–91. World Bank Policy Research Paper #WPS1165.

Milanovic, B. (1999). Explaining the increase in inequality during transition. *Economics of Transition*, 7(2), 299–341.

Myant, M. (2016). Varieties of capitalism in post-socialist countries. In J. Holscher and H. Tomann (eds), *Palgrave Dictionary of Emerging Markets and Transition Economics: Insights from Archival Research*. New York: Palgrave Macmillan, pp.133–152.

National Bank of Georgia (NBG) (2013). Statistics, http://www.nbg.gov.ge.

Nielsen, T.M. and L. Riddle (2010). Investing in peace: the motivational dynamics of diaspora investment in post-conflict economies. *Journal of Business Ethics*, 89, 435–448.

North, D. (1991). Institutions. *Journal of Economic Perspectives*, 5(1), 97–112.

North, D. (2004). *Institutions, Institutional Change and Economic Performance*. Cambridge: Cambridge University Press.

North, D., J.J. Wallis and B.R. Weingast (2009). *Violence and Social Orders*. New York: Cambridge University Press.

Popov, V. (2007). Shock therapy vs. gradualism reconsidered: lessons from transition economies after 15 years of reforms. *Comparative Economic Studies*, 49(1), 1–31.

Puffer, S.M., E.R. Banalieva and D.J. McCarthy (2015). Varieties of communism and risk-taking propensity of Russian entrepreneurs. *Academy of Management Annual Meeting Proceedings*, 2015(1), 11162–11162.

Rehm, P. (2017). *Risk Inequality and Welfare State: Social Policy Preferences, Development, and Dynamics*. New York: Cambridge University Press.

Rodrik, D. (2004). Getting Institutions Right. CESifo DICE Report 2/2004.

Roth, K. and T. Kostova (2003). Organizational coping with institutional upheaval in transition economies. *Journal of World Business*, 38, 314–330.

Schneider, B.R. (2009). Hierarchical market economies and varieties of capitalism in Latin America. *Journal of Latin American Studies*, 41, 553–575.

Schneider, F., A. Buehn and C.E. Montenegro (2010). Shadow economies all over the world: new estimates for 162 countries from 1999 to 2007. World Bank Policy Research Working Paper 5356.

UNDP (2016). Human Development Report, http://hdr.undp.org/en/2016-report.

United Nations Conference on Trade and Development (UNCTAD) (2017). UNCTAD STAT, http://unctadstat.unctad.org, accessed 10 May 2014.

Vonnegut, A. (2010). Institutions and initial conditions in transition: reconciling neo-institutional and neo-classical. MPRA Paper No. 24563.

Wang, D.T., F.F. Gu, D.K. Tse and C.K. Yim (2013). When does FDI matter? The roles of local institutions and ethnic origins of FDI. *International Business Review*, 22, 450–465.

Wood, G. and J.G. Frynas (2006). The institutional basis of economic failure: anatomy of the segmented business system. *Socio-Economic Review*, 4, 239–277.

World Bank (2006). *Armenia – The Caucasian Tiger*. Washington, DC: World Bank.

World Bank (2017a). *2017 Doing Business Report*. Washington, DC: World Bank, http://www.doingbusiness.org.

World Bank (2017b). *2017 Enterprise Surveys*. Washington, DC: World Bank.

World Bank (2017c). World Development Indicators (WDI). Online database. Washington, DC: World Bank, http://databank.worldbank.org.

Zoryan, H. (2005). The measurement of co-circulation of currencies and dollarization in the Republic of Armenia. *European Journal of Competitive Economics*, 2(1), 41–65.

6. Influence of economic and political changes on industrial relations between Turkey and Azerbaijan

Sayım Yorgun

INTRODUCTION

Industrial relations were born as a subsystem of economic and political structures, taking shape accordingly, and becoming a system in line with changes in these domains. In the last four decades, any relevant change and transformation has had a significant impact on these relations, modifying and transforming them. Transition from the industry-dominant social order to a post-industrial society reduces the influence and supervision of national states in economies and trade. The growing influence of international companies in global economies and their utilization of various electronic means, especially the Internet, in production and trade processes including employment relationships, pave the way for a radical change in structure, employment relations, management activities and working styles of organizations (Spooner and O'Neill, 2002, p. 27). Therefore, changes arising from new economic, political, technological, social and cultural conditions elicit serious discussion about, among other things, industrial relations.

Due to the end of the bipolar global order, the principal role of neoliberal policies, and the transition from closed economic structures to a market economy, the following questions emerge: 'Is this the end of industrial relations?' and 'Do industrial relations change and transform?' These questions will be considered with regard to the industrial relations of countries; in particular, the present and future influence of economic and political change and transformation on industrial relations systems between Turkey and Azerbaijan.

Turkey and Azerbaijan are states with people from the same ethnicity; this fact is expressed by the saying, 'single nation and two states'. Indeed, there are strong historical bonds between the two states. Their relationship became even stronger as Azerbaijan gained independence, accepted the

Latin alphabet and took Turkish as its official language; cooperation also accelerated because the countries have the same national and cultural values. Furthermore, as a democratic, secular country with a market economy, Turkey served as a kind of role model for Azerbaijan; moreover, Turkey has provided the latter with assistance during its transition to a democratic system and its establishment of market economy institutions (DPT, 2000, p. 51).

In the light of developments in the economy and systems of political and industrial relations, Turkey and Azerbaijan bear similarities in terms of their transformation, despite having different economic and political histories. Turkey's transformation includes its passage from a mixed to a neoliberal economy; while Azerbaijan is departing from a socialist economy to follow the same track. Turkey underwent a transition period in order to re-establish a democratic political system that was interrupted by the 1980 coup d'état; whereas Azerbaijan is in the process of becoming an independent, democratic country, being freed from its socialist system since 1991. There is one decade between two periods of change; nevertheless, both leave their mark on the respective countries.

Close ties between Turkey and Azerbaijan include industrial relations. The Labour, Social Security and Employment Agreement, signed between the two countries on 13 November 2013, is engendering cooperation between the parties, as well as the sharing of regulations and experiences. Pursuant to Article 2 under the agreement, collaboration shall be established with regard to working life, collective labour agreements, settling of disputes, labour relations, as well as relations between government agencies, employers' organizations and labour unions.[1] As the agreement shows, close cooperation has been initiated between the two countries in order to improve industrial relations.

In consideration of the relations established between the two countries, along with the relevant changes, the question of current process changes or transformations within industrial relations becomes crucial. Indeed, the industrial relations system which emerged in the region has the potential to influence neighbouring countries. Hence, this chapter analyses the economic and political transformation in Turkey and Azerbaijan in the aftermath of 1980 and 1991, respectively; evaluates the industrial relations system; and explores whether the influence of current processes in both countries will lead to change or transformation in terms of industrial relations.

DEVELOPMENTS IN ECONOMIC AND POLITICAL STRUCTURE IN TURKEY AND AZERBAIJAN

Factors such as the congruence of change in both countries in the last 30 years, with globalization processes, a rise in economic and political integration, boundless capital mobility and the influence of global companies on markets, have rendered this period of change and transformation particularly important. Over the last two decades, the economies of Turkey and Azerbaijan have undergone significant transformations which have, in turn, facilitated the development of bilateral ties. While the Turkish economy has experienced both a domestic restructuring and internationalization in terms of overseas trade and investments, Azerbaijan's accumulation of wealth from energy revenues has been the engine of its economic growth, driving its assertive outward investment strategy (Kardaş and Macit, 2015, p. 43). In consideration of the decisive dominance of economic and political structures in industrial relations systems, it is necessary to analyse the economic and political transformations of both countries, as well as the impact of such aspects. Since the changes in both countries are large scale, their impact is expected to be very high.

Turkey is a country in the process of attaining full European Union (EU) membership, serving as a kind of bridge between Europe and Asia, symbolizing the transition between Eastern and Western cultures. Having the sixteenth-biggest economy in the world, Turkey also has close ties with Middle Eastern states and bonds of brotherhood with Turkic Republics. As for Azerbaijan, on the one hand, it reinforces its relations with Turkey and the West; on the other, the country remains a member of the Commonwealth of Independent States (CIS) that emerged after the collapse of the Soviet Union led by the Russian Federation. In this way, Turkey has greater access to the CIS market via Azerbaijan, while Azerbaijan is brought to the gates of Europe through Turkey (Mikail, 2007, p. 1063). Mutual relations, based on the interests of both parties, have become gradually deepened and reinforced.

Economic and Political Structure in Turkey

Changes in the economic and political development of Turkey as of 1980 had an impact on upcoming years and paved the way for a new economic and political layout. Two factors initiated the process: the programme of economic consistency accepted on 24 January 1980, otherwise known as the '24th January Decisions'; and the military coup of 12 September 1980. The 24th January Decisions process was aimed at the fundamental structure of the Turkish economy, while the military coup was aimed at all state and social structures, including the constitutional and legal set-up.

With Notice No. 1 by the National Security Council (NSC),[2] which suspended democracy, the government was terminated (MGK, 1980, p. 4), while Notice No. 7 stopped the activities of political parties (MGK, 1980, p. 6), before all parties were terminated pursuant to the Law on Termination of Political Parties No. 2533 on 16 October 1981. Provisional Article 4 of the Constitution of 1982 brought a political ban of 5–10 years for all politicians of the pre-1980 era.

In the aftermath of the military coup, elections were held on 6 November 1983 in order to ensure transition to a multi-party democratic system once again; the new government was formed in accordance with the popular will. Nevertheless, the Chief of the General Staff, who carried out the coup, became President of the Republic, and the Constitution of 1982 was made in line with this approach; consequently, the country could not evade the effects of this mentality in the upcoming years. The political normalization process began in November 1983, when the political bans were removed and the rights of former politicians were reinstated, whereupon the structure and functioning of Turkish politics began to change.

Notice No. 16 by the NSC adopted previously planned and promulgated economic decisions, touching upon the following issues: 'Economic programs with previous agreements and protocols, which were established in order to rehabilitate and improve the economic condition in our country, shall remain in effect' (MGK, 1980, p. 8). Upon the foregoing provision, neoliberalism, which had been on the agenda and followed in practice in the West since the 1970s, was realized in Turkey by means of the 24th January Decisions and the coup d'état of 12 September, leading to a radical change in the present order.

The Turkish economy, faced with several economic problems such as high inflation, rising energy prices, growing external debt and a trade deficit, stuck at the end of the 1970s, and transitioned from an inward-oriented industrialization structure to an outward-oriented economic policy programme after 1980 within the framework of the Washington Consensus. The most important institutional effect of the liberal economic programme on the development plan of Turkey is in the 1982 Constitution (Saygın and Çimen, 2013, pp. 14–15). The first phase of reforms was followed by a gradual move to trade liberalization in 1984 (which culminated in a Customs Union with the EU 11 years later) and liberalization of the capital account in 1989 (Boratav and Yeldan, 2001, p. 4). The social state, a natural target for neoliberalism, also became a target in Turkey; consequently, an order was planned and actualized whereby the state shrank, the private sector was supported and capital attained a decisive position.

For the development of Turkey, the mixed economic policy was abandoned, a free economic system replaced it, and the share of the state in the economy was reduced. As a result, the rate of state investments rapidly decreased. In 1981–82, the rate of public sector fixed capital investments was 44.1 per cent; this figure fell to 28.4 per cent in 1999–2000 before declining to 23 per cent in 2015. As these figures clearly show, public investment fell by almost 50 per cent as the state withdrew from areas of investment.

In the aftermath of 1980 came a full free market order, bringing with it a regime open to capital mobility where money was entirely convertible (1989) and the planned system came to an end. After 1985, the state economic enterprises (SEEs) were put onto a sales list and no new investments or renewals followed. Accelerating inflation and constant devaluations in the 1990s were followed by an International Monetary Fund (IMF) programme in 1999, SEEs liquidation became a tool in this; about 100 SEEs were closed, while the rest were indiscriminately put up for sale (Kazgan, 2013, p. 16).

Crises in the Turkish economy, those in 1994 and 2001 above all, paved the way for new problems, leaving a negative mark on industrial relations systems in the process. Indeed, changes in the economy caused inconsistency and reduced labour protections. Legal regulations were reformed on the grounds of flexibility instead of worker-friendly adjustments; and regulations on working relations reinforced the tendency to meet market expectations. Flexibility was highlighted in legal regulations, and new laws included provisions towards atypical forms of employment.

Turkey abandoned import-substitution policies for outward-oriented and export-based policies; the protective role of the state was weakened, and neoliberal policy became dominant. All these facts led to radical changes in the economic structure. Moreover, political life was shaped by the military coup: the democratic system was suspended; obstructions in the political system remained intact and unsolved; and, ultimately, changes in these areas also assumed a radical character. Therefore, it became a common opinion that these developments in economic and political life in Turkey paved the way for transformation.

Economic and Political Structure in Azerbaijan

One of the most important incidents of the twentieth century was the disintegration of the Soviet Union and the gaining of independence of countries in the Union. The Azerbaijan Democratic Republic was founded on 27 May 1918, becoming the first ever republic in the East. Soon it joined the Soviet Union and became the Azerbaijan Soviet Socialist

Republic (ASSR), a name which remained in place until 1991. In the wake of independence, the country underwent a re-establishment process of its economic and political systems.

Azerbaijan is a significant country in terms of natural riches, and magnitude of land and population. Azerbaijan has ties of affection with Turkey, thanks to historical and cultural values; upon independence, the country cemented close bonds with Turkey and the friendship was reinforced via economic and political relations. Azerbaijan has significant political experience as a former member of the Union of Soviet Socialist Republics (USSR); nonetheless, the country struggled as a recently independent country under new conditions brought forth by capitalism.

Azerbaijan abandoned the socialist economy for a liberal economic system; moreover, the country adopted a market economy and democratic system based on the separation of powers, as well as the rule of law. Accordingly, the role of the state in its economic, political and social life decreased. But the liberalization of its economic aspect can be reduced to a process of partial or complete reduction of the administrative (administrative-economic) pressure from the government (Gulaliyev et al., 2016, p.9770). For this reason, the effects of liberalization were limited.

Striving for global integration in economic and political terms, Azerbaijan transmitted rich oil and natural gas resources to the European market and strengthened cooperation with many countries; Turkey, the United Kingdom and the United States above all. In 1992, the country became a member of the IMF and World Bank, and accepted the principal rules with regard to the Multilateral Investment Guarantee Agency and International Centre for Settlement of Investment Disputes. On the one hand, Azerbaijan tried to reinforce relations with Western countries; on the other, it became a member of the Commonwealth of Independent States in 1993. With this membership, old habits and structures came to the fore again, and Russia's effectiveness increased.

Simultaneously with ongoing attempts to bring Azerbaijan together with new economic markets, efforts to form the new state were conducted, and the Constitution was accepted following a referendum on 12 November 1995. According to Article 12 of the Constitution of Azerbaijan, the fundamental objective of the state is to ensure human rights and freedom. The state of Azerbaijan is a democratic, legal, secular and unitary republic based on popular sovereignty (Constitution, Art. 7). The new Constitution brought a presidential system, as well as a clear separation of powers (Constitution, Art. 7). Legislative power is now used by the National Assembly (parliament); executive power is used by the President of the State; while judicial power is in the hands of the courts (Zengin, 2010, p.71). But, despite these constitutional regulations, the political change in Azerbaijan has led to authoritarian institutionalization (Alkan, 2010, p. 219). The maxim of the Constitution of Azerbaijan is grounded on the principle of 'strong execution' and bringing a presidential system equipped with broad authority. This constitutional regulation has a negative impact on democratic developments, leading to the gathering of power in the hands of one person.

Under the auspices of the Soviet tradition, and currently the EU, Azerbaijan has tried to find solutions in order to overcome its economic and social crises, which are in line with the socialist Soviet experience and social mentality of Europe. Azerbaijan is looking for solutions to problems such as hunger, poverty and unemployment, with social services and social assistance policies (Zengin, 2010, p. 101). Following the transition from a socialist economic system to a market economy, the free market conditions began to reign; the state-led economy was abandoned, whereupon economic and political crises emerged, bringing hitherto unknown problems. These problems primarily included unemployment, poverty and corruption. Increasing concern for the future, and the proliferation of poverty, led to the exploitation of employees; and of children above all. Consequently, the rise in the grey economy and informal employment deepened the problems.

The process of liberalization of price policy and foreign economic activities abruptly raised prices in Azerbaijan until 1995. The prices of consumer goods increased in 1991 by 2.07 times compared to 1990, and thereafter were growing by several times each year: 10.12 per cent times in 1992, 12.3 times in 1993, and 17.65 times in 1994.[3] During the socialist era, the system applied a full employment policy called 'lifelong employment for all'. Upon transition from a centrally planned economy to a market economy, market factors began to decide the quality and quantity of employment, and unemployment ensued because, in the new order, full employment is not possible, competition and contest are applied in recruitment, and some will inevitably remain unemployed (Zengin, 2010, p. 222). Undoubtedly, the problem of unemployment – which was not a problem in the past – is one of the main problems of the new period.

According to the resource curse theory, the natural resource richness of a country negatively affects its economic, social and political affairs. But the influence of natural resources on Azerbaijan's political and social life seems to be different. Results report that oil rents impact positively upon the health and education sectors. Government efficiency is better with revenue inflows from natural resources (Gasimov, 2014, pp. 101–102). Azerbaijan's economy has grown by 300 per cent in the last ten years; poverty and unemployment have declined; and in 2015, the non-oil industry grew by 8.4 per cent (Aliyev, 2016). Nevertheless the main problem of most natural resource-abundant countries is high-level dependency on natural resources. This problem is experienced in the dependence on oil in Azerbaijan. It means that if governments cannot prepare the economy for this situation, the country may face serious difficulties during coming years. To overcome this danger, policy-makers must apply policies for increasing the share of non-oil sectors and decreasing the degree of oil dependency. First of all, the economy must be diversified. It is clear that investment inflows help the economy to develop. But under the condition of the existing resource curse, this investment mostly flows to resource-abundant sectors, and investors are not interested in investing in other fields (Gasimov, 2014, p. 102). The experience of developing countries that have successfully used their rich natural resources proves that the resource curse is not inevitable (Badeeb et al., 2016, p. 22). As can be understood from these explanations, the Azerbaijan economy is very much influenced by the oil supply. Economic developments are taking place in this sector. However, it is necessary to turn to new sectors, moving away from the economic structure based on oil, to prevent the negative impact this dependency creates.

Prior to 1991, Azerbaijan was a country within the USSR; accordingly, it had no economic relationship with Turkey (Mikail, 2007, p. 1067). Relations between the two countries began to improve in 1991 when Turkey became the first state to recognize the independence of Azerbaijan. During the post-independence era, Turkey tried to reinforce the independence, sovereignty, territorial integrity and new identity of Azerbaijan, contributing to efforts by the latter to introduce itself as an equal member of the international community. Turkey supported efforts by Azerbaijan in order to instil a pluralist democratic structure and to make the market economy functional in every aspect. For Turkey, Azerbaijan has always been an important country, sharing a common language, culture and history. Since day one, Turkey has been the greatest supporter of Azerbaijan on its journey to overcome the challenges of being a new independent republic.

The first agreement between the two countries was signed on 1 November 1992, in order to improve economic and commercial relations between Turkey and Azerbaijan by adopting a market economy model (Zengin, 2010, p. 323). In August 2010, the Agreement on Strategic Partnership and Mutual Support was signed, followed by the decision to establish the High Level Strategic Cooperation Council in September. The Agreement and Council added a new dimension to relations; thereafter, economic cooperation between the countries began to increase. Evidently, such close cooperation is apparent in other domains as well. In consideration of all these facts, Azerbaijan began the process of a radical change in economic and political terms, moving towards transformation into a new system. Although the Azerbaijan economy has a new economic structure, it seems to have stricter economic regulations than the Turkish economy. If liberalization continues, Azerbaijan will strengthen its business alliance with both Turkey and other countries.

DEVELOPMENT OF INDUSTRIAL RELATIONS BETWEEN TURKEY AND AZERBAIJAN

Following the Industrial Revolution, the emerging conditions paved the way for the political economy and 'liberalism' which took hold of countries, causing a change in economic, social and political structures. Nevertheless, the effects were not identical in each country, varying depending upon the level of industrialization, as well as political and social structures. Industrial relations, which can be defined as institutionalized labour relations, sprang forth during industrialization and became a significant factor in forming the economic, political and social structure of countries, while also being shaped through the same structures.

On one hand, an industrial relations system became one of the factors to bring democratic systems to light; on the other, it was nourished by democratic systems as well. Turkey and Azerbaijan are two countries that were affected by the process in different ways. For this reason, the industrial relations of the two countries are emerging in different economic, political and social structures.

Development of Industrial Relations in Turkey

The Ottoman era included almost no industrialization and unionization; the foundation of the Republic of Turkey, however, accelerated industrialization. The first ever regulation for unions was undertaken in laws enacted in 1908 and 1909, whereupon unionization was prohibited in public services. A collective labour agreement entered into Turkish Law under the name of the 'General Contract' through the Code of Obligations and was accepted in 1926. Unfortunately, the prohibition of trade unions prevented collective bargaining (Güzel, 1986, p. 208).

The First Industrial Plan in Turkey came into effect in 1933. Pursuant to this plan, the state was in the market as an investor. Because of state investments, the number of workers soared and the first ever Labour Law was passed in 1936. The law, however, included no provisions in line with requirements of a modern society, especially in terms of collective labour rights. Indeed, the law had seriously rough edges, such as prohibition of strikes and lockouts, lack of any provision on collective agreements, and no mention of labour unions (Güzel, 1986, p. 217). On an individual scale, the definition of a worker was very strict, so the area of execution of the law was notably restricted. The Law of Associations, accepted in 1938, imposed a prohibition on the right to form an association, reflecting the growing tendency to control workers' movements.

The legal regulation process, based upon the prohibition of unions, underwent progress towards union rights in 1946 and 1947, thanks to the amendment of the Law of Associations and the first ever Law on Trade Unions, respectively. The Law on Trade Unions included no right to strike, and workers were banned from political activity. Indeed, the acceptance of this law in the wake of World War II was closely related to the progress of democracy all over the world and the position of Turkey in the Western bloc. This process formed the industrial relations in Turkey, followed by a new era with the military coup in 1960, when began the age of industrial relations with rights to free collective labour bargaining and to strike. Nevertheless, these rights emerged with the military coup and, indeed, lacked sufficient grassroots support. Even so, the post-1960 era heralded a period of significant steps for the institutionalization of labour relations in Turkey. The Constitution of 1961, along with the Law on Trade Unions and the Law on Collective Bargaining Agreement, Strike and Lockout enacted in 1963, enabled proliferation of industrial relations until 1980. Public officials granted the right of organization with the regulation under the Constitution of 1961; nonetheless, the right was removed and prohibited upon an amendment of the Constitution in 1971.

The Trade Unions Act of 1947, and particularly the enactment of collective bargaining legislation in Turkish Labour Law, includes such subjects as:

- trade union freedom;
- the organization, structure and functions of labour unions and employers' unions;
- collective bargaining (competence and authorization, certification, structure and territory of bargaining, legal nature of collective agreements);
- settlement of collective labour disputes (mediation and arbitration);
- strikes and lock-outs;
- exceptions to the right to strike, and recourse to compulsory arbitration;
- workers' participation in management (Dereli, 2013, p. 28).

The system of industrial relations established by statutory regulations continued to exist until 1980, and the use of these rights was relatively widespread. But restrictive interventions have always existed.

The military coup in 1980 and relevant economic changes reformed the industrial relations system. The Constitution of 1982 was made in a reactionary way, putting forth interventions to restrict union-related freedoms. Law No. 2821 on Trade Unions and Law No. 2822 on Collective Bargaining Agreements and Strike, which were prepared in line with foregoing constitutional adjustments, reshaped industrial relations. The 1983 legislation set out to eliminate the abuses and malfunctioning aspects of the previous system, but these 'positive motives' were accompanied by 'negative motives' with respect to several dimensions of union freedoms. Thus, new laws further restricted strikes, expanded the scope of compulsory arbitration, imposed certain limitations on union membership, and instituted heavier penalties for violators (Dereli, 2013, p. 40). Although the union structure was centralized at the industry level, the focus of bargaining was reduced to local levels. At the same time, the requirement that a union, in order to be entitled to bargain on behalf of plant (establishment) or enterprise (company), should represent at least 10 per cent of the workers in the industry (currently 1 per cent) and more than half of the workers in the plant (currently 40 per cent) or company, tended to curb the freedom to bargain without implementation of smaller, newly established unions; a circumstance that has become a major issue in union and International Labour Organization (ILO) circles (Dereli, 2013, p. 41).

The industrial relations system suffered serious effects following the suspension of union activities in 1981–1982 and their subsequent restriction; renewal of collective labour agreements by the High Board of Arbitration due to compulsory arbitration (1980–1983), and limitation and return of acquired rights to unions and collective bargaining via the Constitution of 1982 and laws, was enacted the following year. The Constitution of 1982, in turn, had no explicit provision concerning public officials. Organization of civil servants, initiated by teachers in 1986 based on international documents approved by Turkey, was followed by the right to establish unions and umbrella institutions, as well as to collectively bargain for public officials via a clause added to Article 53 of the Constitution in 1995. In 2001, union rights, albeit limited, were gained upon acceptance of Law No. 4688 concerning Trade Unions for Public Officials; nonetheless, this right was not complemented by the rights to collective agreement and to strike. Amendments in the Constitution on 12 September 2010 transformed the right to collective bargaining into the right to collective agreement, even though the right to strike was yet to be granted. Public officials in Turkey utilized the right to collective agreement without strike (Yorgun, 2011, p. 150).

In order to eliminate the foregoing effects and to establish a more modern and libertarian Turkish law, Law No. 6356 concerning Trade Unions and Collective Bargaining Agreements was accepted in 2012 for the reformation of unions and collective bargaining. This law remains in effect in the country. The law includes certain steps forward; nevertheless, the prohibitions and restrictions within were far from satisfying to the working class. The powers of the Ministry of Labour and Social Security remain substantially preserved, union security is not duly ensured, the authority to double-threshold collective bargaining is maintained, and the level and content of collective labour agreements are limited (Yorgun, 2011, p. 377). According to the International Trade Union Confederation (ITUC) 2012 Turkey Report:

> The law provides limited rights to organise, collective bargaining and strike. The legal protection from acts of interference is weak and sanctions for anti-union discrimination are not dissuasive. The state and the employers make use of various anti-union practices that have weakened trade unions' negotiating rights. Industrial action and protests are often treated with violence and threats. Unions also face increasing judicial harassment. (ITUC, 2012a, p. 6)

In addition, research by the ITUC using 97 indicators in 2015 highlights that Turkey is among the countries where union rights are not under guarantee (ITUC, 2015). According to ITUC reports, only a small number of Turkish workers can use their union rights (unionization rate was 12.18 per cent in January 2017), although most union members cannot use their right to collective bargaining and strike. The rate of unionization among public officials is apparently higher (unionization rate was 72 per cent in July 2016); nevertheless, the troubled situation continues, due to dependency on the government and the lack of the right to strike.

The industrial relations system in Turkey, established in the aftermath of 1980, contributes to the extension of freedoms, albeit partially, by means of amendments in legal regulations, judicial decisions and Constitutional Court decrees. The impact of decisions by the Constitutional Court are indicated as follows: 'Considering the decisions made or to be made by the Constitutional Court in recent years about union rights, we can reasonably modify the common view that "Union rights in Turkey are generally recognised by laws" into "Union rights in Turkey have improved thanks to recent decisions by the Constitutional Court"' (Hekimler, 2015, p. 31). Nevertheless, in spite of certain expansionary decisions with regard to individual freedoms to unionization, the Court maintained the general point of view in the laws when considering collective freedom for unions. In the decisions of the Constitutional Court, the unions are neither expected to be very strong nor completely weak (Yorgun, 2016, p. 1198). Industrial relations in Turkey continue to follow a fluctuating course. The process is shaped through detailed legal regulations, while the state still tends to keep the system under control, even though global impacts are apparent as well.

Development of Industrial Relations in Azerbaijan

Industrial development in Azerbaijan during the late nineteenth and early twentieth centuries brought a boost in the number of workers; accordingly, worker-related problems and reactions began to emerge. Between 1870 and 1920, foreign companies completely disregarded worker rights and interests; as a result, oil workers had to work for 14–15 hours a day without any safety measures, and the situation led to protests. Workers in the Baku oilfield, exploited by world-famous oil-rich Nobel and others, had to fight back in order to boost their prosperity, reduce working hours and improve working conditions in general. In 1903, oil workers went on strike together with the Baku branch of the Russian Social Democratic Party; and the first collective agreement in the country was made following the strike (Salimov, 2014, p. 9). On 30 December 1904, an agreement was signed concerning the petroleum industry; the agreement of 28 articles took labour rights under protection. According to certain sources, agreements were signed with various institutions in 1903 in order to regulate labour relations (Qasımov, 2007, p. 147). Upon signature of these collective agreements, trade unions became a party, and have maintained their existence.

The Labour Code, passed in 1922, was another significant milestone in the journey of the collective labour agreement system in Azerbaijan. The code was applied in Soviet Union countries, and adopted by Azerbaijan without any modification. Collective agreements were contracted within the scope of private property, while a 'Prime Contract' was agreed in government offices; such central agreements restricted the issues and transformed them into official documents. No collective labour agreement was made between 1934 and 1946; during this period, collective bargaining was deprived of its many significant functions; whereas provisions, which aimed at supporting the socialist system in terms of production problems and plans, were added to the agreements (Qasımov, 2007, p. 147).

In 1966, the USSR Council of Ministers and All-Union Central Council of Trade Unions signed an agreement called the 'Conclusion of Collective Agreement in Public Enterprises' in order to determine the institutions with which collective agreements would be made, as well as the content of the collective agreements. It was decided in 1976 to discuss with the Ministries, the USSR Academy of Sciences, Academy of Science in Union Republics of the USSR, and other institutions, the right to negotiate with union committees at central and republic level, and to determine principal provisions of collective agreements at research, engineering, design and technology institutions in consideration of the respective activities of such organizations (USSR KK, 1976). This agreement provides for the signing of collective bargaining agreements at the central level.

In 1984, the 'Directive on Procedure regarding Conclusion of Collective Agreements', approved through the decree by the presidency of All-Union Central Council of Trade Unions and State Committee for Labour and Social Problems, determined the procedure and content of collective agreements. The section concerning agreement content was headed 'Ensuring a socialist work discipline', while the section on liabilities of parties included:

> For economic and social development, implementation of state plan and socialist responsibilities, as well as of improving encouragement with regard to socialist competition and its tangible and intangible incentives; acceleration in productivity rise, cost reduction, improvement of product quality, delivery of orders to contracted sites, introduction of new technologies, inventions, innovations, best practices, production, business and management organisation, mechanisation and automation of main and auxiliary affairs, reduction of manual and labour-requiring activities.

As the foregoing indications show, provisions to ensure assistance to production units were highlighted, while objectives such as training, participation in management, job safety, professional development, and pay rises and bonus payments, were pushed into the background.

The union committee continues to carry out systematic monitoring of timely fulfilment of activities within the scope of collective agreement; it thus regulates the implementation of mutual liabilities and activities together with management. The committee receives quarterly reports of the management about implementation of collective agreement, and asks for elimination of detected flaws; furthermore, it realizes semi-annual and annual reporting on implementation of collective agreements at the general assembly meeting of workers. If necessary, it can add an item to the agenda of the assembly meeting concerning dismissal and punishment of executives who do not fulfil their responsibilities within the scope of collective agreement, breach labour legislation, or allow for delay in bureaucracy and affairs (*Economic Journal*, 1984). Union structures, which existed until the independence of Azerbaijan, were not adversaries to the system; additionally, these organizations assisted the socialist order, and the content of collective labour agreements was determined in this respect.

Following the independence of Azerbaijan, constitutional and legal regulations about industrial relations were reshaped; the beginning of the Azerbaijani Constitution of 1995 included the objective of providing every citizen with an honourable and fair standard of living, in line with economic and social rules. Article 24 in the Constitution guaranteed rights and freedoms, while Article 25 accepted the principle of equality, securing the rights and freedoms of everyone, regardless of whether they were members of unions or any other social associations. The second clause under Article 58 gave citizens the right to establish or become members of existing unions, to participate in union activities and freely carry out such activities.

Article 36 in the Constitution of Azerbaijan secured the right to strike for everyone, indicating:

> Every Person shall have the right to Strike either alone or together with others. The right to Strike of working on Contract basis can be limited only in cases specified by Law. Military and civil Persons serving in the Armed Forces or other armed formations of Azerbaijan Republic shall not go on strike.

Therefore, the right to strike was restricted for military and civil persons in armed formations, but granted to others.

In 1994, the Law on Trade Unions in the Azerbaijani Republic was accepted; the justification of this law was that it was enacted in order to abide by suggestions of the Universal Declaration of Human Rights, ILO conventions and recommendations, and the European Social Charter in order to recognize union rights and to protect economic and social rights and interests of union members. According to Article 3, 'Right of Organisation', employees, the retired and students became able to establish unions on voluntary terms at their sole discretion without obtaining any prior permission; furthermore, such persons now have the right to join unions and carry out union activities in order to protect their legitimate interests, as well as social and economic rights.

Unions, independent from state bodies, enterprises, political parties and social communities, do not have to report to such institutions. Government agencies and officials cannot restrict union rights or hinder activities that are carried out within the scope of the legal framework. Under Article 5 of the law, unions became free to prepare their respective activity programmes and to act in line with provisions in the Constitution (Qasımov, 2007, p. 153). Pursuant to applicable legislation, unions also became able to arrange and carry out strikes, meetings, walk-outs or other mass demonstrations in order to fulfil their objectives and duties (Art. 19). Associations of unions were given the right to enter into collective bargaining and collective agreements in commercial, social and cultural areas with government agencies and other institutions to the extent of their power (Art. 14).

The Law on Collective Bargaining and Agreements, enacted in 1996, became an important milestone in post-independence Azerbaijan with regard to collective bargaining systems. The law brought the right to make high-level agreements above production levels, as well as a provision that social and economic problems concerning workers could be rearranged. According to Article 3 on social collaboration, a collective agreement is an agreement that is made in writing between employer and workers or union in order to regulate conditions about social, economic and subsistence-related aspects of labour (Qasımov, 2007, p. 149).

According to the law on collective agreement, three types of collective agreements are applicable in Azerbaijan. The first is the 'Prime Contract', where general principles of social and economic policies are determined. Hereby, a contract is signed between the Cabinet, Confederation of Unions and employers' associations in Azerbaijan. The second type, known as '*Saha Sazish*', is prepared in order to arrange the conditions and rights of social and economic development and of labour at production level. These agreements are signed between union branches and employer or employers' associations. The third is '*Ərazi (Aayon) Sazish*'. This contract is made between executive bodies and local union associations in order to determine obligations of parties in order to solve social and economic problems (Qasımov, 2007, p. 171). In 1999, this law was removed and replaced by provisions of the Labour Code.

The Labour Code regulates issues regarding both individual and collective labour relations, including provisions for public officials as well as workers. In addition to labour contracts, the law deals with ways to solve collective labour relations, strike and lockout through relevant provisions (Uşan, 2005, p. 1). According to Article 3, working conditions can be decided via collective agreements; it is forbidden to discriminate against workers due to their membership in unions or any other social associations, and the worker has the right to go to court against elimination of such discrimination (Art. 16); labour contracts of the persons assigned in union bodies or participating in collective bargaining negotiations cannot be terminated during their term of duty (Art. 79) (see Uşan, 2005). Another difference between Azerbaijan and Turkish labour laws is that the former incorporate public officials. Therefore, there is no need to distinguish officials and workers in legal terms, with the law including both.

Article 3/16 under the Azerbaijani Labour Code defines an individual labour dispute as 'Individual dissidences between parties during application of the Labour Code or other legislation due to default of fulfilment of respective liabilities arising from labour contracts or collective agreements'. The important point here is that the worker has the power to stop working (strike) at their sole discretion and on their own for settlement of a labour dispute. Nevertheless, unilateral strike action is temporary and cannot exceed one month. A worker may opt for such a method without going to law or terminating the contract. They may go to law during or after the process. Conversely, the employer cannot stop the work or terminate the contract of the worker without a relevant court decision (Uşan, 2005, p. 33).

For successful conduct of the national economy, triple powerful agreements were signed between the Cabinet of the Azerbaijani Republic,

Azerbaijan Trade Unions Confederation and Azerbaijani Republic Association of Entrepreneurs (Employers). These conventions determined the respective responsibilities of each party for developing the labour market and ensuring a guarantee of employment for the population; furthermore, the relevant precautions were prescribed and a significant control mechanism was founded. These conventions contributed to the solution of a social dialogue of problems at the national level.

In the wake of Azerbaijan's independence, unions underwent a reorganization process, whereupon the Azerbaijan Trade Unions Confederation (AHİK) was founded on 5–6 February 1993 at the Congress of Azerbaijani Unions. AHİK is a voluntary alliance of the Nakhchivan Autonomous Republic and 26 union associations, seeking representation and protection of labour, socio-economic rights and the interests of union members. The confederation incorporates 17 430 union associations and around 1.6 million union members.

Azerbaijan has approved conventions No. 87 and 98 under the ILO, called the 'Right to Organise' and 'Right to Organise and Collective Bargaining', respectively; furthermore, the country is open to international audit. According to research on the abuse of union rights by the International Trade Unions Confederation in 2012, in Azerbaijan:

> Trade union rights are adequately protected in the law. Unions are recognised as social partners at all levels, including when adopting social and labour laws and regulations. Freedom of association is secured, and the law prohibits anti-union discrimination. Employers can also in general not dismiss employees without the written consent of the trade union within the enterprise. The right to collective bargaining and the right to strike are guaranteed. Unions may not carry out purely political strikes, but are allowed to protest against the state's socioeconomic policies. Finally, workers in essential services as well as employees of legislative authorities, relevant executive authorities, courts and law enforcement authorities may not go on strike. (ITUC, 2012b)

As the ITUC report indicates, union rights are sufficiently preserved in Azerbaijan; however, intense threats by international companies on unions somehow continue, whereupon union member workers are dismissed. In addition, the employees of the armed forces do not have the right to strike.

CHANGE AND TRANSFORMATION

According to discussions in the relevant literature, the industrial relations system in a country undergoes either a change or a transformation under the influence of economic and political structures in that country, or even preserves its current situation. Nevertheless, it is not easy to detect and evaluate any of these three situations in industrial relations systems. Since the meaning ascribed to concepts of 'change' and 'transformation' can vary greatly, it is necessary, above all, to explain what to understand from these concepts. In this respect, 'change' can be defined as the changes in a period of time, while 'transformation' is, rather, to assume another situation or form from the present one. In other words, change signifies non-radical alterations, while transformation indicates radical alteration. Consequently, it is correct to evaluate the process in industrial relations based on these two concepts (Yorgun, 2007, p. 8). Furthermore, it is important in which areas the change and transformation are examined. For example, we may focus on amendments in laws; nevertheless, the content may also include various areas such as structure, strategies and organization levels of unions, as well as collective bargaining level and issues. Therefore, the content of relevant studies may elicit different outcomes.

Transition from a socialist to a liberal system and democratic developments lead to radical changes in economic and political spheres; therefore, this process equally transforms industrial relations. Likewise, transition from a mixed to a liberal economy can produce various consequences and lead to change or transformation. The history of industrial relations in Turkey and Azerbaijan reveals a different process with dissimilar effects. In the light of these general conclusions, the change or transformation will be analysed with regard to legal regulations, union structures and strategies, collective bargaining level and interest of governments in both countries.

Evidently, there are notable differences in legal regulation of the two countries; in Turkey, this variance was towards restriction and control of unions and union rights after 1980, before improving for a more libertarian approach over the course of time. As for Azerbaijan, changes to expand union rights came to the forefront in the aftermath of independence in 1991. Whether these changes led to a transformation is a crucial question.

As can be seen in Table 6.1, the legal arrangement of industrial relations in Turkey followed a fluctuating course, providing workers with rights to union and collective bargaining in the beginning, adding public officials to the regulatory scope and granting workers the right to strike but depriving civil servants of this right. Furthermore, the definition of public official or civil servant was too broad, including a great number of public employees who actually are workers, within the staff; this fact brought about many negative effects, including problems about the use of union rights.

As Azerbaijan was part of a socialist system prior to 1991, the country had no free collective bargaining before this date. In the socialist system, unions were not adversaries, but only supportive of the system; accordingly, they were not given the right to free collective bargaining. Regulations since 1991 show that, as of 1994, employees were granted the right to a

Table 6.1 Development of industrial relations in Turkey and Azerbaijan

	Turkey before 1980	Turkey after 1980	Azerbaijan before 1991	Azerbaijan after 1991
Trade union rights				
Worker	Y (1946–1980)	Y (1980–1983 activities ceased) (1983–)	Y (socialist system)	Y (1994–)
Public official	Y (1965–1971)	Y (2001–)	Y (socialist system)	Y (1994–)
Collective bargaining				
Worker	Y (1963–1980)	Y (1980–1983 Compulsory arbitration) (1983–)	Y (socialist system) (1934–1946 Collective Agreement is not signed)	Y (1994–)
Public official	N	Y (1995–2010 Collective Bargaining) (2010–Collective Agreement)	Y (socialist system) (1934–1946 Collective Agreement is not signed	Y (1994–)
Strike				
Worker	Y (1963–1980)	Y (1980–1983 forbidden) (1983–)	N	Y (1994–)
Public official	N	N	N	Y (1994–) (Military and civil Persons serving in the Armed Forces other armed formations shall not go on strike)

Note: Y: Yes. N: No.

166

union, collective bargaining and strike. Restrictions on these rights of civil servants are also seen to be limited. Change in union structures and strategies, amendments in legal regulations, level of collective bargaining and changes in government approaches provide us with the results of Table 6.2 with regard to industrial relations in Turkey and Azerbaijan.

In light of these studies, the Turkish industrial relations system arguably underwent two main periods of transformation due to legal amendments and radical changes in union structures and employer strategies, the structure of collective bargaining and relations with the government in the 1960s and 1980s (Yorgun, 2007, p. 26). Changes in 1960 included extending and securing union freedom, while the developments after the 1980s included the restrictive nature with regard to union freedom and rights.

The right to organize and collective bargaining are restricted because of adjustments in favour of central organization through legal regulations, limitations on higher organization models, reduction of collective bargaining to the level of the workplace and enterprise, lack of collective bargaining on a sector basis, and prohibition of multilevel collective bargaining,[4] grounded on the authorization process of organization and collective bargaining at the sector level, as well as the imposition of a double threshold authority system.

Trade unions developed strategies in order to protect their rights, due to the current conditions, while employers endeavoured to take back rights. Governments preferred de-unionization to pro-union protective interventions, and only tolerated yellow unions, causing radical changes in industrial relations. Additionally, the changeable rather than consistent situation of the collective bargaining and collective labour conflict process produced an unstable and insecure industrial relations system in Turkey.

As of 1983, articles under the Law on Trade Unions and Law on Collective Labour Agreements, Strike and Lockout were amended, relatively more libertarian amendments were made, and finally, in 2012, the two laws were combined under the Law on Trade Unions and Collective Labour Agreement. Nevertheless, the improvements were only partial; consequently, the concerns about possible restrictions and prohibitions on union freedoms were far from over. In particular, the delays of strikes have a negative effect on the use of postponed rights by the decisions of the Council of Ministers. As a result, the industrial relations system in Turkey underwent radical changes and finally transformed.

As for Azerbaijan, post-1991 changes in Azerbaijani industrial relations point to a radical shift due to enactment of the right to free organization, grounded on multi-level collective bargaining, provision of a guarantee for union rights, granting the right to strike, providing parties with the right to determine the content of collective bargaining, free determination of

Table 6.2   Structural changes in Turkey's (after 1980) and Azerbaijan's (after 1991) industrial relations systems

Country	Trade union building in exchange			Change in strategy		Legislation change	In the interests of government changes
	Trade Union	Employer	Bargain	Trade Union	Employer		
Turkey	Y	N	Y	Y	Y	Y	Y
Azerbaijan	Y	Y	Y	Y	Y	Y	Y

Note: Y: Yes. N: No.

union strategies, and government support for the process. In particular, the right to free collective bargaining and to strike paved the way for establishment of a new system. Supporters of the current system until then, the unions were now included in the system of free collective bargaining. As a result, union structures and strategies, legal regulations and the governmental approach to the industrial relations system underwent a radical change. The radical changes in industrial relations in the two countries are transforming the system, but it is not yet stabilized. Therefore, we can estimate that the process remains incomplete and is to continue in the forthcoming years.

CONCLUSION

Global economic, technological, political, social and cultural changes are altering and/or transforming industrial relations structures as well as other domains. Such change and transformation processes are taking place on a different basis in each country: in some, laws are amended; while others opt for changes in areas such as the collective bargaining system and level of organization. On the other hand, certain countries are undergoing much more radical changes.

Turkey underwent the mentioned period of change in 1980, followed by Azerbaijan ten years later. Economic and political transformation in the two countries did influence their respective industrial relations and the system was reconfigured. An analysis of several criteria, including union structures and strategies, level of bargaining, legal regulations and governmental approach, point to a radical change whereupon the system was transformed. Such transformation, however, has yet to be completed and remains in progress.

A comparison between the experiences of Turkey concerning the free collective bargaining system and strike, and new legal regulations and applications in Azerbaijan, show that the two systems have characteristics that support one another, and an exemplary industrial relations system can potentially be established between them in the case of effective cooperation.

Pursuant to agreements signed between Turkey and Azerbaijan, the areas of close cooperation include collective labour agreements, settlement of labour disputes, labour relations, and sharing of experiences and knowledge concerning relations between government agencies and employers' associations and trade unions. Such cooperation, which is to cover the entire industrial relations system, will accelerate and even stabilize the transformation process. Therefore, in the light of their history, these two countries are in need of cooperation in industrial relations, as well as other domains. If the cooperation is conducted in a successful manner, these two industrial relations systems can evolve towards a model which can serve as an example for other countries in the region.

NOTES

1. The Government of the Republic of Turkey and the Government of the Republic of Azerbaijan signed the Labour, Social Security and Employment Cooperation Agreement, 13 November 2013.
2. Upon the military coup of 12 September, the National Security Council consisted of the Chief of the General Staff, as well as the Commanders of Land, Air and Naval Forces and Gendarmerie. The Council used its legislative and executive powers until 7 December 1983.
3. Accessed 9 July 2017 at http://www.azerbaijan.az/_Economy/_Reforms/_reforms_e.html.
4. Law No. 6356 on Trade Unions and Collective Labour Agreement, passed in 2012, includes a framework agreement; thereupon, the content of these sector-based agreements between workers and employers' unions that are members of workers' and employers' confederations represented at the Economic and Social Council was limited, with regulations on vocational training, occupational health and safety, social responsibility and employment policies (Art. 2 and Art. 33). Therefore, the framework agreement regulation should not be considered as a sector contract. Since the enactment of the law, nevertheless, no such contract has been signed, which is a proof of the foregoing argument.

REFERENCES

Aliyev, İlham (2016), The future of Azerbaijan's Economy. World Economic Forum. Accessed 6 November 2017 at https://www.weforum.org/agenda/2016/01/azerbaijan.

Alkan, Haluk (2010), Azerbaycan Paradoksu, Azerbaycan'ın İç ve Dış Politikası. Usak Yayınları: 36, Ankara.

Badeeb, Ramez, Lean, Hooi and Clark, Jeremy (2016), The Evolution of the Natural Resource Curse Thesis: A Critical Literature Survey. Working Paper No. 5/2016, Department of Economics and Finance, College of Business and Law, University of Canterbury Christchurch, New Zealand.

Boratav, Korkut and Yeldan, Erinç (2001), *Turkey, 1980–2000: Financial Liberalization, Macroeconomic (In)-Stability, and Patterns of Distribution.* Ankara. Accessed 2 November 2017 at http://yeldane.bilkent.edu.tr/B&YCEPA2002.PDF.

Dereli, Toker (2013), Labour Law and Industrial Relations in Turkey. *International Encyclopaedia for Labour Law and Industrial Relations*, General Editor R. Blanpain. Netherlands, Kluwer Law International.

DPT (2000), Türkiye İle Türk Cumhuriyetleri ve Bölge Ülkeleri İlişkileri. Sekizinci Beş Yıllık Kalkınma Planı, Özel Komisyon Raporu, Ankara.

Economic Journal (1984), No. 45, (Экономическая газета, 1984, No. 45) (Положение О Порядке Заключения Коллективных Договоров, Утверждено Постановлением

Президиума Вцспс И Государственного Комитета Ссср По Труду И Социальным Вопросам От 28 Сентября 1984 Г.)

Gasimov, Ilkin (2014), Resource Curse and Dutch Disease in Azerbaijan: Empirical Analysis. Master of Science in Economics, Eastern Mediterranean University, Gazimağusa, North Cyprus.

Gulaliyev, Mayis G., Ok, Nuri I., Musayeva, Fargana Q., et al. (2016), Economic Liberalization and its İmpact on Human Development: A Comparative Analysis of Turkey and Azerbaijan. *International Journal of Environmental and Science Education*, 11(17), pp. 9753–9771.

Güzel, Ali (1986), 3008 Sayılı İş Yasasının Önemi ve Başlıca Hükümleri, Sosyal Siyaset Konferanslar Dergisi. Sayı: 35–36, ss.165–222.

Hekimler, Banu Uçkan (2015), Anayasa Mahkemesi'nin Sendikal Haklara İlişkin İptal Karalarının Genel Bir Değerlendirmesi. *Çalışma ve Toplum Dergisi*, 2015(4), pp. 11–34.

ITUC (2015), Global Rights Index Names World's Ten Worst Countries for Workers. Geneva. Accessed 9 July 2016 at https://www.ituc-csi.org/ituc-global-rights-index- names?lang=en.

ITUC (2012a), Internationally Recognised Core Labour Standards In Turkey. Report for the WTO General Council Review of the Trade Policies of Turkey, 21–23 February, Geneva. Accessed 9 July 2016 at http://www.ituc-csi.org/IMG/pdf/tpr_turkey-final_.pdf.

ITUC (2012b), Legal Summary- Azerbaijan (2011, 2012), Survey of Violations of Trade Union Rights. Geneva. Accessed 15 May 2016 at http://www.refworld.org/docid/4fd88967c.html.

Kardaş, Şaban and Macit, Fatih (2015), 'Turkey–Azerbaijan Relations: The Economic Dimension', *Journal of Caspian Affairs*, 1(1), pp. 23–46.

Kazgan, Gülten (2013), 2008 Krizi Üsselleşirken Türkiye'nin Sürdürülemez Büyüme Modeli. Türkiye Ekonomi Kurumu Tartışma Metni 2013/4, http://www.tek.org.tr.

Mikail, Elnur Hasan (2007), Türkiye Azerbaycan İlişkileri. 38th ICANAS Uluslararası Asya ve Kuzey Afrika Çalışmaları Kongresi, Ankara, ss.1063–1079. Accessed 15 May 2016 at http://www.ayk.gov.tr/wp-content/uploads/2015/01/ULUSLARARASI-%C4%B0L%C4%B0%C5%9EK%C4%B0LER-3.-C%C4%B0LT.pdf.

Milli Güvenlik Konseyi (MGK) (1980), MGK'nin Onaltı Numaralı Bildirisi. Milli güvenlik Konseyi Tutanak Dergisi. Sayı: 1, Ankara, ss.1–68.

Qasımov, A.M. (2007), Emek HüQuQu. Adiloğlu, Bakı.

Salimov, Latif (2014), Azerbaycan ve Türkiye İş Sağlığı ve Güvenliği Karşılaştırması. Yüksek Lisans Projesi, Ankara Üniversitesi, SBE, Ankara.

Saygın, Hasan and Çimen, Murat (2013), *Turkish Economic Policies and External Dependency*, Cambridge: Cambridge Scholars Publishing.

Spooner, Keri and O'Neill, Brian (2002), Impact of the Internet upon Pluralistic Industrialism. *International Employment Relations Review*, 8(2), pp. 7–34.

Uşan, Fatih (2005), Azerbaycan Hukukunda İş Sözleşmesinin (Emek Mukavelesinin) Temel Özellikleri (Türk Hukukuyla Karşılaştırmalı Olarak). Kamu-İş Dergisi; V:8, I. 3/2005, Ankara, ss.1–34.

USSR KK (1976), No. 24: 123, (О Внесении Изменений И Дополнений В Постановление Совета Министров Ссср И Вцспс От 6 Марта 1966 Г. No. 177 «О Заключении Коллективных Договоров На Предприятиях»).

Yorgun, Sayım (2007), Dirilişin Eşiğinde Sendikalar Yeni Eğilimler Yeni Stratejiler. Ekin Yayınevi, Bursa.

Yorgun, Sayım (2011), Grevsiz Toplu Pazarlık Hakkı ve Aidat Bağımlılığı Kıskacında Memur Sendikaları, *Sosyal Siyaset Konferansları Dergisi*, Sayı: 60, 2011/1, ss. 145–168.

Yorgun, Sayım (2016), Anayasa Mahkemesinin 6356 Sayılı Yasaya İlişkin Kararının Sendikal Özgürlükler Boyutuyla Değerlendirilmesi. Çalışma ve Toplum Dergisi, 2016/3, ss. 1171–1202.

Zengin, Eyüp (2010), Piyasa Ekonomisine Geçiş Sürecinde Azerbaycan. İTO 2010-59, Istanbul.

7. The application of MNC HR policies and practices in the luxury hotel industry: differences and similarities between transitional periphery versus developed economies

Giovanni O. Serafini and Leslie T. Szamosi

INTRODUCTION

International human resource management (IHRM) literature has traditionally centred itself on comparisons within a defined spectrum of developed countries (Peltonen and Vaara, 2012; Tarique and Schuler, 2010), which hampers generalizations at a global level. While this chapter concerns a specific organization at the luxury end of the hotel and hospitality market, it encompasses both advanced and transitional periphery economies (TPEs) thus representing a novel research approach in IHRM. Despite its limitations deriving from focusing only on the upper market segment within a highly varied industry (Kazlauskaite et al., 2011), this study allows for the identification of contextual variations within a mature organizational structure (see Niewiadomski, 2013).

Hence, this research relates to the overseas operations of a United States (US) global hotel company spanning both mature and developing institutional contexts. To safeguard anonymity, the case study hotel industry multinational corporation (MNC) is referred to as 'HotelMNC'. The more mainstream HRM literature has overwhelmingly been focusing on non-hotel-based industry sectors despite its (hotel) labour intensiveness in the broader service sector (Hoque, 2013; Lee-Ross and Pryce, 2010; Baum, 2007; Higgins-Desbiolles, 2006; Marchante et al., 2006). In looking to illustrate the nature of institutional effects impacting upon companies in more fluid national contexts, this study seeks to bring new evidence from the institutional context of TPEs.

To meet the objectives of this study, HR policies and practices are compared across the overseas operations of MNCs, based on evidence gathered from the fully owned overseas subsidiaries of a US MNC luxury hotel chain with locations in both developed economies (the United Kingdom, Germany and Switzerland) and the transitional periphery (Azerbaijan and Kyrgyzstan). Hence, this study analyses and assesses the juxtaposition of HRM implementation according to national capitalist archetypes encompassing liberal market, coordinated market and transitional periphery economies (LMEs, CMEs and TPEs, respectively). The aim is to reveal whether variations and commonalities in HR policies and practices application occur owing to different types of capitalist archetypes, by contrasting more mature, functional and closely knit institutional settings with weaker, less closely coupled and more fluid ones. This analysis is focused on HRM in the hotel industry, which has been relatively understudied (Davidson et al., 2011; Lucas and Deery, 2004) when compared to other sectors such as manufacturing, banking, airlines and retail (Sun et al., 2007; Guerrier and Deery, 1998). Moreover, the research covers economies with weaker institutions, thus adding to our existing knowledge, which has been traditionally focused on studying developed economies such as Central European contexts where institutions are reasonably stable, functional and advanced (Batt and Hermans, 2012; Laruelle and Peyrouse, 2012; Morley et al., 2012; Delbridge et al., 2011).

Contextual peculiarities of differing institutional settings have recently emerged in several instances, namely labour law and the related enforcement capabilities, and the educational system. Further, as our discussion illuminates, in TPEs these were complemented by embedded clanism and clientelism, which appeared to represent a bulwark against the MNC's homogenizing forces.

INSTITUTIONAL CONTEXT

An influential strand of literature (Almond, 2011; Gooderham et al., 2006; Ferner and Quintanilla, 1998; Gooderham et al., 1998; Ferner, 1997) maintains that, regardless of institutional context, US MNCs exert an 'Anglo-Saxonization' pressure on their overseas operations. Initiated by head office, this homogenizing and standardizing process, based on HR policies and practices (Edwards et al., 2016), should affect HotelMNC international subsidiaries in the transitional periphery (Pudelko and Harzing, 2007; Martin and Beaumont, 1998), especially in contexts where union membership is low (Fenton-O'Creevy et al., 2008). Contrariwise, scholars (Cantwell, 2009; Jackson and Deeg, 2008) also suggest that local institutional isomorphic forces pressure US MNC overseas operations to be more likely to accept host country practices, leading, as Meyer et al. (2011, p. 237) put it, to incur 'contextual variations'.

Based on the premise that US MNCs feature a more standardized, formalized and centralized approach than those originating from other countries (Almond, 2011; Harzing and Sorge, 2003), this study aims at exploring whether this central control may vary depending on national contexts in which subsidiaries operate (see Edwards et al., 2007), such as the transitional periphery studied here. In other words, where institutional restraints are weaker, MNCs will have more flexibility to take on board country-of-origin practices. Conversely, where the local institutional environment is more mature, firms will be under greater pressure to adapt what they do, considering local practices and conventions. Efforts to ensure integration of international operations may lead global businesses originating from LMEs (Amable, 2003), such as the US, to resort to tighter central controls, particularly in countries with weakly regulated and fluid labour markets (Belizon et al., 2013), versus the transitional periphery (Serafini et al., 2017; Serafini and Szamosi, 2015).

HRM IN THE HOSPITALITY INDUSTRY

Scholarly recognition about the 'multiplier effect' contribution of tourism to the welfare of local economies worldwide (Pender, 2005, p. 8) provides additional support for its further study and understanding (Tang and Tan, 2013; Brida and Risso, 2009). Although research is advancing, there is a substantive lack outside of the developed economies, despite the wide proliferation of the sector into other economic structures such as the TPE. Reflecting the sector, the case study firm has a highly segmented workforce. This is the result of efforts to accommodate the labour costs within a highly volatile and seasonal business (Riley et al., 2002; Reisinger, 2001). Firstly, there is the differentiation between managerial, core, 'well-paying professional jobs', and 'low-wage, low-skill' blue-collar jobs (Otis, 2009, p. 54). Secondly, there is a demarcation between blue-collar workers employed directly by the hotel through standard contracts, and the subcontracted or outsourced external workforce which varies depending on the location and institutional structures. As Ferus-Comelo (2015, p. 72) argues: 'Despite the rising quantity of jobs, tourism-related employment is overwhelmingly seasonal translating into under-employment for most hotel workers . . . and the dramatic rise of precarious work for the majority of the five-star hotel staff, representative of changing employment practices in the new economy'.

This multiple-tier HRM approach results from the nature of the industry as a whole which, although being labour-intensive, features particularly high cyclicality and seasonality that mandates the application of mechanisms to promote numerical flexibility (Lai and Baum, 2005). Inevitably, this affects both the extent of employer–employee interdependence (Whitley, 1999) and the propensity of the organization to invest in its people (Yang, 2010).

Further, this research hints at the role of the HR manual, which is typical of the kind found in global organizations spanning many and diverse host countries, towards the goal of maintaining consistency and alignment to corporate identity, policies and practices across overseas subsidiaries (Lucas and Deery, 2004). As is common practice, the MNC under examination deploys its globally centred HR manual as a mechanism for seeking to create corporate alignment (see Morris et al., 2009) in subsidiaries operating in varying institutional contexts, with disparate managerial teams, and in some instances employing few or no parent-country nationals as expatriates. It could be argued that HR manuals would be less important if the organization were making greater usage of parent-country expatriates, and if foreign MNC operations were limited to home-country-like regions of the English-speaking world within the Anglo-Saxon context.

RESEARCH EVIDENCE

This chapter offers new insights into HRM practice in a major MNC, whose activities span a very diverse set of contexts. Evidence discussed originates from seven overseas subsidiaries which were examined, with a focus on the transitional periphery, through research methods employed in a process of triangulation, encompassing qualitative data analysis with small sample inferential statistics, document analysis and participant observation. In particular, information from overseas subsidiaries was collected from HR executives through quantitative questionnaires and in-depth interviews looking at similarity and diversity according to Whitley's (1999) defining national features of employment and work relations: employer–employee interdependence and employee delegation.

Host-Country Specific Factors Determining the Application of HRM Practices in MNC Hotel Chain Subsidiaries

In terms of key differences across national capitalist archetypes, HR policies and practices implementation in CMEs and LMEs was primarily impacted upon by the national labour law. Evidence reveals that firm sensitivity to its 'liability of newness' (see Hillman and Wan, 2005, p. 325; Stinchcombe, 1965, p. 148), together with the need to safeguard reputation, urge overseas operations towards conformity with the local labour law in emerging TPEs. This leads to HotelMNC applying an arm's-length approach with its subsidiaries in relation to labour relations issues, as well as casual employment and job protection directives. Thus, while in CMEs and LMEs the intense utilization of well-established casual work arrangements was instrumental in attaining payroll cost containment, in TPEs these employment agreements have been introduced lately in the labour law, arguably due to the more recent influx of MNCs and the need to attract further levels of foreign direct investment (Bitzenis and Szamosi, 2009).

Further, in the case of TPEs, an additional influential contextual feature was an educational system failing to supply a workforce trained and exposed to modern customer service associated with world-class hospitality. In fact, in the post-communist countries under consideration, respondents indicated that study curricula have mostly remained unchanged since the Soviet era, presenting critical areas of concern for the company. Consequently, it appears that subsidiaries operating in those economies needed to highlight and focus on employee training courses aimed specifically at embedding a quality customer service attitude, which is essential in world-class hotels (Lam and Chen, 2012). Indeed, the Soviet-era study curriculum in Commonwealth of Independent States (CIS) countries still focuses on ambitious agendas involving scientific knowledge and technical skills rather than training basic skills required at the organizational level, in this case service occupational training such as waitressing or guestroom attending (Sondergaard and Murthi, 2012). There was a perceived gap in terms of customer service skills and attitude training (see Das et al., 2010), which TPE subsidiaries needed to compensate. Instead, overseas operations located in CMEs benefited from an efficient state educational system duly preparing apprentices for industrial placements to obtain professional qualifications. As well as the dearth of an appropriate workforce educated by the system itself, in TPEs the lack of other international property management companies means that there was no industry-trained portfolio of workers. Evidence also showed that TPE hotel properties operated in a context featuring a widespread presence of unofficial forms of labour, which indicates poor labour law enforcement capabilities, as opposed to CME- and LME-based operations.

Delegation to Employees

Given the limited opportunities for mobility offered to TPE employees, due to also their geographic distance from the corporate centre as compared to CME and LME employees, research evidence shows that candidates were much more interested in building careers within the local facility itself from a bottom-up perspective. In terms of internal communication, HotelMNC applied a comprehensive system reflecting the scale and scope of the MNC, whereby functional standardization was paramount. A case in point was the whistleblower procedure, whose application was challenged by the local legal framework. As observed by the research participant, the whistleblower system was particularly indicative of the challenges between firm intentions and application. Besides the fact that the European Union (EU) legal dispositions opposed anonymous claims and allegations (see Deutsche Welle, 2015), the utilization of the whistleblowing policy was further hampered by the absence of a 'reporting culture' (see Schultz and Harutyunyan, 2015, p. 92). The uncertainty experienced by people in emerging TPE weak institutional settings thus discouraged employees from speaking, for fear of being exposed and left unprotected. In settings characterized by powerful social ties, such as tribes and clans in Azerbaijan and Kyrgyzstan for example, it was highly unlikely that an employee would make an allegation, even anonymously, due to concerns of retribution or being 'cast out'. Therefore, limited legal protection prevented the system's productive application, especially in CME subsidiaries; while in TPEs the deeply rooted local clan system, with tight social ties, would be highly unlikely to approve of any anonymous allegation process. This would then allow the company to indicate that it had a system in place to root out activities at odds with specified controls, but would not likely ever be activated, due to the clan system, thereby providing a false sense of organizational security and due diligence. This further impacted on the application of grievance procedures, which varied depending on the institutional context. The advanced CMEs and LMEs appeared to safeguard employees in their quest for justice, while wary TPE employees were reluctant to use formal upward communication avenues out of fear of retaliation by those exposed (see Bjørkelo, 2013).

Consequently, similarly to what emerged with open door policies, the reasons for these formal communication breakdowns in TPEs, particularly with the lower workforce tier, most often lay in the relationship blue-collar workers established with their respective departmental supervisors, who planned their shifts and directly influenced their quality of work. Since the HR department is perceived as a rather distant entity representing HotelMNC head office in the hotel subsidiary, employees tend to consider HRM practice as fundamentally enforced by departmental leadership. Accordingly, the most critical communication link from an employees' viewpoint occurred between them and their supervisors, thus relegating HR and its management team and executives to a rather auxiliary role, as administration specialists to consult for procedural reasons. This evidence supports observations about the increasingly prominent role line managers play in the implementation of HR policies and practices (see Renwick, 2003).

Employer–Employee Interdependence

In terms of training and development, the evidence illustrates the relative capability that overseas HotelMNC properties had in adjusting training actions to local realities, regardless of institutional setting. Although it could have been simpler, or more cost-effective, to stick to core company materials and develop economies of scale, subsidiary HR executives sought to add a stronger, more locally relevant component into their training portfolio. There were two main reasons for this. Firstly, the uneven preparation of the workforce in hospitality professions across different contexts compelled TPE hotel properties to compensate for the dearth of education and training when compared to LME and CME subsidiaries. Secondly, the substantially higher yearly voluntary turnover rates recorded in developed economy subsidiaries as opposed to transitional periphery hotels meant that a large proportion of training in the former focused on basic induction training. Much of this revolved around the customer, and enhancing customer experience in line with the expectations of HotelMNC.

Next, an investigation of security of tenure revealed the usage of large amounts of outsourced labour to impart numerical flexibility in developed economies, thus enabling subsidiaries in LMEs and CMEs to optimize the accommodation of payroll to business levels. Thus, findings suggest a widespread deployment of highly contingent labour, meaning that in developed economies a considerable number of employees covered vulnerable positions. Contrariwise, TPE subsidiaries suffered a more rigid and inflexible labour cost due to the limited availability of contingent labour matching the TPE subsidiary quality requirements. Nonetheless, from an organizational viewpoint, this gave HotelMNC in the TPEs the opportunity to develop more organizationally centric employees, trained to their specifications, according to their standards. Next, all participating HR executives shared relatively similar approaches related to compulsory redundancies. They maintained that it was critical to avoid any hard measures in addressing workforce 'rightsizing', because of the labour law rigidities related to such matters and the potential negative repercussions on the subsidiaries' reputations in the local labor markets (see Meyer, 2004).

Thus, the common methods across subsidiaries, including those located in TPEs, related to low-impact measures such as non-renewal of fixed-term contracts, except in one circumstance. In fact, evidence emerged about a limited-scale downsizing in the CME context of Switzerland, due to a large drop in business volume, which was accompanied by outplacement services to line employees as dictated by law. The latter appears indicative of the strength of country-of-domicile and institutional pressures in the name of employment protection. It could be assumed that this would have been highly unlikely to occur in neoliberal and deregulated LME or weakly enforced and fluid TPE institutional settings. Thus, TPE subsidiaries suffered from much less flexibility than CME and LME properties. Lastly, the job loss ratio over total standard workforce was highest in TPE hotel properties, as opposed to LME and CME subsidiaries. These variations across institutional contexts revealed a higher volatility in the TPE versus the more stable and labour-flexible LME and CME developed economies.

In summary, the local legal framework and its enforcement, together with the educational system, appear to affect HR policies and practices implementation differently according to locale. Furthermore, host-country informal norms and social ties of TPE nations in the Caucasus and Central Asia regions opposed the homogenization forces exerted by HotelMNC. Lastly, regardless of locale, the imperative for labour cost efficiencies translated into wage compression and limited work security arrangements. To counter the high voluntary turnover rates affecting casual and blue-collar workers, overseas operations located in the CMEs and LMEs resorted to applying intensive outsourcing and subcontracting practices. Consequently, it appears that the advanced HR policies and practices were more applicable to white-collar and key managerial personnel.

CONCLUSIONS

There are two main implications resulting from the research. Firstly, this study contributes to knowledge by addressing the MNC as a partially institutionally rooted international actor that responds to pressures affected by varying institutional contexts to attain its set global business strategy. Here, the findings point towards significant investment in a comprehensive HRM infrastructure in an attempt to ensure seamless control and global alignment across operations. Yet, the institutional context of the TPE does not appear to support this as expected, due to host-country-specific factors. Another area characterized by attempts towards homogenization includes anti-union measures undertaken to head off efforts in the formation of employee representative bodies in the TPE. The suggested 'powers' of MNCs to employ such tactics may appear counterintuitive to the clan system, but are in line with the overall approach implemented. In other areas, however, the MNC had to adapt to local realities and nuances, most notably in having to conform with local labour law and informal conventions, leading to an arm's-length approach vis-à-vis overseas subsidiaries.

Secondly, the application of HR policies and practices encounters pressures across differing institutional contexts. In terms of labour law and vocational education, these show the effect of fluid and weak regulation and enforcement capabilities within the TPE. Most critically, although previous research and literature underline the strong homogenizing effect of US MNCs, the research findings indicate that in TPEs the legal and educational system, as well as the predominant clientelism and clanism, resist such effects and to a large extent create a strong barrier that may, in certain situations, force MNCs to adapt or hinder further foreign direct investment into the system. Thus, the chapter contributes original knowledge to the growing body of international business research on the very novel concept of the TPE capitalist archetype (Wood and Demirbag, 2015).

The focus of this research is on the luxury hotel industry, which offers superior product-branded services on a standardized global basis. The research evidence gleaned emanates from hotel properties representing all wholly owned and operated subsidiaries in the European division of HotelMNC. Focusing on hotel properties over which head office exerts full control avoids addressing subsidiaries affected by complex agency challenges posed by relationships of the hotel firm with individual property franchisees and owning companies, respectively. Furthermore, the study involves only overseas subsidiary HR executives, thereby focusing on a distinct category of executives to the exclusion of other stakeholders such as, for instance, managers from other departments or line employees, which may have limited the variety of input sources. Due to HotelMNC's binding instructions there was no possibility to expand the sample beyond HR executives to encompass managers in other departments, or to include line employees. Again, as the hotels were largely non-unionized, it was not possible to develop a basis of comparative data through interviewing union representatives. Lastly, this research considered country-of-domicile pressures, while not investigating parent-country institutional forces. This boundary was dictated by the need to render the study manageable. Since it was exploring a single organizational case, the researchers could not ascertain whether procedures implemented in the country of origin were typical of the US paradigm or not, which was also not the focus of the research. Hence, the study is not of country-of-origin effects, but of how practices vary according to country of domicile, and whether this variation can be explained by differences in institutions.

Future research within the TPE in relation to MNC influence should begin to analyse the variances between the international investments and those from the local level. Understanding this transitional effect as the countries of the TPE evolve will aid in better explaining the devolution and evolution of HR policies and practices application in the area. Broadening out from the hospitality industry in such circumstances would also add a fresh perspective towards the diffusion and expansion of professional HR within the region as a whole. Lastly, drawing from the work of Brewster and Wood (2015), another recommendation concerns the further exploration of measures implemented by MNCs to attain alignment to corporate HR policies and practices across subsidiaries.

REFERENCES

Almond, P. (2011) Re-visiting 'country of origin' effects on HRM in multinational corporations. *Human Resource Management Journal*, 21(3), pp. 258–271.

Amable, B. (2003) *The Diversity of Modern Capitalism*. Oxford: Oxford University Press.

Batt, R. and Hermans, M. (2012) Global human resource management: bridging strategic and institutional perspectives. In: Martocchio, J.J., Laio, H. and Joshi, A. (eds) *Research in Personnel and Human Resources Management*. Bingley: Emerald Group Publishing, pp. 1–52.

Baum, T. (2007) Human resources in tourism: still waiting for change. *Tourism Management*, 28(6), 1383–1399.

Belizon, M.J., Gunnigle, P. and Morley, M. (2013) Determinants of central control and subsidiary autonomy in HRM: the case of foreign-owned multinational companies in Spain. *Human Resource Management Journal*, 23(3), pp. 262–278.

Bitzenis, A. and Szamosi, L.T. (2009) Entry modes and the determinants of foreign direct investment in a European Union accession country: the case of Albania. *Journal of East–West Business*, 15(3/4), pp. 189–209.

Bjørkelo, B. (2013) Workplace bullying after whistleblowing: future research and implications. *Journal of Managerial Psychology*, 28(3), pp. 306–323, https://doi.org/10.1108/02683941311321178.

Brewster, C. and Wood, G.T. (2015) Comparative HRM and international HRM. In: Collings, D.G., Wood, G. and Caligiuri, P.M. (eds) *The Routledge Companion to International Human Resource Management*. Abingdon: Routledge, pp. 121–137.

Brida, J.G. and Risso, W.A. (2009) Tourism as a factor of long-run economic growth: an empirical analysis for Chile. *European Journal of Tourism Research*, 2(2), pp. 178–185.

Cantwell, J. (2009) Location and the multinational enterprise. *Journal of International Business Studies*, 40(1), pp. 35–41.

Das, A., Kumar, V. and Saha, G.C. (2010) Retail service quality in context of CIS countries. *International Journal of Quality and Reliability Management*, 27(6), pp. 658–683.

Davidson, M.C.G., McPhail, R. and Barry, S. (2011) Hospitality HRM: past, present and the future. *International Journal of Contemporary Hospitality Management Volume*, 23(4), pp. 498–516.

Delbridge, R., Hauptmeier, M. and Sengupta, S. (2011) Beyond the enterprise: broadening the horizons of International HRM. *Human Relations*, 64(4), pp. 483–505.

Deutsche Welle (2015) Most of Europe has no whistleblower protection. Available

from: http://www.dw.com/en/most-of-europe-has-no-whistleblower-protection
/a-16942870 (accessed 27 August 2015).

Edwards, T., Colling, T. and Ferner, A. (2007) Conceptual approaches to the transfer of employment practices in multinational companies: an integrated approach. *Human Resource Management Journal*, 17(3), pp. 201–217.

Edwards, T., Sánchez-Mangas, R., Jalette, P., Lavelle, J. and Minbaeva, D. (2016) Global standardization or national differentiation of HRM practices in multinational companies? A comparison of multinationals in five countries. *Journal of International Business Studies*, 47(8), pp. 997–1021, https://doi.org/10.1057/s41267-016-0003-6.

Fenton-O'Creevy, M., Gooderham, P. and Nordhaug, O. (2008) Human resource management in US subsidiaries in Europe and Australia: centralisation or autonomy? *Journal of International Business Studies*, 39(1), 151–166, https://doi.org/10.1057/palgrave.jibs.8400313.

Ferner, A. (1997) Country of origin effects and HRM in multinational companies. *Human Resource Management Journal*, 7(1), 19–37, https://doi.org/10.1111/j.1748-8583.1997.tb00271.x.

Ferner, A. and Quintanilla, J. (1998) Multinationals, national business systems and HRM: the enduring influence of national identity or a process of 'Anglo-Saxonization'. *International Journal of Human Resource Management*, 9(4), pp. 710–731.

Ferus-Comelo, A. (2015) Labour geographies in India's hotel industry. In: Jordhus-Lier, D. and Underthun, A. (eds) *A Hospitable World? Organising Work and Workers in Hotels and Tourist Resorts*. Abingdon: Routledge, pp. 67–83.

Gooderham, P.N., Nordhaug, O. and Ringdal, K. (1998) When in Rome, do they do as the Romans? HRM practices of US subsidiaries in Europe. *Management International Review*, 38, pp. 47–64.

Gooderham, P.N., Nordhaug, O. and Ringdal, K. (2006) National embeddedness and calculative human resource management in US subsidiaries in Europe and Australia. *Human Relations*, 59(11), pp. 1491–1513.

Guerrier, Y. and Deery, M. (1998) Research in hospitality human resource management and organizational behaviour. *International Journal of Hospitality Management*, 17(2), pp. 145–160.

Harzing, A.-W. and Sorge, A. (2003) The relative impact of country of origin and universal contingencies on internationalization strategies and corporate control in multinational enterprises: worldwide and European perspectives. *Organization Studies*, 24(2), pp. 187–214.

Higgins-Desbiolles, F. (2006) More than an 'industry': the forgotten power of tourism as a social force. *Tourism Management*, 27(6), 1192–1208.

Hillman, A.J. and Wan, W.P. (2005) The determinants of MNE subsidiaries' political strategies: evidence of institutional duality. *Journal of International Business Studies*, 36(3), pp. 322–340.

Hoque, K. (2013) *Human Resource Management in the Hotel Industry: Strategy, Innovation and Performance*. London: Routledge.

Jackson, G. and Deeg, R. (2008) Comparing capitalisms: understanding institutional diversity and its implications for international business. *Journal of International Business Studies*, 39(4), pp. 540–561.

Kazlauskaite, R., Buciuniene, I. and Turauskas, L. (2011) Organisational and psychological empowerment in the HRM–performance linkage. *Employee Relations*, 34(2), 138–158.

Lai, P.-C. and Baum, T. (2005) Just-in-time labour supply in the hotel sector: the role of agencies. *Employee Relations*, 27(1), pp. 86–102.

Lam, W. and Chen, Z. (2012) When I put on my service mask: determinants and outcomes of emotional labor among hotel service providers according to affective event theory. *International Journal of Hospitality Management*, 31(1), pp. 3–11.

Laruelle, M. and Peyrouse, S. (2012) The challenges of human security and development in Central Asia. In: Amer, R., Swain, A. and Öjendal, J. (eds) *The Security–Development Nexus: Peace, Conflict and Development*. London: Anthem Press, pp. 137–160.

Lee-Ross, D. and Pryce, J. (2010) *Human Resources and Tourism: Skills, Culture and Industry*. Bristol: Channel View Publications.

Lucas, R. and Deery, M. (2004) Significant developments and emerging issues in human resource management. *International Journal of Hospitality Management*, 23(5), pp. 459–472.

Marchante, A.J., Ortega, B. and Pagán, R. (2006) Determinants of skills shortages and hard-to-fill vacancies in the hospitality sector. *Tourism Management*, 27(5), 791–802.

Martin, G. and Beaumont, P. (1998) Diffusing 'best practice' in multinational firms: prospects, practice and contestation. *International Journal of Human Resource Management*, 9(4), pp. 671–695.

Meyer, K.E. (2004) Perspectives on multinational enterprises in emerging economies. *Journal of International Business Studies*, 35(4), pp. 259–276.

Meyer, K., Mudambi, R. and Narula, R. (2011) Multinational enterprises and local contexts: the opportunities and challenges of multiple-embeddedness. *Journal of Management Studies*, 48(2), pp. 235–252.

Morley, M.J., Minbaeva, D. and Michailova, S. (2012) The transition states of Central and Eastern Europe and the Former Soviet Union. In: Brewster, C. and Mayrhofer, W. (eds) *Handbook of Research on Comparative Human Resource Management*. Cheltenham, UK and Northampton, MA, USA: Edward Elgar Publishing, pp. 550–575.

Morris, S.S., Wright, P.M., Trevor, J., et al. (2009) Global challenges to replicating HR: the role of people, processes, and systems. *Human Resource Management*, 48(6), pp. 973–995.

Niewiadomski, P. (2013) The globalisation of the hotel industry and the variety of emerging capitalisms in Central and Eastern Europe. *European Urban and Regional Studies*, 23(3), pp. 267–288.

Otis, E. (2009) Labor of luxury: gender and generational inequality in a Beijing Hotel. In: Davis, D. and Feng, W. (eds) *Creating Wealth and Poverty in Post-Socialist China*. Stanford, SA: Stanford University Press, pp. 54–68.

Peltonen, T. and Vaara, E. (2012) Critical approaches to comparative HRM. In: Brewster, C. and Mayrhofer, W. (eds) *Handbook of Research on Comparative Human Resource Management*. Cheltenham, UK and Northampton, MA, USA: Edward Elgar Publishing, pp. 69–89.

Pender, L. (2005) Managing the tourism system. In: Pender, L. and Sharpley, R. (eds) *The Management of Tourism*. London, SAGE, pp. 1–13.

Pudelko, M. and Harzing, A.-W. (2007) Country-of-origin, localization, or dominance effect? An empirical investigation of HRM practices in foreign subsidiaries. *Human Resource Management*, 46(4), pp. 535–559.

Reisinger, Y. (2001) Unique characteristics of tourism, hospitality, and leisure services. In: Kandampully, J., Mok, C. and Sparks, B. (eds) *Service Quality*

Management in Hospitality, Tourism, and Leisure. Binghamton: Haworth Press, pp. 15–50.

Renwick, D. (2003) Line manager involvement in HRM: an inside view. *Employee Relations*, 25(3), pp. 262–280.

Riley, M., Ladkin, A. and Szivas, E. (2002) *Tourism Employment: Analysis and Planning.* Bristol: Channel View Publications.

Schultz, D. and Harutyunyan, K. (2015) Combating corruption: the development of whistleblowing laws in the United States, Europe, and Armenia. *International Comparative Jurisprudence*, 1(2), 87–97, https://doi.org/10.1016/j.icj.2015.12.005.

Serafini, G.O. and Szamosi, L.T. (2015) Five star hotels of a multinational enterprise in countries of the transitional periphery: a case study in human resources management. *International Business Review*, 24(6), pp. 972–983.

Serafini, G.O., Wood, G.T. and Szamosi L.T. (2017) IHRM application in transitional periphery countries: lessons from the luxury hotel industry. Paper presented at the British Academy of Management 2017 Conference, 5–7 September, University of Warwick, UK.

Sondergaard, L. and Murthi, M. (2012) *Skills, Not Just Diplomas: Managing Education for Results in Eastern Europe and Central Asia.* Washington, DC: World Bank Publications.

Stinchcombe, A. (1965) Social structure and organizations. In: March, J. (ed.) *Handbook of Organizations.* Chicago, IL: Rand-McNally, pp. 142–193.

Sun, L.-Y., Aryee, S. and Law, K.S. (2007) High-performance human resource practices, citizenship behavior, and organizational performance: a relational perspective. *Academy of Management Journal*, 50(3), pp. 558–577.

Tang, C.F. and Tan, E.C. (2013) How stable is the tourism-led growth hypothesis in Malaysia? Evidence from disaggregated tourism markets. *Tourism Management*, 37, pp. 52–57.

Tarique, I. and Schuler, R.S. (2010) Global talent management: literature review, integrative framework, and suggestions for further research. *Journal of World Business*, 45(2), 122–33.

Whitley, R. (1999) *Divergent Capitalisms: The Social Structuring and Change of Business Systems.* Oxford, Oxford University Press.

Wood, G.T., and Demirbag, M. (2015) Business and society on the transitional periphery: comparative perspectives. *International Business Review*, 24(6), pp. 917–920.

Yang, J.-T. (2010) Antecedents and consequences of job satisfaction in the hotel industry. *International Journal of Hospitality Management*, 29(4), pp. 609–619.

PART III

Other transitional periphery

8. The state and company managements in Belarus

Hanna Danilovich and Richard Croucher

INTRODUCTION

Drawing on Zartman and Rubin's (2000) theory of power and negotiation, this chapter analyses investment decisions made by private and quasi-private Belarusian firms, despite state direction. The first two decades of transition in the former Soviet economies were characterised by institutional fluidity, the dominance of informal business interest groups, business networks and ethnic clans resulting from weakened government structures (e.g., Wedel, 2001; Yakovlev and Zhuravskaya, 2006; Melnykovska, 2008; Closson, 2009; Ledeneva, 2009). The *raison d'être* behind domestic firms' investment decisions at the time was often determined by the desire to secure firms' financial futures by complying with the unwritten 'rules of the game'.

The decline of formal institutions' legitimacy and the prevailing informality of state–firm relations in the region has its roots in *blat*: informal networks within Soviet society which provided enterprise directors with access to limited economic resources, the task only being possible through well-established political connections. The adoption of new laws during *perestroika*[1] did not weaken *blat* but, rather, gave it a new dimension. With the de facto denationalization and privatization of the Soviet economy, informal business and ethnic interest groups could access resources previously controlled by the state. By 1991, politically connected individuals and insiders from the Communist political elite assumed ownership of at least two-thirds of Russian industrial enterprises (e.g., McFaul, 1995), forming oligarchic groupings with strong lobbying power. Formal state institutions had to either cede to informal networks (e.g., Yakovlev and Zhuravskaya, 2006; Viktorov, 2015) or merge with them, creating authoritarian neo-patrimonial regimes (e.g., Ilkhamov, 2007; Özcan, 2010; Laruelle, 2012; Lewis, 2012).

However, the last two decades have seen the state largely recovering the position it lost in the 1980s–1990s. The most notable example is Russia, where the government managed to subdue oligarchic lobbying groups using the formal 'rules of the game'. The new model is believed to be characterized by considerable state involvement in the economy, clientelism and corruption, and has hence been labelled 'patrimonial state capitalism' (e.g., Easter, 2008; Robinson, 2011; Becker, 2013). Nonetheless, informal practices remain embedded in the business routines of small and medium-sized Russian companies (Vasileva, 2017), indicating a similarity between the current Russian political-economic model and its Soviet predecessor in terms of the power of informality in state–business relations.

This chapter focuses on Belarus, another example of continuity between Soviet and contemporary models of state–business relations. The Belarusian state has emphasized the need for stability and has sought to avoid the disastrous social consequences of major change which occurred in Russia. This in turn has allowed it to build a degree of societal acquiescence to a highly authoritarian regime. Thus, unlike most of its post-Soviet neighbours, Belarus did not experience institutional fluidity after the collapse of the Soviet Union. The government's attempt to maintain a Soviet regulatory model through a multitude of Presidential Decrees and government enactments has led to ever-increasing state involvement in the economy (Danilovich and Croucher, 2015; Adarov, 2016). It has been argued that an imbalanced institutional and political environment in Belarus, characterized by extreme concentration of directive power in government institutions, fluid non-governmental structures, and the indirect state ownership of many industrial and service companies, negatively affects the ability of domestic firms' senior management to make economically rational investment decisions. This causes further attempts at intervention by the state. Despite the efforts of external lending organizations to encourage a state-independent private sector, industry has largely remained in the state's hands, preserving the dominance of industrial ministries, or *kontsern*, over management's decision-making in state-owned and quasi-privatized companies.

However, unlike in Russia, the degree of informality in day-to-day business activities seems to have decreased. The state's desire to reduce the role of informality for individual businesses has led to the partial Westernization of business practices in industries dominated by private companies, particularly the information technology (IT) industry. For others, however, informal relations with government institutions have remained a significant part of operations. Nonetheless, one may argue that even under these conditions, the senior managements of Belarusian companies manage to preserve a certain degree of independence in decision-making, and their concerns are able to profit thereby. Thus the Belarusian regulatory model has evolved, demonstrating a certain flexibility.

We assess the degree of independent decision-making by Belarusian enterprise directors with regard to investment, despite the increasing concentration of power in formal institutions. We highlight important institutional differences between Belarus and other economies on the transitional periphery, most of which are characterized by considerable institutional fluidity and the dominance of clan politics. We assess the extent to which the capacity of businesses to act independently is suppressed by the single powerful state, forcing these organizations to find ways around the formal 'rules of the game'. We then discuss whether state–business relations are one of the factors contributing to the ability of the Belarusian economy to stay afloat despite massive external debt and an outdated industrial base. We therefore contribute to the debate on the nature of the institutional and socio-economic transformation on the transitional periphery.

We start by deriving our research questions from a critical analysis of existing literature on post-Soviet transition trajectories. We then explain our research methodology. The chapter continues by analysing primary and secondary data on enterprise decision-making, informality and institutional development in Belarus. We conclude by showing the central patterns of state–business relations in Belarus and assessing the effect they have on the development of the country's socio-economic model.

THEORY AND RESEARCH QUESTIONS

The effect of national economic elites on the direction of transition trajectories in former Soviet economies has been much studied (e.g., Wedel, 2001; Frye, 2002, 2010; Hellman et al., 2003; Iwasaki and Suzuki, 2007; Junisbai, 2010). Three main models of state–business relations in the post-Soviet space have been identified: oligarchic state-capture, ethnic-clan neopatrimonialism and indirect negotiated influence with the authoritarian state.

Oligarchic state-capture occurred in Russia, the Ukraine, Moldova and some of the economies of the Caucasus, where collaborating oligarchic business structures had a strong influence on the formation of the new economic and political environment. Such businesses achieved this by merging with weakened formal institutions and using newly created ties to divert considerable economic resources towards themselves (Olson, 2000; Fries et al., 2003; Guriev and Rachinsky, 2006; Closson, 2009; Pyle, 2011), forcing the governments to use coercive methods of corporate exploitation (licensing, inspections, and so on) to retain some control over the economy (Johnson et al., 2002; Iwasaki and Suzuki, 2007).

At the beginning of transition, the process was dominated by criminal organizations and oligarchs who grew out of the old Soviet elite (Aslund et al., 2001). After 2005, these groups gradually lost their influence and were replaced with merged power networks between new business elites and top government bureaucrats (e.g., Frye, 2002; Viktorov, 2015). While business elites in the Ukraine, Moldova and the Caucasian economies continued to dominate economics and politics (Closson, 2009; Fisun, 2016; Markus and Charnysh, 2017), in Russia the state managed to reclaim a large share of its bargaining power by suppressing its business allies (e.g., Hoffman, 2011). This led to the formation of a new type of negotiation-based state–business relations with both parties holding relatively equal perceived bargaining power, and being forced to assume a common motivational orientation in order to function efficiently.

At the same time, non-oligarchic business entities in Russia lack negotiating power with state bodies and are therefore forced to resort to corruption. Recent research into the entrepreneurial orientation and investment decisions of Russian small and medium-sized enterprises (SMEs) found that operating in an unstable institutional environment characterized by a large 'shadow economy' compels many companies to make decisions based on information obtained from informal, sometimes illegal, contacts developed with local officials (Wales et al., 2016). Large inconsistencies in informal relations, combined with the limited protection of private property rights, leave many Russian companies exposed to private raiding, creating fundamental threats to their existence (Levina et al., 2016).

Ethnic-clan neopatrimonialism is a key feature of socio-political transition in Central Asia, where certain nationalities and ethnic clans managed to preserve and further accumulate wealth and political influence due to a lack of pressure 'from below'. The absence of 'critical junctures', together with the Soviet legacy, has led to the establishment of rent-seeking, authoritarian regimes across Central Asia. The emergence of the entrepreneurial class in these countries occurred under direct political patronage, forcing business to negotiate its position with the ruling political elite in order to secure property rights, which resulted in high levels of government corruption (e.g., Özkan, 2010; Pomfret, 2012; Kubicek, 2016).

Similarly to the cases of Russia and the Ukraine, SMEs in Central Asia and Caucasus suffer from widespread corruption and base investment decisions on insider information from informal sources. Corruption and strong ties between the business elite and officialdom have resulted in the emergence of 'frozen states', with no visible institutional or socioeconomic dynamics (Gallina, 2010). Özkan's (2010) study of entrepreneurs in Uzbekistan demonstrated a low estimate by business of the quality of the country's legal system and the judiciary. The majority of entrepreneurs would prefer to seek solutions by using their network of family and friends rather than go through official channels. Informal ties seem to be working best if both parties are of the same ethnic origin or clan. A more recent inquiry into SME financing in Uzbekistan further confirmed the importance of informal connections with government bureaucracy for entrepreneurs when securing formal financing (Ruziev and Midmore, 2015). Thus one can argue that, although on the surface the two models that emerged across the post-Soviet region differ in that they give the upper hand to opposite parties (the state in Russia and ethnic clans in Central Asia), they are essentially similar. Effective business operations within both models require companies to maintain high levels of informal personal connections with government bureaucracies.

The model of state–business relations that has developed in Belarus in the last two decades assumes the leading role of the state as the main economic and political actor. Because the government managed to keep a tight grip on the country's industrial base, a Russian-style powerful oligarchic lobby has never developed. The dominance of certain ethnic clans in the economy and politics was also impossible in Belarus due to a relatively homogeneous ethnic composition of the population. Hence, the literature on the Belarusian transition identifies a 'pseudo-market' transition model where the government has made continuous attempts to preserve Soviet institutional structures and socialist-style state–business relations (e.g., Brixiova and Volchok, 2005; Fritz, 2008; Wilson, 2012; Favaro et al., 2012; Cuaresma et al., 2012; Danilovich and Croucher, 2015; Dabrowski, 2016). The result is a potentially unsustainable model wherein the state possesses overwhelming control over the economy, and superficial changes only occur to allow positive international ratings, such as that in the World Bank's Doing Business report.

Indeed, although for the first few years of independence the Belarusian economy and society were undergoing a transition 'from plan to market' similar to that experienced by the rest of the former Soviet Union, since the mid-1990s reforms have stalled and reversed. Unlike in Russia, where such 'involuntary retroregression' (Burawoy, 2001) led to the establishment of powerful state-capturing oligarchic structures, in Belarus, the consolidation of power occurred around formal institutional structures. Chief among these structures have been the executive (presidential) branch which preserved control over the economy and subordinate newly created economic elites which were forced to establish strong ties to the governmental and presidential structures in order to continue their economic activities (e.g., Wilson, 2012). The Belarusian government thus acts as a capitalist corporatist interest group and occupies the same niche that oligarchs and ethnic clans have in the rest of the region, but while maintaining a certain amount of social continuity and stability by ensuring living standards.

At the same time, private property rights in Belarus are weakly protected.

There is no independent judiciary; regulation is unpredictable, since the country is run by Presidential Decrees which supersede the law. Industry is still represented by fully state-owned or quasi-privatized enterprises with an excessively large government share (more than 90 per cent in some cases). Since the majority of the population outside the capital, Minsk, is employed in these companies, the government retains indirect control over wages, creating an artificial sense of equality among much of the population and thus avoiding large-scale social unrest (Bell and Bell, 2015). However, a few recent legal Acts, particularly the controversial 'Law on Social Parasites' (which in effect taxes the most vulnerable groups), have caused mass protests which were suppressed by the police.

The private sector accounts for about a quarter of all businesses and predominantly consists of small and medium-sized service companies, with a total output of 20.6 percent of gross domestic product (GDP) in 2015 (Shimanovich, 2016). The largest share of output from private companies comes from the IT sector, which has received a considerable boost in the last few years, with its output reaching US$1120 million in 2015 (Uniter, 2016). Despite being united in a few employers' and entrepreneurs' associations, private Belarusian companies have so far failed to create an industrial lobby strong enough to influence government policy-making.

The largest share of domestic investments in Belarus is initiated by the government. These investments are undertaken either by state-owned or quasi-privatized enterprises, or are delivered through government investment programmes such as the industry modernization programme aimed at replacing outdated machinery and equipment in the country's manufacturing enterprises (e.g., Sokolova, 2009; Ministry of Economics of the Republic of Belarus, 2012). Despite the fact that the actual rate of investment in Belarus was higher than in the rest of the Commonwealth of Independent States (CIS) until 2016, centralized control over the size and distribution of investment funds negatively affected their effectiveness. State-owned and quasi-privatized enterprises still follow the Soviet-type centrally planned system of output-based targets developed by industry ministries in order to meet government growth standards (e.g., Bell and Bell, 2015; Dabrowski, 2016; Dobrinsky et al., 2016). The targets are set extremely high and impossible to reach given the current state of the industry. One example is the government requirement for enterprises to cut production costs by 25 percent by the end of 2016 (Zlotnikov and Loewy, 2017) and simultaneously increase output to achieve planned GDP growth rates.

Previous studies found that enterprise directors had little say in the way the investment funds were used, and had to comply with state policies, under the threat of criminal prosecution (Dabrowski, 2016). The latest criminal cases against businesses proved the same to be true for private investors, some of whom were accused of mismanaging funds and not reaching impossibly high production targets. For example, the private investor who bought the Motovelo bicycle and motorcycle factory was given an 11-year prison sentence. All of his property, including the company shares, was confiscated by the state (Sputnik, 2017).

The Weaknesses of International Indices

One of our aims is to give perspective on the composite ratings created by international organizations, which are widely used by practitioners. The main question is whether (despite claiming objectivity) they actually present a comprehensive picture of current relations. We analysed two of the most influential, the World Bank's Doing Business (DB) rating and Transparency International's Corruption Perception Index (CPI), with respect to the Belarusian economy and the institutional environment for business.

Belarus showed positive dynamics in both ratings over the years, demonstrating easing in terms of overcoming formal barriers to registering and starting the business, getting credit (also as a result of better access to information on public finance), dealing with contract enforcement, insolvencies, and being more protected from bribery and extortion due to improved judiciary and law enforcement (Table 8.1). Although better ratings can be an indicator of improved institutional environment, one still wonders whether these changes are derived from the actual relationships between the state and the enterprises.

Unfortunately, none of the indices provide separate estimations for enterprises of different forms of ownership. The analysis of the methodology used for calculating the indices shows that they were based on the influence that the institutional environment has on purely private companies, which in the case of Belarus are less than a quarter of the total number of companies, mostly SMEs, not covered by the system of production targets and government programmes, thus reducing their contact with government officials to a minimum.

Another problem with the indices when applied to Belarusian reality is that the indicators they use reflect changes in the law, not in real-life practices. A 'getting credit' indicator (part of the Doing Business rating), for example, reflects legal changes to the rights of borrowers and lenders, the ease of obtaining information on available credit, existence of the centralized credit database, as well as the introduction of some new formal elements into the system. Such innovations include the launch of the unitary secured transactions system or the right of creditors to

*Table 8.1   The dynamics of Doing Business and Corruption Perception
             Index ratings for Belarus*

Year	Doing Business rating (183 countries)	Corruption Perception Index rating (176 countries)
2006	124	151
2007	129	150
2008	110	151
2009	85	139
2010	58	127
2011	68	143
2012	60	123
2013	58	123
2014	63	119
2015	57	107
2016	50	79
2017	37	n/a

Sources: Doing Business; Corruption Perception Index.

recover funds through the court if the borrower goes into administration. Although these elements are easy to introduce (and have been introduced in Belarus for rating purposes), they do not reflect the actual availability of credit to Belarusian companies, since: (1) most of the commercial banks in the country are de facto state-owned (e.g., Bell and Bell, 2015) and operate under the same government rules which limit the availability of credit to purely private companies; and (2) the majority of the country's industrial core is also directly or indirectly owned by the government, and is financed outside of the traditional banking credit system through either state investment programmes or direct subsidies from the ministries, neither of which are included in the 'getting credit' indicator.

Another example of the limited coverage of the Doing Business rating is the 'protecting minority investors' indicator. Under the conditions of market economy, the protection of the interests of minority shareholders from company directors' arbitrary decisions represents an important element. The data are collected from corporate and securities accounts and show respective changes in company codes and the relevant legislature (both laws and court rulings). However, these formal sources do not manifest the actual state of the problem in Belarus. The only minority shareholders at quasi-privatized and private companies in the country are the workers (the labour collective). While quasi-privatized enterprises are controlled by the government and workers are deprived of a voice

(Danilovich, 2017), no conflict of interests with respect to the management's decisions can occur. Private companies of any potential value to the state are often renationalized. One of the most striking cases was the renationalization of the pharmaceutical company Belmedpreparaty. The enterprise was first privatized by the workers and the management in 1995. It was returned to state ownership by court ruling in 2004 when the company was about to attract potential foreign investors, something the government was not likely to allow.

A similar pattern is apparent in the case of the wood processing and furniture producer Pinskdrev, which was fully privatized in the 1990s. However, in 2011 it was renationalized by a special Presidential Decree which appointed the state *kontsern* Bellesbumprom as Pinskdrev's management company, under the pretext of protecting the interests of the labour collective after an accident took place on company premises.

Another blow to early Belarusian privatization was Presidential Decree No.107 (14 March 2011) which limited free circulation of company shares in the securities market, and established state observing committees at private companies with a government share of 50 percent and less. The observing committees were granted the right to start the renationalization process at these companies if they were concerned that the rights of minority shareholders were threatened. The most well-known recent case induced by Decree No.107 was the renationalization of the confectionery companies Spartak and Kommunarka, whose shares were seized from the American investor who bought them in the 1990s. The court found violations in the initial privatization procedure and ruled in favour of the state, regardless of the fact that a ten-year limitation period on those shares had expired long before then (Manenok, 2016). Once again, the official reason offered by the state was the need to protect the interests of minority shareholders.

The Corruption Perception Index also relies on a number of formal measurements. The use of a survey of businesses as the main data collection method makes it more reliable than the Doing Business rating. At the same time, when applied to Belarus rather than traditional market democracies, the CPI suffers from the same problems as the DB. Its survey takes into account the perceptions of private companies, leaving state-owned and quasi-privatized enterprises outside of the analysis, thus adversely affecting the validity and generalizability of the final scores. Moreover, the personal perceptions of selected analysts, experts and businessmen on corruption may differ quite considerably from day-to-day business practice. Also, the CPI does not account for the multiple forms that corruption can take. For example, private companies in Belarus do not need to bribe government officials on a daily basis, but may have to provide non-monetary favours or services (for example, sponsor certain events) in order to reduce the amount of red tape. Further, it does not account for the extensive informal connections businesses must develop in order to survive. It also does not account for the amount of corruption-induced nepotism (for example, hiring or promoting workers with certain governmental connections), which has been very common in Belarus (Danilovich and Croucher, 2015). Thus one can argue that the indices developed by international organizations fail to fully capture the reality of the relationships between the business and its institutional environment in this particular 'pseudo-market' economy.

Hence, when analysing the Belarusian 'pseudo-market' transition model, there is a question concerning the role of the state in relation to enterprise managements, and another concerning the scope for independent company-level decision-making. Our questions therefore are: to what degree (if any) can senior managements of Belarusian state-owned, quasi-privatized and private companies act autonomously with respect to company investment? And what methods (if any) do they use to push their companies' agenda?

RESEARCH APPROACH

Problems with conducting primary research in Belarus have been highlighted by earlier studies (e.g., Mandell, 2004; Danilovich and Croucher, 2015; Danilovich et al., 2016). The most common issues include the lack of reliable data on enterprise policies due to lack of documentation, since Belarusian enterprises only routinely collect data they need for state reporting; and scarce secondary data on state–enterprise relations and on company decision-making in general.

For our inquiry, the main problem was the reluctance of senior management to participate in the research and grant researchers access to company data and personnel. The system of ideological control at Belarusian enterprises is even stronger than it was in the Soviet era. Senior managers fear disclosing potentially sensitive information contradicting the official position. Chief executive officers (CEOs) of private companies, to our surprise, were much more accommodating, a dramatic change from previous years when they were as hostile to researchers as their counterparts from state-owned and quasi-privatized enterprises. However, we were able to obtain information from some representatives of the senior management of state-owned and quasi-privatized enterprises.

Sample

Our sample included senior managers of nine state-owned and quasi-privatized manufacturing enterprises (four deputy directors, three chief financial officers and six planning managers) as well as the CEOs of eight private companies, representing service, retail and IT sectors. Though some may argue that the different statuses of the senior managers from both categories of the state-controlled enterprises may have impacted upon the reliability of the information, the senior management of Belarusian enterprises is rather knowledgeable of the actual state of the relations between their directors and their superiors in branch ministries and other governmental institutions. None of the company directors themselves participated in the study, which can be explained by their unwillingness to open themselves up to anything that could potentially compromise their informal relationships with governmental organizations. By contrast, the CEOs of private companies were much more open to conversation. We believe that the reason for this openness was that none of their companies were what the Belarusian authorities would deem 'strategically important'.

Measurements

Finding measurements which reflect both formal and informal state–business relations in Belarus is a challenging exercise. On the one hand, formal relations are supposed to be largely captured by the World Bank Doing Business indicators – which cover a number of areas, from starting a business, registering property and getting credit, to contract enforcement and insolvencies – and the Transparency International Corruption Perception Index. However, in our view, these indicators do not cover key indicators of informal relations between enterprise directors and government officials. Hence, in addition to using these two sets of indices, we add others, namely:

- negotiated changes in output targets;
- areas of independent investment-related decision-making;
- amount of state investment funding received;
- amount and dynamics of government subsidies received (these funds are different from investment funding since they are aimed not at the improvement of the production process, but at debt repayment and elimination of wage arrears);
- the dynamics of annual number of inspections by various government bodies;
- amount of 'social welfare burden' on the company's books.

Direct government influence on companies was also assessed through analysis of the strength of the ideological control at individual companies.

Methods

Semi-structured interviews were used and were supplemented by analysis of company statistics. The choice of interviews as the main research method was dictated by the unwillingness of the respondents to fill in questionnaires (hence the interviews allowed the collection of rich first-hand data).

Each interview took between 45 and 60 minutes. Interviews were conducted at the workplaces. Those with senior managers of state-owned and quasi-privatized companies had to be recorded manually since the subjects refused to have their voices recorded, which shows the degree of their fear of being compromised in any way. The CEOs of private companies were more open to recording the interviews, although some preferred to have the interviews conducted outside of their workplaces. The data received were manually analysed in relation to questions asked.

The statistical analysis involved analysing the figures on company output as well as statistics on enterprise expenditure. The statistical data from state-owned and quasi-privatized enterprises proved valuable in two ways: (1) as a control tool for some of the interview data; and (2) as a separate source allowing us to, at least partially, trace the dynamics of the relations between the state and each individual company. Similar data from private companies was far patchier and much less useful in this respect.

FINDINGS

The empirical study aimed to fill the gaps in our understanding of the relationships between the state and companies in Belarus left by the indices developed by international organizations. We found clear differences between the management's level of autonomy at state-controlled (state-owned and quasi-privatized) and private companies in a number of areas (Table 8.2).

Although, by law, every domestic company has absolute freedom over the distribution of funds and in making investment deals, in reality the need to obtain permissions and constantly negotiate with the branch ministry or managing *kontsern* makes enterprise management the weaker party in state–business relations. Deputy directors interviewed for the study assert that obtaining the ministry's consent on attracting external investors or reinvesting profits into new projects, for example, depends on 'certain special relations' the enterprise has with its institutional superiors. These relations, they admit, are largely based on the enterprise being 'in the

Table 8.2 Level of independence in company decision-making in Belarus, by ownership type

Type of ownership	Areas of decision-making					
	Attracting outside investments	Retaining profit	Reinvesting profit	Changes in the level of output	Managing internal labour markets
State-owned	Permission from the *kontsern* needed, involves a large degree of informality	Only profits in Belarusian roubles may be retained, currency is to be sold to the government	Permission from the *kontsern* needed for every new project, has to be negotiated	Set centrally, have to be negotiated	According to the Labour Code and Presidential Decrees
Quasi-privatized	Permission from the *kontsern* needed, involves a large degree of informality	Only profits in Belarusian roubles may be retained, currency is to be sold to the government	Permission from the *kontsern* needed for every new project, has to be negotiated	Set centrally, have to be negotiated	According to the Labour Code and Presidential Decrees
Fully private	No government control	Only profits in Belarusian roubles may be retained, currency is to be sold to the government, if not a resident of a free economic zone	No government control, but is subject to inspections by state controlling bodies 'for crime prevention reasons'	No government control	According to the Labour Code and Presidential Decrees

Sources: Interview data and company archives.

ministry's good books' by continuously achieving set output targets and not asking for subsidies.

Good personal relationships between the enterprise director and 'the people above' also play an important role. As one of them put it:

> If they see that an enterprise is doing fine, no labour conflicts, deficits or anything of the kind, then they know that the director can be trusted. Yes, it takes a lot of persuasion every time because no one wants to be blamed if thing [*sic*] don't exactly work out as promised.

When asked whether such negotiations have elements of informality, the senior managers usually resort to phrases like, 'well, you should understand, things are never just done', 'good people eventually always understand each other', 'good human relations between people is the key to success', and so on. They never openly admitted to offering bribes to government officials or being asked for any. Instead, deputy directors usually referred to 'negotiations'. At the same time, some interviewees mentioned that there exists a certain degree of mutual dependency between their companies and branch ministries or *kontserns*, since the latter are ultimately responsible for ensuring that the government-set targets for their industries are met. The responses therefore implicitly confirm that in certain areas the enterprise management of successful companies have a lot of leverage with their superiors in government institutions, which strengthen their bargaining position.

However, things change dramatically if the enterprise is bidding for funds from one of the government investment programmes. In the words of the planning manager of a wood processing plant, 'these are a curse rather than a blessing because control over the money is so strict that you never know when and in what you find yourself guilty'. Her peer from a machine-building plant said in his 'kitchen interview':

> State money always comes with the plan signed you know where [he pointed at the ceiling], so we can't really go sideways. Even when it was obvious for us that the return won't be what they thought in the Ministry it would be, we could not really do anything but go with the flow. The director and our department tried to negotiate with them so that the money would be better used for other purposes, but it was like bumping into a wall: you got money for modernisation, so go on and modernise. Modernise how, and what to do with all these people [excess personnel after modernisation], there was no instruction. Just, the President gave you the money, which means he trusts you, don't betray his trust! And this is the worst thing of all: fine, you get those lathes; stick them onto the shop floor and then what?! Same people, same targets, same materials, no orders, so how do we show all this profit they expect to see? Now we have a new director and the deputy directors were all removed from office, luckily not to prison, and we are still no better off, so who knows how long these new ones are going to remain.

When asked whether there was a way to circumnavigate the rules, the common answer was 'of course there are and quite a few, but not with the state investment, it is too much risk'. Thus, to use Zartman and Rubin's (2000) explanation, when the Belarusian government uses its superior position as the sole institutional investor, it treats the enterprise receiving the funds in ways which deprive the latter of any opportunity to negotiate the conditions and use of the funds provided.

Private companies which are not subordinated to ministries or *kontserns* report very little use of informal connections and need for negotiation in these areas. They are usually free to choose and attract investors or reinvest their profits, provided they can prove to the controlling government bodies that the funds are not used for illegal deals or to fund anything outside their primary economic activity (that is, funding political opposition or sponsoring independent civil society organizations). Private companies have very little access to state investment programmes unless the government sees them as strategically valuable, in which case state investments may be forced upon private companies as a means of gaining control over them. The CEOs of private IT companies admitted that they use their informal connections most on the rare occasions when they bid for state contracts. This relative independence from the state gives successful private companies a stronger bargaining position in negotiations with government institutions, thus largely shielding them from petty corruption.

Both state-controlled and private companies have received much more freedom in the area of intra-firm investments in recent years, when compared to previous research findings (see Danilovich and Croucher, 2011, 2015; Danilovich et al., 2016). The most significant changes have taken place in the area of investment in personnel. Presidential Decree No.5, 'On the Intensification of the Requirements on Senior Managers and Workers in Organisations' (15 December 2014), considerably widened the rights of the employer with regards to the workforce. The employer gained the right to fire at will under the newly introduced 'discriminating circumstances' definition,[2] as well as the right to change the working conditions (including pay) in individual contracts with a seven-day notice given to workers. If the worker refuses to accept the new working and pay conditions, the employer has the right to dismiss them without pay. These 'innovations' resulted in a considerable reduction of enterprise expenditure on the workforce, particularly of investments in training and retraining. Training budgets for the personnel in highly skilled technical and managerial positions (previously the main recipients of work-related training) were slashed, and training of blue-collar workers is now limited to in-house health and safety training. As the labour planning manager of one of the machine-building plants put it:

Of course, we understand everything, and we feel for workers. At the end of the day, we are all workers and all in the same situation. But these are hard times, the enterprise cannot afford to give that much to people and people should understand that. And they do: if earlier we had many people coming requesting and even insisting [on training], now we don't. And they usually don't scream about this, because no one wants to become a parasite [in this, she referred to another 'innovation', the Presidential Decree No.3 (2 April 2015), widely known as the 'Law on Social Parasites', which requires the unemployed to pay US$245/ year to finance the state welfare].

Company statistics confirm a continued practice of rehiring existing employees on new contracts to avoid paying for training, or hiring 'from the street' on short-term fixed contracts, a trend noticed in our earlier research (Danilovich and Croucher, 2015). The data show that the overall investment in training has fallen below 0.1 per cent of the total expenditure on personnel at eight out of nine state-controlled companies in the sample.

Private companies have always enjoyed more freedom in dealing with their personnel, and their investments in training were traditionally lower than at state-controlled enterprises. Since the introduction of new legislation, the statistical data on retail and service private companies in the sample show that they have stopped making investments in training and retraining altogether. IT companies still have some funds allocated for these investments, but rarely use them as the management encourages employees to self-study.

With regard to their day-to-day economic activities, neither state-controlled nor private companies admit the need to regularly use their informal connections, thus giving a certain credibility to the conclusions of the Corruption Perception Index and the Doing Business ratings. Informal connections and negotiating favours are used in daily activities only in dealing with certain inspecting bodies, such as the fire inspection and the sanitary control committee. The companies that are affected the most are private retail and service companies, due to the nature of their business. The CEO of one of the private retail companies even admitted having a small 'investment budget for greasing things up'. State-controlled enterprises that have special labour protection engineers on their payroll are much less affected. At the same time, the CEOs of two IT companies interviewed for the study did not see much informality in their daily operations. Their use of informal connections is low, limited to the periodic visits from fire and sanitary inspection, and the relations with individual tax inspectors when submitting quarterly and yearly figures.

DISCUSSION AND CONCLUSION

It has previously been argued that the fluidity of formal institutions which followed the collapse of the Soviet Union led to informal oligarchic structures dominating the state across the post-Soviet space. Our analysis only partially confirms this thesis. Indeed, the first decade of post-Soviet transition was characterized by the destruction of the Soviet institutional system and the emergence of business and ethnic interest groups which subsequently captured and colonized the majority of formal government institutions. However, subsequent economic changes in the region limited the influence of informal business lobbying networks.

Our literature analysis shows that although the majority of the economies are characterized by varying degrees of institutional fluidity, the reality of state–business relations differs quite considerably across the region. However, significant changes to the transition path over the last two decades, notably the declining number of liberal reforms and the recentralization of economic and political apparatus, indicate that the majority of former Soviet economies have been gradually transitioning towards much less liberalized regulatory regimes. As dysfunctional as they may sound, these new regulatory modes frequently provide development opportunities for businesses within the game's new, stricter rules.

Unlike in other post-Soviet states, business in Belarus never reached the level of power that would have allowed it to directly influence government economic policy. The preservation of Soviet-type state–business relations is shown in the high degree of control in state hands, manifested in direct government control over the majority of the companies either through direct ownership or through a controlling stake. Thus, in order to maintain a certain degree of autonomy over their investment decisions and to compensate for their weaker negotiating position, managers of state-controlled companies are forced to establish close informal connections with their governmental superiors.

The largest increase in enterprise autonomy in recent years has manifested itself via investments in personnel, particularly expenditure on training and retraining, which was made unnecessary by the latest changes in labour law. In a sense, this makes intra-firm employment relations more 'capitalist', but can also be seen as evidence of the failure of state ideology since the state voluntarily removed its responsibility to protect the labour collective from employer despotism, one of the cornerstones of the Belarusian 'social market economy'.

In other areas, such as access to financial resources, reinvesting profits, attracting outside investment and negotiating output targets, informal personal relationships with government institutions still play a crucial role for state-controlled companies. Some areas, such as the utilization of the investment funds provided by the government, remain outside of company management's control, and even good informal relationships with ministries or *kontserns* cannot change the situation.

Thus, despite the authoritarian political regime and management being the weaker party in negotiations with government structures, both state-controlled and private domestic Belarusian companies demonstrate a certain degree of bargaining power in relation to their government counterparts. They indirectly influence state policies and manage to maintain a certain degree of autonomy in their investment decisions.

Increasing differences in state–business relations for private and state-controlled companies have led to two disparate economies. The first is a highly controlled economy of state-owned and quasi-privatized enterprises, predominantly in manufacturing. This is characterized by centrally-set targets, where enterprise directors are often pushed to resort to their extensive informal connections in order to obtain certain economic benefits. The second is the much less controlled economy of private companies, operating predominantly in high-tech and service sectors, where government control is limited to overseeing reporting and tax payments, company management is free in its day-to-day operations, and informal connections are utilized less and at a much more individual level.

The ability of the majority of individual economic actors to act independently is suppressed within the Belarusian 'pseudo-market' system, and the Soviet institutional legacy still largely determines state–business relations. However, state-controlled companies still manage to exert indirect influence on the government, by having established informal connections with the formal institutions that oversee them and using the concentration of control and agenda-setting to their advantage.

NOTES

1. The situation started to change in 1987 when the 'Law on State Enterprise' granted the working collective the ability to fully dispose of profits, while assets remained state property. It was followed by the introduction of five major laws: 'On Cooperation in the USSR' (1988), 'The Foundations of the Rent in the USSR' (1989), 'On Property in the RSFSR' (1990), 'On the General Foundations of Entrepreneurship for the Citizens of the USSR' (1991) and 'On the Privatization of State and Municipal Enterprises in RSFSR' (1991).
2. 'Discriminating circumstances' refer to any circumstances which an employer deems damaging, or potentially damaging, to the company and its reputation. In the Belarusian context, this definition is usually used to describe workers openly voicing their dissatisfaction with their jobs, or unauthorized trade union activity.

REFERENCES

Adarov, A. (2016) 'The Belarus economy: the challenges of stalled reforms', Vienna Institute for International Economic Studies Research Report No. 413. Available at: http://www.wiiw.ac.at/the-belarus-economy-the-challenges-of-stalled-reforms-dlp-4032.pdf, accessed 16 January 2017.

Aslund, A., Boone, P. and Johnson, S. (2001) 'Escaping the under-reform trap', *IMF Staff Papers*, 48, Special Issue. Available at: https://www.researchgate.net/profile/Peter_Boone/publication/5222004_S_Escaping_the_Under-Reform_Trap/links/5654105508ae4988a7afca9a.pdf, accessed 18 December 2016.

Becker, U. (2013) 'Measuring change of capitalist varieties: reflections on method, illustrations from the BRICs', *New Political Economy*, 18 (4): 503–532.

Bell, H. and Bell, R. (2015) 'Post-crisis Belarus: Marxism and the lender of last resort', *Journal of Eurasian Studies*, 6 (2): 153–160.

Brixiova, Z. and Volchok, V. (2005) 'Labour markets in Belarus', *Problems of Economic Transition*, 48 (1): 56–67.

Burawoy, M. (2001) 'Transition without transformation: Russia's involutionary road to capitalism', *East European Politics and Societies*, 15 (2): 269–290.

Closson, S. (2009) 'State weakness in perspective: strong politico-economic networks in Georgia's energy sector', *Europe–Asia Studies*, 61 (5): 759–778.

Cuaresma, J.C, Oberhofer, H. and Vincelette, G.A. (2012) 'Firm growth and productivity in Belarus: new empirical evidence from the machine-building sector', World Bank Policy Research Working Paper No.6005. Available at: http://library1.nida.ac.th/worldbankf/fulltext/wps06005.pdf, accessed 15 July 2016.

Dabrowski, M. (2016) 'Belarus at a crossroads', *Bruegel Policy Contribution* 2016 (2). Available at: http://aei.pitt.edu/71017/, accessed 12 December 2016.

Danilovich, H. (2017) 'Struggling to be heard: the past and present of employee voice in Belarus', in Pyman, A., Gollan, P.J., Wilkinson, A., Xu, C. and Kalfa, S. (eds), *Employee Voice in Emerging Economies*, pp. 105–135. Bingley: Emerald Group Publishing.

Danilovich, H. and Croucher, R. (2011) 'Labour management in Belarus: transcendent retroregression', *Journal of Communist Studies and Transition Politics*, 27 (2): 241–262.

Danilovich, H. and Croucher, R. (2015) 'Investment in personnel and FDI in Belarusian companies', *International Business Review*, 24 (6): 966–971.

Danilovich, H., Croucher, R. and Makovskaya, N. (2016) 'Compulsory reduced working time in Belarus: incidence, operation and consequences', *Economic and Industrial Democracy*. Available at: http://journals.sagepub.com/doi/full/10.1177/0143831X15586071, accessed 3 January 2017.

Dobrinsky, R., Adarov, A., Bornukova, K., et al. (2016) 'The Belarus economy: the challenges of stalled reforms', Vienna Institute for International Economic Studies Research Report 413. Available at: http://wiiw.ac.at/the-belarus-economy-the-challenges-of-stalled-reforms-dlp-4032.pdf, accessed 6 January 2017.

Easter, G. (2008), 'The Russian state in the time of Putin', *Post-Soviet Affairs*, 24 (3): 199–230.

Favaro, E., Smits, K. and Bakanova M. (2012) 'Structural challenges for SOEs in Belarus: a case study of the machine building sector', World Bank Policy

Research Working Paper, No.6010. Available at: https://openknowledge.world-bank.org/bitstream/handle/10986/19871/WPS6010.pdf?sequence=1, accessed 15 July 2016.

Fisun, O. (2016) 'Ukrainian constitutional politics: neopatrimonialism, rent-seeking, and regime change', in Hale, H.E. and Orttung, R.W. (eds), *Beyond the Euromaidan: Comparative Perspectives of Advancing Reform in Ukraine*, pp. 105–123. Stanford, CA: Stanford University Press.

Fries, S., Lysenko, T. and Polenac, S. (2003) 'The 2002 business environment and enterprise performance survey: results from a survey of 6100 firms', European Bank of Reconstruction and Development Working Paper No.84. Available at: https://www.researchgate.net/publication/241755940_The_2002_Business_Environment_and_Enterprise_Performance_Survey_Results_from_a_Survey_of_6100_Firms, accessed 13 December 2016.

Fritz, V. (2008) *State-Building: A Comparative Study of Ukraine, Lithuania, Belarus and Russia*. Budapest: Central European University Press.

Frye, T. (2002) 'Capture or exchange? Business lobbying in Russia', *Europe–Asia Studies*, 54 (7): 1017–1036.

Frye, T. (2010) *Building States and Markets after Communism: The Perils of Polarized Democracy*. Cambridge: Cambridge University Press.

Gallina, N. (2010) 'Puzzles of state transformation: the cases of Armenia and Georgia', *Caucasian Review of International Affairs*, 4 (1): 20–34.

Guriev, S. and Rachinsky, A. (2006) 'The evolution of personal wealth in the former Soviet Union and Central and eastern Europe', UNU-WIDER, United Nations University Working Paper No. 2006/120. Available at: https://www.econstor.eu/bitstream/10419/63536/1/52139225X.pdf, accessed 5 February 2017.

Hellman, J.S., Jones, G. and Kaufmann, D. (2003) 'Seize the state, seize the day: state capture and influence in transition economies', *Journal of Comparative Economics*, 31 (4): 751–773.

Hoffman, D.E. (2011) *The Oligarchs: Wealth and Power in the New Russia*, 3rd edn. New York: Public Affairs.

Ilkhamov, A. (2007) 'Neopatrimonialism, interest groups and patronage networks: the impasses of the governance system in Uzbekistan', *Central Asian Survey*, 26 (1): 65–84.

Iwasaki, I. and Suzuki, T. (2007) 'Transition strategy, corporate exploitation, and state capture: an empirical analysis of the former Soviet states', *Communist and Post-Communist Studies*, 40 (4): 393–422.

Johnson, S.H., McMillan, J. and Woodruff, C.M. (2002) 'Property rights and finance', *American Economic Review*, 92 (5): 1335–1356.

Junisbai, B. (2010) 'Improbable oppositions: personalist rule, privatisation and elite defection in the post-Soviet autocracies', paper prepared for the 2010 Annual Conference of the American Political Science Association. Available at: https://papers.ssrn.com/sol3/papers2.cfm?abstract_id=1642507, accessed 14 December 2016.

Kubicek, P. (2016) 'Applying the democratization literature to post-Soviet Central Asian statehood', in Kavalski, E. (ed.), *Stable Outside, Fragile Inside? Post-Soviet Statehood in Central Asia*, pp. 37–51. London: Routledge.

Laruelle, M. (2012) 'Discussing neopatrimonialism and patronal presidentialism in the Central Asian context', *Demokratizatsiya*, 20 (4): 301–324.

Ledeneva, A. (2009) 'From Russia with *blat*: can informal networks help modernize Russia?', *Social Research: An International Quarterly*, 76 (1): 257–288.

Levina, I., Kisunko, G., Marques, I. and Yakovlev, A.A. (2016) 'Uncertainty as a factor in investment decisions: the case of the Russian Federation's regions', World Bank Policy Research Working Paper No. 7806. Available at: https://papers.ssrn.com/sol3/papers2.cfm?abstract_id=2836556, accessed 6 January 2017.

Lewis, D. (2012) 'Understanding the authoritarian state: neopatrimonialism in Central Asia', *Brown Journal of World Affairs*, 19 (1): 115–130.

Mandell, D. (2004) *Labour after Communism*. Montreal, Canada; New York, USA; London, UK: Black Rose Books.

Manenok, T. (2016) 'Высокая позиция Беларуси в рейтинге ВБ: утешение для власти или позитивный сигнал для инвесторов?' (High position of Belarus in the WB rating: comfort for the authorities or a positive signal to investors?) *Belrynok*, 31 October. Available at: http://www.belrynok.by/ru/page/economics/4054/, accessed 16 December 2016.

Markus, S. and Charnysh, O. (2017) 'The flexible few: oligarchs and wealth defence in developing democracies', *Comparative Political Studies*, 50 (12): 1632–1665.

McFaul, M. (1995) 'State power, institutional change, and the politics of privatisation in Russia', *World Politics*, 47 (2): 210–243.

Melnykovska, I. (2008) 'Colour revolutions or soft authoritarianism? Different ways to cope with similar challenges in the globalised world', paper presented at the workshop The Colour Revolutions, CEELBAS, 30 April, Cambridge.

Ministry of Economics of the Republic of Belarus (2012) Program of the development of the industrial complex of the Republic of Belarus. Available at: http://www.economy.gov.by/nfiles/001146_12850_Programma.pdf, accessed 6 October 2016.

Olson, M. (2000) *Power and Prosperity: Outgrowing Communist and Capitalist Dictatorships*. New York: Basic Books.

Özcan, G.B. (2010) *Building States and Markets: Enterprise Development in Central Asia*. London: Palgrave Macmillan.

Pomfret, R. (2012) 'Central Asia after two decades of independence', in Roland, G. (ed.), *Economic Transition: The Long-Run View*, pp.400–429. London: Palgrave Macmillan.

Pyle, W. (2011) 'Organised business, political competition, and property rights: evidence from the Russian Federation', *Journal of Law, Economics and Organisation*, 27 (1): 2–31.

Robinson, N. (2011) 'Russian patrimonial capitalism and the international financial crisis', *Journal of Communist Studies and Transition Politics*, 27 (3/4): 434–455.

Ruziev, K. and Midmore, P. (2015) 'Connectedness and SME financing in post-communist economies: evidence from Uzbekistan', *Journal of Development Studies*, 51 (5): 586–602.

Shimanovich, G. (2016) Тенденцииразвитиямалого и среднегобизнеса в Беларуси (SME development trends in Belarus). IPM Research Paper PDP/16/04. Available at: http://www.research.by/webroot/delivery/files/pdp2016r04.pdf, accessed 28 December 2016.

Sokolova, G.N. (2009) 'Belorusskaya model innovatsionnogorazvitiya v social-nomizmerenii' (Social dimension of the Belarusian innovation development model), in Proleskovsky, O.V. and Osipov, G.V. (eds), *Belarus and Russia: Social Sphere and Socio-Cultural Dynamics*, pp.60–79. Minsk: IAC.

Sputnik (2017) Акции «Мотовело» –стране, Минпрому и ГКИ – замечание ('Motovelo' shares – to the country, and the reprimand to the Ministry of Manufacture and the State Industrial Committee), *Sputnik. by*, 30 January. Available at: https://sputnik.by/society/20170130/1027211391/prigovor-muravevu-akcii-motovelo-strane-minpromu-i-gki-zamechanie.html, accessed 3 February 2017.

Transparency International (2016) 'Corruption Perception Index 2016'. Available at: www.transparency.org/country/BLR#, accessed 14 February 2017.

Uniter (2016) 'IT-рынок в Беларуси' (IT-market in Belarus). Available at: http://www.uniter.by/upload/iblock/68e/68ec0d19a876e84896dccbca0ae4cf60.pdf, accessed 10 January 2017.

Vasileva, A. (2017) 'Trapped in informality: the big role of small firms in Russia's statist-patrimonial capitalism', *New Political Economy*. Available at: http://www-tandfonline-com.ezproxy.mdx.ac.uk/doi/pdf/10.1080/13563467.2017.1349090?n eedAccess=true, accessed 3 October 2017.

Viktorov, I. (2015) 'The state, informal networks, and financial market regulation in post-Soviet Russia, 1990–2008', *Soviet and Post-Soviet Review*, 42: 5–38.

Wales, W.J., Shirokova, G., Sokolova, L. and Stein, C. (2016) 'Entrepreneurial orientation in the emerging Russian regulatory context: the criticality of interpersonal relations', *European Journal of International Management*, 10 (3): 359–382.

Wedel, J.R. (2001) 'Clans, cliques and captured states: rethinking "transition" in Central and Eastern Europe and the former Soviet Union', World Institute for Development Economics Research Discussion Paper No.2001/58.

Wilson, A. (2012) *Belarus: The Last Dictatorship in Europe*. New Haven, CT, USA and London, UK: Yale University Press.

World Bank (2017) *Doing Business: Measuring Business Regulations*. Washington, DC: World Bank Group. Available at: www.doingbusiness.org/rankings/, accessed 14 February 2017.

Yakovlev, E. and Zhuravskaya, E. (2006) 'State capture: from Yeltsin to Putin', Centre for Economic and Financial Research at the New Economic School Working Paper No.94. Available at: http://www.cefir.org/papers/WP94_Zhuravskaya_Yakovlev.pdf, accessed 14 December 2016.

Zartman, I.W. and Rubin, J.Z. (2000) 'The study of power and the practice of negotiation', in Zartman, I.W. and Rubin, J.Z. (eds), *Power and Negotiation*, pp.3–28. Ann Arbor, MI: University of Michigan Press.

Zlotnikov, V. and Loewy, D.J. (2017) 'Sizing up markets – and your investment strategy'. Available at:https://blog.alliancebernstein.com/post/en/2017/07/sizing-up-markets-and-your-investment-strategy, accessed 16 November 2017.

9. Equity commitment and company resources: evidence from Nordic multinational enterprise strategies in transitional periphery economies

Ahmad Arslan, Jorma Larimo and Shlomo Y. Tarba

INTRODUCTION

The transitional periphery of the European Union (EU) is defined as those countries which are located in its immediate neighbourhood, such as the Balkan countries and some former Soviet states (Demekas et al., 2005, 2007; Aslund, 2012). In the academic context, the term 'transitional periphery' was coined by those sociologists, political analysts and economists who had an interest in analysing these countries, which, although in close proximity to the EU, present significantly differing socio-political and economic characteristics (Barry, 2004; Galego et al., 2004; Balkir et al., 2013). In one way or another, most transitional periphery countries adopted the communist model of economic and state governance during the twentieth century. Once the Soviet bloc had been dismantled, these countries started transitioning (in some cases, very slowly) towards a market economy. However, despite more than two decades of transition, they still present issues linked to political and economic instability, problematic legal systems, corruption of officials, crime, lack of information about market conditions, and uncertainty due to events such as the recent civil war in Ukraine (Demekas et al., 2007; Bitzenis, 2009; Estrin and Uvalic, 2013, 2014; Kuznetsov, 2016).

It is important to mention that, despite their similarities – stemming from having been part of the communist bloc at some point in their history – these transitional periphery economies represent different economic bases and reform speeds. For example, the economic and political conditions found in Belarus are very different from those prevalent in Ukraine or in Balkan countries such as Bosnia, Croatia and Serbia, which were the scene of political turmoil that eventually led to civil war. Similarly, the economic structures and bases of these countries also tend to vary significantly. For example, Kazakhstan is a resource-rich economy – especially in terms of oil – and has attracted a significant amount of foreign direct investment (FDI) and foreign multinational enterprise (MNE) activity, primarily in that sector. On the other hand, countries such as Belarus or Georgia lack significant resources, but their strategic location and occasionally favourable investment policies have been the driving force behind FDI inflows by foreign MNEs. Moreover, Ukraine received a significant amount of FDI from Western MNEs from the 1990s onwards due to its attractive market size and location, until political uncertainty and civil war erupted in 2014 (Diez et al., 2016).

The term 'transitional periphery' is also linked to the idea of significant economic, political and social reforms, and to the aspirations of at least some of these countries – for example, Bosnia, Serbia and Ukraine – to achieve full EU membership at some point. Some transitional periphery economies – such as that of Croatia, which became a full member of the EU in 2014 – have successfully implemented the required reforms. Earlier research showed that Western MNEs tend to face significant entry and operational challenges in these economies (Uvalic, 2010; Arslan et al., 2015). However, despite such challenges, several Western MNEs have entered these economies and continue to operate within them, with varying degrees of success (for example, Umland, 2016; Diez et al., 2016). MNEs' interest to enter these economies is fuelled by prospects for future market and business growth, and by the location advantages presented by the presence in low-cost economies adjacent to the EU (Treisman, 2014; Ledyaeva et al., 2014).

Specific market entry and international business (IB) studies somewhat ignored transitional periphery economies because they mostly focused upon those Central and Eastern European (CEE) countries – such as Poland, Hungary, Estonia, Lithuania, Latvia, the Czech Republic, Slovakia and Slovenia – that joined the EU in 2004 (e.g., Dikova and Van Witteloostuijn, 2007; Arslan and Larimo, 2010; Dikova, 2012). It is also important to mention that the results of those few earlier studies that focused on the transitional periphery were influenced by the inclusion of the Russian Federation in their samples (e.g., Arslan et al., 2015). As the Russian Federation is a large and resource-rich economy that receives a significant amount of FDI and attention from Western MNEs, the specificities of other transitional periphery countries – such as Belarus, Bosnia, Georgia, Kazakhstan, Serbia, Ukraine and Uzbekistan – were ignored in the quantitative analysis due to their low representation in the overall samples. However, earlier research revealed that, in some instances, MNE investment choices made in these economies tend to differ from the ones undertaken in the Russian Federation (e.g., Arslan et al., 2015). Therefore, this chapter is aimed at focusing specifically on relatively ignored transitional periphery economies in a rather interesting context.

We aim at analysing the equity commitment made by MNEs from Nordic countries at the time of market entry in transitional periphery economies. It is an established fact that extensive market entry studies have been undertaken in IB research (e.g., Datta et al., 2002; Brouthers and Hennart, 2007; Dikova and Van Witteloostuijn, 2007; Slangen and Hennart, 2008; Arslan and Larimo, 2011; Hernandez and Nieto, 2015; Hennart and Slangen, 2015). However, despite such extensive research, the need remains for a better understanding of the determinants of entering company choices (for example, equity commitment) in ignored contexts such as the transitional periphery. Moreover, the analysis of the MNE entry strategies in transition periphery economies involved significant attention being paid to the influences of external environmental factors (for example, institutions) (e.g., Arslan et al., 2015; Drahokoupil et al., 2015; Diez et al., 2016). This is understandable in view of the unique context of these economies and of their development of market economy institutions. However, along with external factors, the IB literature has established that the specific resources of the investing companies do play a significant role in their entry choices (e.g., Isobe et al., 2000; Meyer et al., 2009; Sui and Baum, 2014; Klier et al., 2017). Due to the uncertainties associated with changing institutional dynamics, the investing companies' resources become even more important in the context of emerging and transition economies (e.g., Estrin et al., 2009; Zoogah et al., 2015; Meyer and Peng, 2016).

Moreover, earlier studies analysing market entry in the transitional periphery addressed equity ownership as a dichotomous variable; that is, a choice between joint ventures and wholly owned subsidiaries (e.g., Arslan et al., 2015). However, the IB literature has established that control dynamics vary significantly in different joint venture categories; that is, minority, 50:50 or majority ones (e.g., Liu et al., 2014). Moreover, some transitional periphery economies do not allow the establishment of wholly owned subsidiaries in certain industries and sectors (e.g., Croucher, 2015). For this reason, we argue that it is important to consider the specific equity commitment at the time of market entry, rather than taking the rather simplistic dichotomous choice view. Therefore, we intend to address the specific resources of investing MNEs in relation to their equity commitments at time of market entry.

This chapter contributes to the market entry and transitional periphery-specific literature by addressing the influence of factors such as the investing MNEs' sizes, levels of diversification, and international and host country-specific experience. The empirical part of this chapter is based on market entries undertaken by companies from open and highly internationalized Nordic economies (that is, Denmark, Finland, Norway and Sweden) in the transitional periphery economies of Belarus, Bosnia, Croatia, Georgia, Kazakhstan, Serbia, Ukraine and Uzbekistan. The rest of this chapter is organized as follows. The next section addresses the key resources owned by the investing MNEs, which leads to the development of the study hypotheses. Then, as part of the detailed analysis and discussion of the findings, we describe the data sources, the empirical sample and the research methodology. The chapter concludes with a discussion on contributions, limitations and managerial applications.

THEORETICAL DISCUSSION AND STUDY HYPOTHESES

The resource-based view of companies (RBV) has gained prominence in management and marketing studies because it offers a comparatively sound explanation of the competitive advantage held by companies in relation to their strategy choices (Newbert, 2007; Cavusgil and Knight, 2015). The RBV addresses companies as bundles of resources (Penrose, 2009 [1959]; Grant, 2005) and emphasizes the 'value maximization of a firm through pooling and utilizing valuable resources' (Das and Teng, 2000, p. 36). These resources are developed, evolved and improved over time by companies (Andreu et al., 2017). In the foreign market entry context, the RBV offers a relatively 'unique opportunity to explain entry mode choices from the perspective of a firm's resource endowment and deployment' (Sharma and Erramilli, 2004, p. 6). As this chapter focuses upon the influence wielded by the investing MNEs' resources on their equity commitment in transitional economies, we consider the RBV to be a theoretical lens suited to the exploration of this phenomenon. A review of earlier studies revealed the key MNE resources to be size (e.g., Ekeledo and Sivakumar, 2004; Zeng et al., 2013; Anil et al., 2014), product diversity or level of diversification (e.g., Slangen and Hennart, 2008; Larimo and Arslan, 2013; Su and Tsang, 2015), international experience (e.g., Tsang, 2000; Barney et al., 2001; Mohr and Batsakis, 2014; Andreu et al., 2017) and host country experience (Delios and Beamish, 2001; Fang et al., 2007; Arslan and Dikova, 2015; Peng and Beamish, 2016). We theoretically address the influence wielded by these specific resources on the equity commitment at market entry of Nordic MNEs in the transitional periphery, as follows.

MNE Size

MNE size is an important variable linked with the RBV in earlier IB studies (e.g., Anil et al., 2014). The size of an investing MNE is a good indication of both its tangible and intangible resources and can be employed for strategic purposes (Wernerfelt, 1984, 1995; Bloodgood, 2014), including equity commitment at market entry (Wooster et al., 2016). MNE size has been associated with the availability of the financial resources required to undertake market entry, which in many cases is an expensive venture (e.g., Kogut and Singh, 1988; Drogendijk and Slangen, 2006; Anil et al., 2014). Moreover, the irreversibility of the FDI mode means that market entry through this mode requires investing MNEs to commit even more sizeable financial resources to it (Wooster et al., 2016). Therefore, MNE size is an important factor to consider in this concern.

The earlier literature has shown that large MNEs tend to prefer modes that afford higher degrees of control (Sanchez-Peinado et al., 2007). Higher-control modes can only be achieved by committing more equity at the time of market entry (Trevino and Grosse, 2002; Andreu et al., 2017). It is especially important to consider this aspect as, in transitional periphery economies, political and economic uncertainty is even higher that it is in other emerging economies (e.g., Demirbag et al., 2015; Umland, 2016). Despite this uncertainty, large MNEs can undertake high equity commitment, as they have enough resources to finance such a venture. Even if host transitional periphery economies do not allow wholly owned subsidiaries at the time of entry, such large MNEs can achieve a high degree of control in subsidiary management (that is, majority joint ventures). This choice can offer an investing MNE the possibility to pursue the strategies of its choice, despite not having full ownership (e.g., Yan and Luo, 2016). This control can further enable an MNE to transfer the required organizational practices and to make the necessary adjustments to operational strategies to manage its transitional periphery subsidiaries effectively (Chi and Zhao, 2014; Lo, 2016). Therefore, we expect large-sized Nordic MNEs to commit more equity at times of market entry in the transitional periphery:

Hypothesis 1:   *MNE size is positively associated with higher equity commitment at the time of market entry in transitional periphery economies.*

MNE Product Diversity

The product diversity of MNEs was used in earlier studies as a key indicator of those companies' operational strategies (e.g., Nath et al., 2010;

Su and Tsang, 2015). The IB literature reports that highly concentrated companies tend to own the necessary product-specific knowledge (e.g., Burgel and Murray, 2000) and, especially in emerging markets, are hesitant to share it with partners due to intellectual property issues (Zhao, 2006). However, when the degree of diversification of a company increases, it becomes aware of the lack of required product-specific knowledge in all the fields and industrial sectors in which it operates (Larimo and Arslan, 2013). Such lack of product-specific knowledge can become a hindrance to managing a foreign subsidiary (Larimo, 2003), especially if the latter is located in an uncertain and relatively risky transitional periphery economy (Demirbag et al., 2015). The earlier literature also mentioned that, in new markets, MNEs with diversified product portfolios tend to prefer partial ownership (that is, joint ventures) with local partners that possess particular product knowledge (e.g., Luo, 2002; Yan and Luo, 2016). This collaborative approach with a local partner also enhances any product-specific competitive advantage, as well as offering access to the networks required for production in the host country (Lin and Wu, 2014; Hiratsuka, 2016). Therefore, in the context of equity commitment at the time of market entry in the transitional periphery, it is reasonable to expect that, compared to a more concentrated one, a highly diversified Nordic MNE would prefer a lower equity commitment. Therefore, we hypothesize:

Hypothesis 2:   *MNE product diversity is negatively associated with higher equity commitment at the time of market entry in transitional periphery economies.*

MNE International Investment Experience

A substantial number of earlier IB studies addressed international experience as a key resource for internationalizing MNEs (e.g., Jung et al., 2010). From the RBV, as companies accumulate international investment experience, their organizational capabilities (Dierickx and Cool, 1989) to manage uncertain and unfamiliar contexts in new international markets increase (Chang, 1995; Das and Teng, 2000; Larimo and Arslan, 2013). International experience also equips investing MNEs with organizational capabilities to deal appropriately with risky situations while making FDI decisions (e.g., Buckley et al., 2016). It has also been argued that companies lacking international investment experience benefit from partnerships with others that possess useful knowledge of local environments (Yan and Gray, 1994; Jung et al., 2010). Therefore, joint ventures with a reputable local partner offer such MNEs the possibility to fill the gap generated by the lack of this key resource. The earlier IB research yielded conflicting results with regard to the influence of international investment experience, with some studies finding that it led to choosing high equity modes (e.g., Desai et al., 2004; Jung et al., 2010). Furthermore, a number of studies investigating entry strategies in transitional and emerging economies found international investment experience to be non-significant (e.g., Li and Meyer, 2009; Arslan et al., 2015). This last finding was explained by referring to the peculiarities of these host economies, which render generic international experience rather ineffective in devising local strategies (Dikova and Van Witteloostuijn, 2007; Li and Meyer, 2009). Based on these conflicting findings, we present two hypotheses: one which suggests that a high degree of international experience leads to higher equity commitment, and another which views it as being non-significant. Therefore, we hypothesize that:

Hypothesis 3a: *MNE international investment experience is positively associated with higher equity commitment at the time of market entry in transitional periphery economies.*

Hypothesis 3b: *MNE international investment experience is non-significantly associated with higher equity commitment at the time of market entry in transitional periphery economies.*

MNE Host Country Investment Experience

Host country-specific investment experience has been reported to be an important resource for internationalizing companies (Meyer et al., 2009; Arslan and Dikova, 2015). Such experience provides MNEs with important knowledge of local market dynamics (Larimo and Arslan, 2013) and of the key players in the industrial sectors in which the MNEs operate (Lindsay et al., 2015). Host country experience can also offset some of the effects of uncertainty stemming from institutional differences, and offer information on any attractive local companies in terms of collaboration or acquisition (Arslan and Dikova, 2015). The earlier IB research mentioned that a lack of host country experience can force MNEs to pay more for potential acquisition deals (e.g., Chakrabarti and Mitchell, 2013), to establish joint ventures with unsuitable partners (e.g., Shenkar and Yan, 2002), or to choose unsuitable locations for greenfield investments (e.g., Ascani et al., 2016). All these mistakes can lead to high operational costs and to the risk of potential failure in the new market. Such risks become even higher in transitional periphery economies – such as those of Belarus, Kazakhstan or Uzbekistan – in which many companies in key sectors are still publicly owned (e.g., Griffith et al., 2001; Panibratov, 2017). In such cases, the issue of equity commitment requires delicate handling by MNE managers. It is reasonable to expect that, by taking into account practical contingencies including infrastructure and utilities issues (e.g. Gurkov, 2016), MNEs with prior investment experience in particular transition economies will be better equipped to deal with pre-agreement negotiations (e.g., Basuil and Datta, 2015), reduce bureaucratic hurdles (Arslan and Dikova, 2015) and speed up the start of production in cases of greenfield investments. Finally, such experienced MNEs will understand the market potential and, especially, future growth opportunities despite the risks and uncertainties associated at time of market entry. Therefore, they may opt for higher equity commitment despite the risks involved in the case of transitional periphery economies. Based on this discussion, we hypothesize that:

Hypothesis 4:   *MNE host country investment experience is positively associated with higher equity commitment at the time of market entry in transitional periphery economies.*

RESEARCH METHODOLOGY

Data Sources

The data used in this chapter are primarily based on an internal FDI databank developed and constantly updated over the course of roughly 30 years by one of the authors. This manufacturing sector Nordic MNE FDI activity database is based on annual reports, corporate websites and stock release information, and articles and information found in leading business magazines (*Kauppalehti, Talouselämä, Dagens Industri, Veckans Affärer* and *Borsen*). Moreover, historical reports published by national investment agencies such as Finnfund, Swedfund and IFU (Denmark) were used in compiling and updating the dataset. The data were further supplemented with information drawn from the Thompson One database. Such data consist of basic investing company and FDI-related information such as year of investment, field of industry, location, ownership and establishment mode information at entry, and subsequent changes (if applicable). The dataset is almost unique and is representative of the FDIs made by Nordic MNEs in the manufacturing sector.

Operationalization of Study Variables

- MNE equity share. This variable is based on the percentages of actual equity shares owned by investing MNEs at the time of market entry.

- MNE international experience. We operationalized international experience by the number of earlier FDIs undertaken by the investing companies in different international markets (Shaver et al., 1997; Larimo and Arslan, 2013).
- MNE host country experience. We operationalized host country experience using the number of years of presence in host countries, calculated from the first manufacturing investment in each particular market (Hennart and Park, 1993; Larimo, 2003; Arslan and Dikova, 2015).
- MNE product diversity. We used the number of four-digit Standard Industrial Classification (SIC) codes of the products in which the investing companies had been operating, based on company annual reports and websites (Hennart and Larimo, 1998; Harzing, 2002; Chung et al., 2013).
- MNE size. We used the investing companies' natural log of global sales for the year preceding the investment, converted to euros (e.g., Hennart and Park, 1993; Taylor et al., 1998; Dow and Larimo, 2011).
- MNE establishment mode choice. We operationalized the establishment mode choice as a dichotomous variable, in which 0 stands for greenfield investment and 1 stands for acquisition, at the time of market entry.

Sample Description

The study sample includes 71 FDIs made by Nordic (Danish, Finnish, Swedish and Norwegian) MNEs in the transitional periphery economies of Belarus, Bosnia, Croatia, Georgia, Kazakhstan, Serbia, Ukraine and Uzbekistan between 1990 and 2009. The host countries were chosen based on two criteria. Firstly, they had to be in the EU's transitional periphery; therefore, other emerging and transition economies were not included. Secondly, the host economies were not to have been EU members during the period under study. Therefore, Croatia (which joined the EU in 2014) was included. The key aspects of the study sample are explained as follows.

Home countries of investing MNEs
The study sample includes 71 FDIs: 20 undertaken by Danish MNEs (28.2 per cent), 17 by Finnish MNEs (23.9 per cent), 14 by Norwegian MNEs (19.7 per cent) and 20 by Swedish MNEs (28.2 per cent). It is important to mention that we took into account the ownership of each investing company at the time of investment when determining its home country. Therefore, later changes in MNE ownership (for example, due to

acquisition of the investing MNEs by other MNEs) were not considered in the analysis.

Number of FDIs in host countries

The study sample includes: 36 FDIs made in Ukraine (50.7 per cent), 14 in Croatia (19.7 per cent), 8 in Kazakhstan (11.3 per cent), 6 in Serbia (8.5 per cent), 3 in Belarus (4.2 per cent), 2 in Uzbekistan (2.8 per cent), 1 in Bosnia (1.4 per cent), and 1 in Georgia (1.4 per cent). As Ukraine is the destination of the highest number of FDIs, we offer a more in-depth analysis of this particular transitional periphery economy, alongside a general analysis of the others.

Investing MNEs

The study sample includes FDIs undertaken by both well-known and lesser-known Nordic MNEs. The largest investors in transitional periphery economies during the period under study include: Orkla (a Norwegian conglomerate), with 11 FDIs; Carlsberg (a Danish brewing MNE), with 10 FDIs; ABB (a Swedish–Swiss Electrical MNE), with 6 FDIs; and Rautaruukki (a Finnish metal industry MNE) with 5 FDIs. Alongside these large transitional periphery investors are also well-known Nordic MNEs including Danfoss (Denmark), Ericsson (Sweden), Elopak (Norway), Hartwall (Finland), Hidling Anders (Sweden), Kemira (Finland) and Nokia (Finland).

Equity ownership at the time of entry

The study sample includes equity ownership percentages at the time of entry that range from 11 per cent (minimum) to 100 per cent. If we use 95 per cent equity ownership as a cut-off point (that is, we consider equity ownerships of 94 per cent or less as joint ventures), then the sample includes 53 joint ventures (74.6 per cent) and 18 wholly owned subsidiaries (25.4 per cent).

Establishment mode

The study sample includes 27 greenfield investments (38 per cent) and 44 acquisitions (62 per cent). It is important to mention that most acquisitions are partial (with equity share percentages of 94 per cent or less).

International and host country experience

The study sample includes MNEs with a range of international and host country experience. The minimum international experience in the sample is a single instance of FDI, while the maximum is 156 prior FDIs (the highly experienced ABB Swedish MNE). We also observe that the host country experience of most companies is very low, that is, zero years. At the other end of the spectrum, the highest host country experience in the sample is nine years (Rautaruukki, a Finnish MNE with multiple FDIs in Ukraine starting from the 1990s).

MNE size and product diversity
The sample presents a significant degree of heterogeneity; it includes significantly large MNEs – such as ABB, Orkla, Carlsberg, Kone and Nokia – and relatively smaller ones, such as ZinkTeknik. We can also observe a variance in the product diversity (diversification) of investing MNEs, as the sample includes highly diversified conglomerates – such as Orkla – and a number of more industry or business sector-focused companies.

Statistical Analysis Technique

We used a correlation matrix along with descriptive statistics to understand the strength of the relationship between equity commitment at the time of market entry and selected company resources. Due to the limited sample size (71), we were unable to perform a more sophisticated statistical analysis, such as general linear regression. However, as we were interested in the association or relationship between the chosen companies' resources and their equity commitments, rather than specific causation, we reckoned that correlation analysis would offer sufficient insights into this phenomenon. In order to better understand the strategies of Nordic MNEs, we aimed at analysing the relationship between establishment mode and equity commitment at market entry time, as well as performing a sub-sample analysis of the major FDI destination – that is, Ukraine. We also carried out a sub-sample analysis based on the time of investment by dividing the FDIs into those undertaken in the 1990s versus those undertaken in the 2000s.

RESULTS

The Pearson correlation results for the full sample of study are presented below. As our focus was on the interrelationship between equity commitment and the chosen companies' resources and establishment modes, only those statistics are presented. Table 9.1 presents the correlations between company resources and equity commitment for the full sample of the study.

The correlation results show that establishment modes are non-significantly associated with equity commitments at the time of market entry. This result is interesting, as some earlier studies inferred that establishment and ownership decisions are interrelated (e.g., Larimo and

*Table 9.1   Full sample Pearson correlations:equity commitment and MNE
              resources*

	N	Mean	S.D.	Correlations
Equity commitment	71	54.33	31.54	1
Establishment mode	71	0.62	0.49	–0.006 (0.963)
MNE size	71	6.39	1.73	0.203 (0.090)
MNE product diversity	71	10.73	10.51	–0.208 (0.042)*
MNE international experience	71	45.45	43.85	–0.221 (0.188)
MNE host country experience	71	2.39	1.87	0.062 (0.006)**

Note: * Significant at the p < 0.05 level. ** Significant at the p < 0.01 level.

Arslan, 2013). However, the non-significance of establishment modes can be explained by referring to the specificities of transitional periphery economies, where establishment mode choices can be hindered by the lack of availability of suitable acquisition targets, or by the need for significant restructuring linked to brownfield strategies (Meyer, 2002, 2005). On the other hand, equity commitments are associated with the MNEs' evaluations of risk and uncertainty in the environment, and their willingness to commit financial and human resources to their subsidiaries.

We also observe that the correlation between MNE size and equity commitments is non-significant. Therefore, hypothesis 1 of our study is not supported. It has been mentioned that FDI entry modes are irreversible, as they involve significant financial commitments (Wooster et al., 2016). Moreover, transitional periphery economies such as those of Croatia, Serbia, Kazakhstan and Ukraine presented high degrees of uncertainty and political change during the period under study (e.g., Lam and Zhang, 2014; Estrin and Uvalic, 2014). Therefore, the detailed analysis of the sample reveals that even large MNEs such as Carlsberg, Ericsson, Nokia and Orkla established some minority joint ventures or partial acquisitions at the time of market entry into these economies. Later, in some cases, we observe higher equity commitments, as the result of either the MNEs increasing their shares of the same subsidiaries or by subsequent investments on their part in the same transitional periphery economies (e.g., Carlsberg in Ukraine). Hence, it can be argued that the traditional argument of MNE size being a key driver for higher equity commitments is not fully valid in transitional periphery economies.

Table 9.1 also shows a medium-strength negative correlation between the MNEs' product diversity and equity commitments at the time of their market entries into transitional periphery economies. This finding supports hypothesis 2 of our study. For highly diversified MNEs, the lack of product-specific knowledge is a hindrance to the smooth running of foreign subsidiaries (Larimo, 2000), especially in highly uncertain transitional periphery economies (e.g., Arslan et al., 2015). Therefore, such companies may choose to establish joint ventures with partners that have the required specific product knowledge (e.g., Yan and Luo, 2016). Moreover, given the high levels of uncertainty found in transitional periphery economies, these MNEs may prefer not to have majority stakes in their subsidiaries, and opt for lower equity commitments at the time of market entry. However, as transitional periphery economies offer interesting location and growth possibilities, diversified MNEs may still opt to establish a presence there. This is shown by large MNEs such as Carlsberg and Orkla choosing to set up minority control subsidiaries on different occasions, in the transitional periphery economies of Croatia, Kazakhstan, Serbia and Ukraine.

We further observe that international experience is non-significantly correlated with equity commitments at the time of market entry in transitional periphery economies. This finding supports hypothesis 3b of our study, as well as the findings of those earlier studies that pointed to the lack of significance of generic international experience in the specific context of transitional and emerging economies (e.g., Li and Meyer, 2009; Arslan et al., 2015).

Finally, Table 9.1 shows that MNE host country experience has a medium-strength positive correlation with equity commitments at the time of market entry. This finding supports hypothesis 4 of our study. Host country experience is important in all international entry decisions, but its importance increases in the case of emerging and transitional economies (e.g., Arslan and Dikova, 2015; Arslan et al., 2015). Experienced MNEs leverage their understanding of the local market dynamics and their knowledge of the key players in their industrial sectors when establishing joint ventures with local companies or acquiring them (Lindsay et al., 2015). These MNEs are not likely to make mistakes such as overpaying for acquisitions (e.g., Chakrabarti and Mitchell, 2013) or choosing unsuitable locations for new greenfield investments (e.g., Ascani et al., 2016) in transitional periphery economies. High equity commitments can enable experienced MNEs to better integrate their subsidiaries in their global strategies, even in cases of partial ownership such as majority joint ventures (Yan and Luo, 2016). Moreover, they can speed up the start of production in cases of greenfield investments by taking into account practical contingencies such as infrastructure and utilities issues (e.g., Gurkov, 2016).

Table 9.2   FDIs in the Ukraine sub-sample: correlations between equity commitments and MNE resources

	N	Mean	S.D.	Correlations
Equity commitment	36	59.13	31.07	1
Establishment mode	36	0.64	0.487	−0.046 (0.790)
MNE size	36	6.84	1.54	0.090 (0.600)
MNE product diversity	36	12.44	10.54	−0.181 (0.029)*
MNE international experience	36	52.22	46.45	−0.216 (0.205)
MNE host country experience	36	3.06	2.23	0.105 (0.42)*

Note: *Significant at the $p < 0.05$ level. ** Significant at the $p < 0.01$ level.

In order to increase our understanding of equity commitments in transitional periphery economies, we analysed FDIs made in Ukraine (which received the largest share of FDIs among the sample destination countries). The correlations for the Ukrainian sub-sample are presented in Table 9.2.

Table 9.2 shows relationships between company resources and equity commitments similar to those observed in the full sample. Therefore, from this perspective, we do not observe any specificity linked to the Ukrainian context. The IB literature established that, during the 1990s, both the transitional periphery and other CEE economies went through a series of changes that also had an influence on MNE strategies (e.g., Meyer, 2002; Peng, 2003). Earlier studies also found differences in MNE strategies in these economies during the 1990s and the 2000s (e.g., Larimo and Arslan, 2013). Therefore, we next present the correlations between equity commitments and MNE resources in host transitional periphery economies during the 1990s.

Table 9.3 shows that the correlations between equity commitments and MNE resources are non-significant in all cases. This finding differs from that yielded by the full sample. We can explain this by referring to the specificities of the economic contexts of the transitional periphery economies during the 1990s, which was a decade of high turbulence during which those countries were ranked as risky for market entry (Peng, 2003; Euromoney country risk ratings, https://www.euromoney-countryrisk.com/). Transitional periphery economies opened to foreign MNE operations for the first time during the 1990s. In such circumstances, MNE strategies based on their experiences in other markets were less applicable to this context due to its uniqueness. Therefore, the non-significance of factors such as MNE size, general international experience and product diversity is understandable. Moreover, most MNEs lacked host country experience as they only made their first FDIs in these economies during the 1990s. Therefore, the non-significance of host country experience is also logical. For example, the FDIs made by MNEs such as Carlsberg or Hartwall in the 1990s were their first ones in the transitional periphery context; for example, in Ukraine. Subsequent FDIs and strategic subsidiary management choices made by Nordic MNEs included increasing equity shares and diversification.

Table 9.4 presents the correlations between MNE equity commitments and resources for FDIs made during the 2000s. For this sub-sample, we can observe an interesting finding concerning MNE size; it has a

Table 9.3 FDIs during the 1990s sub-sample: Pearson correlations between equity commitments and MNE resources

	N	Mean	S.D.	Correlations
Equity commitment	37	50.28	26.98	1
Establishment mode	37	0.68	0.475	0.099 (0.562)
MNE size	37	6.44	1.87	0.087 (0.608)
MNE international experience	37	46.03	48.07	0.026 (0.877)
MNE host country experience	37	2.24	1.21	−0.060 (0.726)
MNE product diversity	37	11.22	10.92	0.017 (0.920)

Note: * Significant at the $p < 0.05$ level. ** Significant at the $p < 0.01$ level.

Table 9.4 FDIs during the 2000s sub-sample: Pearson correlations between MNE equity commitments and resources

	N	Mean	S.D.	Correlations
Equity commitment	34	58.74	35.76	1
Establishment mode	34	0.56	0.504	−0.057 (0.748)
MNE size	34	6.34	1.60	0.319 (0.046)*
MNE international experience	34	44.82	39.449	0.482 (0.400)
MNE host country experience	34	2.56	2.402	0.098 (0.045)*
MNE product diversity	34	10.21	10.174	−0.403 (0.018)*

Note: *Significant at the $p < 0.05$ level. ** Significant at the $p < 0.01$ level.

medium-strength positive correlation with equity commitments. Therefore, we can argue that large MNEs opted for high equity commitments that gave them a high degree of control over their subsidiaries (e.g., Andreu et al., 2017) in transitional periphery economies during the 2000s. This aspect can also be linked with the fact that transitional periphery economies – especially Croatia, Serbia, Kazakhstan and Ukraine – posted positive growth figures, removed restrictions and enacted other reforms during the first decade of the twenty-first century (e.g., Gwartney et al., 2009).

Therefore, it can be argued that even large MNEs tend to be careful in committing equity in host economies during times of reforms and political changes leading to uncertainty (that is, during the 1990s). However, once the environment is more stable, these MNEs become willing to increase their equity commitments (that is, during the 2000s).

IMPLICATIONS, LIMITATIONS AND FUTURE RESEARCH DIRECTIONS

The transitional periphery of the EU is an under-researched context in IB studies. This chapter presents an attempt to go beyond the analysis of institutional factors and the transition to a market economy by bringing in an analysis more geared towards company strategies. We address the influences of key company resources on the equity commitments at the time of market entry made by Nordic MNEs in transitional periphery economies. We identified 71 FDIs made by Nordic MNEs in the transitional periphery economies of Belarus, Bosnia, Georgia, Kazakhstan, Serbia, Ukraine and Uzbekistan between 1990 and 2009. Using the RBV as the theoretical basis and descriptive statistics along with correlation analysis, our study uncovers interesting theoretical and managerial implications.

Firstly, rather than concentrating solely on the role played by the external environment made up of institutions, this study highlights the importance of the role played by MNE resources in the important decisions concerning equity commitments (e.g., Drahokoupil et al., 2015; Diez et al., 2016). We therefore extend the earlier IB studies that analysed the strategies adopted by MNEs in transitional countries and highlight the importance of MNE resources (e.g., Isobe et al., 2000; Meyer et al., 2009; Sui and Baum, 2014; Zoogah et al., 2015; Meyer and Peng, 2016). Secondly, as suggested by Hennart and Slangen (2015), this chapter highlights the importance of analysing the entry strategies adopted in less-researched geographical contexts such as the transitional periphery. In this vein, we also aim at addressing equity commitments specifically, rather than treating them as a dichotomous choice between joint ventures (JVs) and wholly owned subsidiaries (WOSs), with minority and majority JV dynamics being rather ignored in the analysis.

Our findings also have several implications for managerial audiences. Firstly, while focusing on company resources, this chapter's findings emphasize the importance of context and uncertainty. We found that MNE size is non-significantly associated with equity commitments in both the full sample and sub-samples, with the exception of FDIs made in the 2000s. This finding shows that even large MNEs were cautious in regard to making high equity commitments in transitional periphery economies, due to the high degree of uncertainty associated with social, political and economic changes. However, when these economies appeared to have stabilized during the 2000s, large companies opted for high equity commitments. This finding further highlights minority JVs as an important entry mode choice in high-risk environments. The cost of lost opportunity can be high in international business; thus, MNE managers should consider minority equity stakes at entry time in such environments. Once they will have accumulated enough host country-specific experience, they will be able to decide whether to increase their equity commitments in the same subsidiaries, or to make further entries by establishing new ones. This aspect has also been shown by the choices made by Nordic MNEs, as we found that those with host country-specific experience tended to make high equity commitments at time of entry, even though their subsidiaries may still be JVs. Such high equity commitments enable high degrees of control, facilitating subsidiary management, transfer of practices, and other operations. Moreover, on the basis of this study's findings, the managers of highly diversified MNEs are also recommended to consider minority JVs as a suitable entry mode, especially in host economies characterized by relatively high levels of uncertainty, such as transitional periphery ones.

MNE managers also need to be careful in regard to generalizing their international experience into new markets, such as transitional periphery ones, that present changing dynamics. Earlier research uncovered MNE inertia, leading to a preference for mimicking their existing successful strategies in new international markets (e.g., Ferreira et al., 2007; Ang et al., 2015). However, such mimicking requires a careful analysis of the host country context, as lessons learned in previously accessed markets may not apply specifically to new host economies, in which the transitional dynamics and opportunities for investing MNEs can be significantly different. Finally, our study found a non-significant correlation between establishment mode choice and equity commitments in transitional periphery economies. This finding has important implications for managers to also consider the specificities of entry mode choices despite their being related, as mentioned in some studies. In the case of transitional periphery and other emerging economies, the entry mode options can be limited by the lack of suitable local companies to acquire. Therefore, managers are advised to look at the overall costs associated with the establishment and operation of greenfield subsidiaries, as acquiring unsuitable local companies may lead to higher overall costs linked to restructuring.

Like any other research endeavour, this chapter does have certain limitations. Firstly, our sample size (71) was rather limited, which hindered the use of advanced statistical analysis techniques. However, despite such sample size limitations, our study does expand the understanding of the company-level strategies adopted in the chosen countries, because we did not include the large economies of Russia or of older EU member states in the sample, as earlier studies had. Moreover, unlike those studies that used few cases to analyse the strategies adopted in these economies, our sample is large enough to allow us to perform some basic statistical analysis, as well as to refer to specific cases in the discussion. Future research can expand MNE samples from Nordic countries to include the study of other small and highly internationalized European countries – such as Austria, Belgium and the Netherlands – over longer periods of time, in order to analyse similarities or differences with Nordic MNEs' strategies. Another limitation of this study stems from its use of basic statistical tools such as descriptive statistics and correlations. Although these tools do not offer any clear direction of influence, they are able to shed light on the strength of the relationship that exists between company resources and equity commitments. By selecting large enough samples for their analyses, future studies can employ advanced tools such as regression. Finally, human resources, including both experienced expatriates and local employees, are an important asset for internationalizing MNEs, one which our study did not address. Therefore, future studies can analyse different aspects of human resources, and link them to experience and influence on equity commitments and other MNE strategies adopted in transitional periphery economies.

REFERENCES

Andreu, R., Claver, E., and Quer, D. (2017). Firm-specific factors and entry mode choice: an analysis of Chinese hotel chains. *Tourism Economics*, 23(4), 756–767.

Ang, S.H., Benischke, M.H. and Doh, J.P. (2015). The interactions of institutions on foreign market entry mode. *Strategic Management Journal*, 36(10), 1536–1553.

Anil, I., Tatoglu, E. and Ozkasap, G. (2014). Ownership and market entry mode choices of emerging country multinationals in a transition country: evidence from Turkish multinationals in Romania. *Journal for East European Management Studies*, 19(4), 413–452.

Arslan, A. and Dikova, D. (2015). Influences of institutional distance and MNEs' host country experience on the ownership strategy in cross-border M&As in emerging economies. *Journal of Transnational Management*, 20(4), 231–256.

Arslan, A. and Larimo, J. (2010). Ownership strategy of multinational enterprises and the impacts of regulative and normative institutional distance: evidence from Finnish foreign direct investments in Central and Eastern Europe. *Journal of East–West Business*, 16(3), 179–200.

Arslan, A. and Larimo, J. (2011). Greenfield investments or acquisitions: impacts of institutional distance on establishment mode choice of multinational enterprises in emerging economies. *Journal of Global Marketing*, 24(4), 345–356.

Arslan, A., Tarba, S.Y. and Larimo, J. (2015). FDI entry strategies and the impacts of economic freedom distance: evidence from Nordic FDIs in transitional periphery of CIS and SEE. *International Business Review*, 24(6), 997–1008.

Ascani, A., Crescenzi, R. and Iammarino, S. (2016). Economic institutions and the location strategies of European multinationals in their geographic neighborhood. *Economic Geography*, 92(4), 401–429.

Aslund, A. (2012). *How Capitalism was Built: The Transformation of Central and Eastern Europe, Russia, the Caucasus, and Central Asia*. New York: Cambridge University Press.

Balkir, C., Bolukbasi, H.T. and Ertugal, E. (2013). Europeanisation and dynamics of continuity and change: domestic political economies in the 'southern periphery'. *South European Society and Politics*, 18(2), 121–137.

Barney, J., Wright, M. and Ketchen Jr, D.J. (2001). The resource-based view of the firm: ten years after 1991. *Journal of Management*, 27(6), 625–641.

Barry, F. (2004). Enlargement and the EU periphery: introduction. *World Economy*, 27(6), 753–759.

Basuil, D.A. and Datta, D.K. (2015). Effects of industry- and region-specific acquisition experience on value creation in cross-border acquisitions: the moderating role of cultural similarity. *Journal of Management Studies*, 52(6), 766–795.

Bitzenis, A. (2009). *The Balkans: Foreign Direct Investment and EU Accession*. Farnham: Ashgate Publishing.

Bloodgood, J. (2014). Enhancing the resource-based view of the firm: increasing the role of awareness. *Strategic Management Review*, 8(1), 61–75.

Brouthers, K.D. and Hennart, J.F. (2007). Boundaries of the firm: insights from international entry mode research. *Journal of Management*, 33(3), 395–425.

Buckley, P.J., Chen, L., Clegg, L.J. and Voss, H. (2016). Experience and FDI risk-taking: a microfoundational reconceptualization. *Journal of International Management*, 22(2), 131–146.

Burgel, O. and Murray, G.C. (2000). The international market entry choices of start-up companies in high-technology industries. *Journal of International Marketing*, 8(2), 33–62.

Cavusgil, S.T. and Knight, G. (2015). The born global firm: an entrepreneurial and capabilities perspective on early and rapid internationalization. *Journal of International Business Studies*, 46(1), 3–16.

Chakrabarti, A. and Mitchell, W. (2013). The persistent effect of geographic distance in acquisition target selection. *Organization Science*, 24(6), 1805–1826.

Chang, S.J. (1995). International expansion strategy of Japanese firms: capability building through sequential entry. *Academy of Management Journal*, 38(2), 383–407.

Chi, T. and Zhao, Z.J. (2014). Equity structure of MNE affiliates and scope of their activities: distinguishing the incentive and control effects of ownership. *Global Strategy Journal*, 4(4), 257–279.

Chung, C. C., Lee, S.H., Beamish, P.W., Southam, C. and Nam, D.D. (2013). Pitting real options theory against risk diversification theory: international diversification and joint ownership control in economic crisis. *Journal of World Business*, 48(1), 122–136.

Croucher, R. (2015). National and international labour relations in oil and gas trans national corporations in Kazakhstan. *International Business Review*, 24(6), 948–954.

Das, T.K. and Teng, B.S. (2000). A resource-based theory of strategic alliances. *Journal of Management*, 26(1), 31–61.

Datta, D.K., Herrmann, P. and Rasheed, A.A. (2002). Choice of foreign market entry mode: critical review and future directions. In M.A. Hitt and J.L.C. Cheng (eds), *Managing Transnational Firms: Resources, Market Entry and Strategic Alliances*, Advances in International Management, Vol. 14 (pp. 85–153). Amsterdam: JAI Press.

Delios, A. and Beamish, P.W. (2001). Survival and profitability: the roles of experience and intangible assets in foreign subsidiary performance. *Academy of Management Journal*, 44(5), 1028–1038.

Demekas, D.G., Horváth, B., Ribakova, E. and Wu, Y. (2005). Foreign direct investment in South-Eastern Europe: what do the data tell us?. In Klaus Liebscher (ed.), *European Economic Integration and South-East Europe* (pp. 209–241). Cheltenham, UK and Northampton, MA, USA: Edward Elgar Publishing.

Demekas, D.G., Horvath, B., Ribakova, E. and Wu, Y. (2007). Foreign direct investment in European transition economies: the role of policies. *Journal of Comparative Economics*, 35(2), 369–386.

Demirbag, M., McGuinness, M., Wood, G. and Bayyurt, N. (2015). Context, law and reinvestment decisions: why the transitional periphery differs from other post-state socialist economies. *International Business Review*, 24(6), 955–965.

Desai, M.A., Foley, C.F. and Hines Jr, J.R. (2004). The costs of shared ownership: evidence from international joint ventures. *Journal of Financial Economics*, 73(2), 323–374.

Dierickx, I. and Cool, K. (1989). Asset stock accumulation and sustainability of competitive advantage. *Management Science*, 35(12), 1504–1511.

Diez, J.R., Schiller, D. and Zvirgzde, D. (2016). Doing business in Ukraine: multinational companies in the trap of regional institutions? *Environment and Planning C: Government and Policy*, 34 (4), 638–655.

Dikova, D. (2012). Entry mode choices in transition economies: the moderating effect of institutional distance on managers' personal experiences. *Journal of East–West Business*, 18(1), 1–27.

Dikova, D. and van Witteloostuijn, A. (2007). Foreign direct investment mode choice: entry and establishment modes in transition economies. *Journal of International Business Studies*, 38(6), 1013–1033.

Dow, D. and Larimo, J. (2011). Disentangling the roles of international experience and distance in establishment mode choice. *Management International Review*, 51(3), 321–355.

Drahokoupil, J., Myant, M. and Domonkos, S. (2015). The politics of flexibility: employment practices in automotive multinationals in Central and Eastern Europe. *European Journal of Industrial Relations*, 21(3), 223–240.

Drogendijk, R. and Slangen, A. (2006). Hofstede, Schwartz, or managerial perceptions? The effects of different cultural distance measures on establishment mode choices by multinational enterprises. *International Business Review*, 15(4), 361–380.

Ekeledo, I. and Sivakumar, K. (2004). International market entry mode strategies of manufacturing firms and service firms: a resource-based perspective. *International Marketing Review*, 21(1), 68–101.

Estrin, S., Baghdasaryan, D. and Meyer, K.E. (2009). The impact of institutional and human resource distance on international entry strategies. *Journal of Management Studies*, 46(7), 1171–1196.

Estrin, S. and Uvalic, M. (2014). FDI into transition economies. *Economics of Transition*, 22(2), 281–312.

Estrin, S. and Uvalic, S.E. (2013). Foreign direct investment into transition economies: are the Balkans different?. Discussion paper, London School of Economics/European Institute, http://www.lse.ac.uk/europeanInstitute/LEQS%20Discussion%20Paper%20Series/LEQSPaper64.pdf.

Fang, Y., Wade, M., Delios, A. and Beamish, P.W. (2007). International diversification, subsidiary performance, and the mobility of knowledge resources. *Strategic Management Journal*, 28(10), 1053–1064.

Ferreira, M.P., Li, D. and Jang, Y.S. (2007). Foreign entry strategies: strategic adaptation to various facets of the institutional environment. Available at https://www.iconline.ipleiria.pt/handle/10400.8/24 (accessed 17 February 2017).

Galego, A., Vieira, C. and Vieira, I. (2004). The CEEC as FDI attractors: a menace to the EU periphery? *Emerging Markets Finance and Trade*, 40(5), 74–91.

Grant, R.G. (2005). *Contemporary Strategy Analysis: Concepts, Techniques, Applications*. Hoboken, NJ: Wiley.

Griffith, D.A., Zeybek, A.Y. and O'Brien, M. (2001). Knowledge transfer as a means for relationship development: a Kazakhstan–foreign international joint venture illustration. *Journal of International Marketing*, 9(2), 1–18.

Gurkov, I. (2016). Against the wind: new factories of Russian manufacturing subsidiaries of Western multinational corporations. *Eurasian Geography and Economics*, 57(2), 161–179.

Gwartney, J.D., Lawson, R., Grubel, H., de Haan, J. and Zandberg, E. (2009). *Economic Freedom of the World 2009 Annual Report*. Vancouver, BC: Fraser Institute.

Harzing, A.-W. (2002). Acquisitions versus greenfield investments: international strategy and management of entry modes. *Strategic Management Journal*, 23(3), 211–227.

Hennart, J.F. and Larimo, J. (1998). The impact of culture on the strategy of multinational enterprises. Does national origin affect ownership decisions? *Journal of International Business Studies*, 29(3), 515–538.

Hennart, J.F. and Park, Y.R. (1993). Greenfield vs. acquisition: the strategy of Japanese investors in the United States. *Management Science*, 39(9), 1054–1070.

Hennart, J.F. and Slangen, A.H. (2015). Yes, we really do need more entry mode studies! A commentary on Shaver. *Journal of International Business Studies*, 46(1), 114–122.

Hernández, V. and Nieto, M.J. (2015). The effect of the magnitude and direction of institutional distance on the choice of international entry modes. *Journal of World Business*, 50(1), 122–132.

Hiratsuka, D. (2016). Production networks in Asia: a case study from the hard disk drive industry. In G. Wignaraja (ed.), *Production Networks and Enterprises in East Asia* (pp. 139–157). Tokyo: Springer Japan.

Isobe, T., Makino, S. and Montgomery, D.B. (2000). Resource commitment, entry timing, and market performance of foreign direct investments in emerging economies: the case of Japanese international joint ventures in China. *Academy of Management Journal*, 43(3), 468–484.

Jung, J.C., Beamish, P.W. and Goerzen, A. (2010). Dynamics of experience, environment and MNE ownership strategy. *Management International Review*, 50(3), 267–296.

Klier, H., Schwens, C., Zapkau, F.B. and Dikova, D. (2017). Which resources matter, how and where? A meta-analysis on firms' foreign establishment mode choice. *Journal of Management Studies*, 54(3), 304–339.

Kogut, B. and Singh, H. (1988). The effect of national culture on the choice of entry mode. *Journal of International Business Studies*, 19(3), 412–432.

Kuznetsov, A. (2016). Russian direct investment as a factor of Eurasian integration. *Problems of Economic Transition*, 58(4), 348–361.

Lam, S.S. and Zhang, W. (2014). Does policy uncertainty matter for international equity markets? ACSEP Basic Research Working Paper No. 3. National University of Singapore. Available at: https://bschool.nus.edu.sg/Portals/0/images/ACSEP/Publications/ACSEP-Working-Paper-14-03.pdf.

Larimo, J. (2000). Organizational structure in foreign markets: the impact of ownership and location specific determinants on the foreign direct investment behavior of Nordic firms. AIB Annual Conference in Phoenix, AZ.

Larimo, J. (2003). Form of investment by Nordic firms in world markets. *Journal of Business Research*, 56(10), 791–803.

Larimo, J. and Arslan, A. (2013). Determinants of foreign direct investment ownership mode choice: evidence from Nordic investments in Central and Eastern Europe. *Journal for East European Management Studies*, 18(2), 232–263.

Ledyaeva, S., Karhunen, P., Kosonen, R. and Wörz, J. (2014). FDI in Russia from CESEE and Central Asia: a micro-level perspective. NUS Working Paper. Available at: https://bschool.nus.edu.sg/Portals/0/images/ACSEP/Publications/ACSEP-Working-Paper-14-03.pdf.

Li, P.Y. and Meyer, K.E. (2009). Contextualizing experience effects in international business: a study of ownership strategies. *Journal of World Business*, 44(4), 370–382.

Lin, Y. and Wu, L.Y. (2014). Exploring the role of dynamic capabilities in firm performance under the resource-based view framework. *Journal of Business Research*, 67(3), 407–413.

Lindsay, V. J., Rod, M. and Ashill, N. (2015). SME entry into an emerging market: a resource-based and institutional approach. Available at: http://ro.uow.edu.au/cgi/viewcontent.cgi?article=1698&context=dubaipapers.

Liu, X., Vredenburg, H. and Steel, P. (2014). A meta-analysis of factors leading to management control in international joint ventures. *Journal of International Management*, 20(2), 219–236.

Lo, F.Y. (2016). Intra-MNE advantage transfer and subsidiary innovativeness: the moderating effect of international diversification. *Journal of Business Research*, 69(5), 1712–1717.

Luo, Y. (2002). Product diversification in international joint ventures: performance implications in an emerging market. *Strategic Management Journal*, 23(1), 1–20.

Meyer, K.E. (2002). Management challenges in privatization acquisitions in transitions economies. *Journal of World Business*, 37(4), 266–276.

Meyer, K. (2005). *Foreign Direct Investment in Emerging Economies*. Oxford: Templeton College.

Meyer, K.E. and Peng, M.W. (2016). Theoretical foundations of emerging economy business research. *Journal of International Business Studies*, 47(1), 3–22.

Meyer, K.E., Estrin, S., Bhaumik, S.K. and Peng, M.W. (2009). Institutions, resources, and entry strategies in emerging economies. *Strategic Management Journal*, 30(1), 61–80.

Mohr, A. and Batsakis, G. (2014). Intangible assets, international experience and the internationalisation speed of retailers. *International Marketing Review*, 31(6), 601–620.

Nath, P., Nachiappan, S. and Ramanathan, R. (2010). The impact of marketing capability, operations capability and diversification strategy on performance: a resource-based view. *Industrial Marketing Management*, 39(2), 317–329.

Newbert, S.L. (2007). Empirical research on the resource-based view of the firm: an assessment and suggestions for future research. *Strategic Management Journal*, 28(2), 121–146.

Panibratov, A. (2017). Russian oil and gas MNEs investing in China: the role of government in value creation. In S. Marinova, J. Larimo and N. Nummela (eds), *Value Creation in International Business* (pp. 279–306). Basingstoke: Springer International Publishing.

Peng, M.W. (2003). Institutional transitions and strategic choices. *Academy of Management Review*, 28(2), 275–296.

Peng, G.Z. and Beamish, P. (2016). Sequential entry timing and the survival of MNC subsidiaries. *Academy of Management Proceedings*, 2016(1), p. 15064. Briarcliff Manor, NY: Academy of Management.

Penrose, E.T. (2009 [1959]). *The Theory of the Growth of the Firm*. Revised edn. Oxford: Oxford University Press.

Sanchez-Peinado, E., Pla-Barber, J. and Hebert, L. (2007). Strategic variables that influence entry mode choice in service firms. *Journal of International Marketing*, 15(1), 67–91.

Sharma, V.M. and Erramilli, M.K. (2004). Resource-based explanation of entry mode choice. *Journal of Marketing Theory and Practice*, 12(1), 1–18.

Shaver, J., Mitchell, W. and Yeung, B. (1997). The effect of own-firm and other-firm experience on foreign direct investment survival in the United States, 1987–92. *Strategic Management Journal*, 18(10), 811–824.

Shenkar, O. and Yan, A. (2002). Failure as a consequence of partner politics: learning from the life and death of an international cooperative venture. *Human Relations*, 55(5), 565–601.

Slangen, A.H. and Hennart, J.F. (2008). Do multinationals really prefer to enter culturally distant countries through greenfields rather than through acquisitions? The role of parent experience and subsidiary autonomy. *Journal of International Business Studies*, 39(3), 472–490.

Su, W. and Tsang, E.W. (2015). Product diversification and financial performance: the moderating role of secondary stakeholders. *Academy of Management Journal*, 58(4), 1128–1148.

Sui, S. and Baum, M. (2014). Internationalization strategy, firm resources and the survival of SMEs in the export market. *Journal of International Business Studies*, 45(7), 821–841.

Taylor, C.R., Zou, S. and Osland, G.E. (1998). A transaction cost perspective on foreign market entry strategies of US and Japanese firms. *Thunderbird International Business Review*, 40(4), 389–412.

Treisman, D. (2014). Twenty-five years of market reform: the political economy of change after communism. Discussion Paper, Department of Political Science, University of California, Los Angeles, National Bureau of Economic Research, International Center for the Study of Institutions and Development (Moscow), http://www.sscnet.ucla.edu/polisci/faculty/treisman/Daniel'sNEWPAPERS/Buda pest%20paper%20June%201%202014.pdf (accessed 15 January 2017).

Trevino, L.J. and Grosse, R. (2002). An analysis of firm-specific resources and foreign direct investment in the United States. *International Business Review*, 11(4), 431–452.

Tsang, E.W. (2000). Transaction cost and resource-based explanations of joint ventures: a comparison and synthesis. *Organization Studies*, 21(1), 215–242.

Umland, A. (2016). Political risk insurance for FDI in Ukraine. *Harvard International Review*, 37(1), 31–35.

Uvalic, M. (2010). Transition in Southeast Europe: understanding economic development and institutional change. Working Paper, No. 2010, 41, World Institute for Development Economics Research.

Wernerfelt, B. (1984). A resource-based view of the firm. *Strategic Management Journal*, 5(2), 171–180.

Wernerfelt, B. (1995). The resource-based view of the firm: ten years after. *Strategic Management Journal*, 16(3), 171–174.

Wooster, R.B., Blanco, L. and Sawyer, W.C. (2016). Equity commitment under uncertainty: a hierarchical model of real option entry mode choices. *International Business Review*, 25(1), 382–394.

Yan, A. and Gray, B. (1994). Bargaining power, management control, and performance in United States–China joint ventures: a comparative case study. *Academy of Management Journal*, 37(6), 1478–1517.

Yan, A. and Luo, Y. (2016). *International Joint Ventures: Theory and Practice*. London: Routledge.

Yildirim, C. (2017). Turkey's outward foreign direct investment: trends and patterns of mergers and acquisitions. *Journal of Balkan and Near Eastern Studies*, 19(3), 276–293.

Zeng, Y.P., Shenkar, O., Song, S. and Lee, S.H. (2013). FDI experience location and subsidiary mortality. *Management International Review*, 53(3), 477–509.

Zhao, M. (2006). Conducting R&D in countries with weak intellectual property rights protection. *Management Science*, 52(8), 1185–1199.

Zoogah, D.B., Peng, M.W. and Woldu, H. (2015). Institutions, resources, and organizational effectiveness in Africa. *Academy of Management Perspectives*, 29(1), 7–31.

10. Lessons in nonmarket strategy from Eastern Europe and Central Asia: moving beyond the 'compared to what' question

Yusaf H. Akbar and Maciej Kisilowski

INTRODUCTION

The post-Soviet periphery, which we define as 19 countries of Eastern Europe and Central Asia that remain outside the European Union, and which we herein refer to as 'the EECA'[1] are known for their close entanglement of governments and the economy. It thereby is quite surprising that systematic research on strategic interactions of businesses with their nonmarket environment in these countries remains relatively sparse compared with other parts of the world. The only exception here is the voluminous research on EECA corruption. While this line of research is important, the sole focus on this one type of nonmarket strategy, chosen by researchers a priori, may be skewing our picture of what exactly EECA businesses do in order to 'improve [their] performance by managing the institutional or societal context of economic competition' (Mellahi et al., 2016, p. 143).

In all candour, this research gap may in large part be a consequence of theoretical and even conceptual challenges that surround the topic of nonmarket strategy, even in the context of developed countries. Even a basic question – what kind of business activities constitute the generic nonmarket strategies? – remains debated, even in the Western context. This is a problem for those studying the transitional periphery. After all, the West has, for better or for worse, become a de facto benchmark for those studying numerous phenomena in international business and strategy. We make sense of business practices in the transitional periphery in large part by comparing those practices to what we understand about the ways businesses operate in the West. If that latter understanding is ambiguous, we instantly encounter conceptual challenges.

In this chapter we try to overcome this 'compared to what' challenge by contrasting the results of our original empirical research in the EECA countries with one specific stream of the nonmarket strategy literature: the theoretical framework explaining corporate political activity, developed by Hillman and Hitt (1999) and empirically tested in the Western European context in Hillman (2003). The most important contribution of these authors was to postulate a threefold taxonomy of corporate political activities, which consists of informational strategies, financial strategies and constituency-based strategies. We demonstrate that this framework is insufficient to adequately explain nonmarket activity in the transitional periphery. We thus extend that framework to incorporate the particularities of the EECA institutional context, focusing specifically on two other important types of nonmarket strategies which we term 'relational strategies' and 'procedural strategies'.

Our chapter is organized as follows. In the next section we briefly examine the conceptual problems in the nonmarket strategy literature. The chapter then outlines the most important aspects of the institutional context of the transitional periphery. Next, it identifies the limitations of the threefold Hillman–Hitt framework as applied to the transitional periphery, and goes on to extend that framework. The final section concludes.

CONCEPTUAL CHALLENGES IN THE STUDY OF THE NONMARKET STRATEGIES

Despite the rising importance of nonmarket strategy within scholarly developments around international business (IB) and strategy (Doh et al., 2012; Doh et al., 2015), a more granular notion of what constitutes nonmarket strategy remains somewhat vague (Boddewyn, 2003). We still face considerable uncertainty about the types of activities that constitute nonmarket strategies. Doh et al. (2012), for instance, offer some examples of 'nonmarket actions', including 'building coalitions' or 'lobbying legislators or regulators' (ibid., p.23), as well as indicating that 'corporate philanthropy' is 'a nonmarket strategy' (ibid., p.29). We will argue below that this is in part due to the fact that most research on nonmarket strategy focuses on political strategies in the United States (US) (Baysinger and Woodman, 1982; Mattingly, 2007) or European contexts (Hillman and Wan, 2005; Jimenez, 2010; Taminiau and Wilts, 2006; Tenbücken, 2002), which by its nature restricts the kinds of nonmarket strategies practised by firms because of the relatively developed institutional context. This is despite the relatively obvious fact that due to differences in the institutional environments confronting foreign firms in developed versus developing contexts, both the importance and nature of nonmarket strategies are likely to vary between developed and developing countries (Brewer, 1983; Kostova et al., 2008).

Further adding to this conceptual ambiguity is the coexistence of the notion of 'nonmarket strategy' and some other terms such as 'corporate political activity'. The latter examines corporate attempts to influence political institutions and actors in ways favourable to the firm (Hillman et al., 2004; Lux et al., 2011). The term is clearly narrower than the concept of nonmarket strategy, but conceptual arguments for singling out strategies targeting the political process from the broader class of nonmarket strategies have not, to our knowledge, been offered. Indeed, such focus on only one arena of corporate nonmarket activity may be introducing significant bias to our understanding of the nonmarket behaviour of businesses, especially in the EECA context.

Contrast this with the traditional field of business ('market') strategy. While scholars may differ on emphases and nuances, including achievement of competitive advantage (resource-based view of strategy versus positioning view) (Casadesus-Masanell and Ricart, 2010) and the utility of strategic planning as a technique (Mintzberg and Waters, 1985), most would agree that there exists a certain range of common approaches that businesses choose at the strategic level (such as cost leadership, core competence development, market positioning and dynamic capabilities).

A rare exception in the nonmarket strategy literature has been the influential papers by Hillman and Hitt (1999) and Hillman (2003). Political strategy formulation in the model developed and tested in these two papers is based on three distinct choices: approach (transactional or relational), participation level (individual or collective), and strategy (information, financial incentive and constituency building). By the transactional approach, Hillman and Hitt (1999) argue that firms react once specific issues emerge, before trying to influence political decision-makers. This approach also tends to be ad hoc, they argue. In the relational approach, firms invest resources and time in cultivating relationships in order to be able to respond when issues arise. This means that when problems arise, they have mechanisms in place to manage the situation. Participation refers to how they engage in the political realm in terms of pursuing independent initiatives or by working with other firms.

For our purposes, however, the most important aspect of the Hillman–Hitt framework is their taxonomy of corporate political strategies. Their approach, grounded in a rational choice framework, models politics as a market of repeated transactions between self-interested politicians and organized interest groups (see, generally, Stigler, 1971; Shepsle and Bonchek, 1997). Based on this framework, the authors essentially focused on identifying ways with which businesses 'pay' for favourable policies provided by politicians. They identified three such approaches or 'currencies' used in Western political markets. These are: data and insight needed in the policy-making process ('informational strategies'), resources made available to political parties or individual politicians ('financial strategies'), and efforts to influence voters who elect a given politician ('constituency-based strategies'). Informational strategies imply the provision of information as a good to political decision-makers through lobbying. Financial strategies are essentially financial inducements to align the interests of political decision-makers through activities such as election campaign donations, hiring political figures to directorships and using political consultants. Lastly, constituency-based strategies aim at engaging the broader community in supporting the political goals of the company by outreach to communities and citizens. Examples of such initiatives would be advocacy based advertising and support for grassroots social movements supportive of the interests of firms.

As we will argue below, while Hillman and Hitt's (1999) typology and Hillman's (2003) application to US multinational enterprises (MNEs) operating in Western Europe is a valuable conceptual and empirical contribution to understanding nonmarket strategy, in the specific context of the transitional periphery it misses a range of centrally important nonmarket strategies. Before we discuss these shortcomings in specific detail, let us briefly outline the major institutional peculiarities of the region under our consideration.

THE TRANSITIONAL PERIPHERY: AN INSTITUTIONAL PICTURE

The post-Soviet countries of the EECA comprise a broad range of countries linked principally by a shared history of central planning and communism in the twentieth century. After 1991, all EECA countries began a transition from a centrally planned economy towards varying forms of mixed economy. The term 'transition economy' was first used in the early 1990s as academics and practitioners around the world confronted an unprecedented natural experiment in institutional and market-based reforms. Economic, political, legal and social policies were developed from scratch, and while significant ideas were imported from policy-makers and scholars in North America and Western Europe, these approaches were adapted and revised to reflect new insights, regional specificities and political realities exposed by the transition experience itself.

The transition to a capitalist-centred mixed economy began with far-reaching reforms in governance (especially, changes in ownership of key sectors of the economy through privatization). Yet while, almost without exception, the EECA countries committed to reforms, one generation later the result of this transformation has varied substantially across countries in the EECA region. One of the most interesting facets of transition and post-transition, and perhaps the best explanation for transition outcomes, has been the incomplete and uneven nature of institutional development across the region. In the early days of the transition process in the EECA, the debate over 'shock therapy' and 'gradualism' (Balcerowicz, 1993; Healey, 1991; Rybczynski, 1991) appears with hindsight to have been a false dichotomy, predicated on an assumption about the importance of the redundancy of states and the capacity for markets to replace centrally planned economic structures. A generation on from the changes in 1989, it is now clear that neither the view that the preservation of some aspects of pre-existing institutions from the state socialist system would be useful for market economy functioning (gradualism), nor the view that markets would spontaneously develop in response to liberalization (shock therapy), appear to be valid.

What is clear, instead, is that in the longer term, the depth and consistency with which Western liberal institutions have been adopted turned out to be more important than the issues of initial staging or sequencing of reforms. This is perhaps most visible when we compare the economic development of our 19 transitional periphery countries with the so-called 'EU-11' post-socialist member states of the European Union (EU). Figure 10.1 presents this comparison. As one can notice, at the outset of the transition, the future EU-11 countries were on average significantly poorer

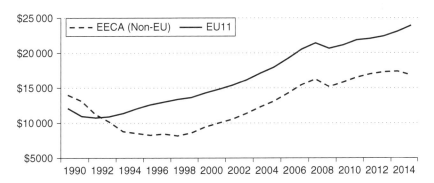

Figure 10.1   GDP per capital in the EU-11 and non-EU EECA countries (PPP, constant 2011 dollars)

than their eastern neighbours. This lower starting point reflected some objective disadvantages of the EU-11 bloc, including the comparatively limited endowments of natural resources and the fact that Central Europe was in many ways in itself a periphery within the Soviet bloc. And yet, a quarter-century later, the average per capita gross domestic product (GDP) within the EU-11 is more than 40 per cent higher than in the 19 'east of the EU' countries. It is difficult not to see the institutional dynamics beyond this significant economic divergence. Since the mid-1990s, most of the EU-11 countries have been subject to increasingly stringent conditionality, introduced as part of their long process of accession to the European Union.

Schimmelfennig and Sedelmeier (2004, p. 662) sum up this concept of conditionality: 'The dominant logic underpinning EU conditionality is a bargaining strategy of reinforcement by reward, under which the EU provides external incentives for a target government to comply with its conditions.' These rewards are manifold. First, they include direct financial transfers of regional aid (EU Structural Funds) and infrastructural support mechanisms (EU Cohesion Funds). These transfers represent important contributions to the EU-11 economies; up to 5 per cent of GDP (EU Commission, 2016). A clear illustration of this material reward was the withdrawal of EU funds to Bulgaria because of its failure to tackle organized crime and its role in distorting the conduct of the Bulgarian judiciary (BBC, 2008).

A second 'reward' for compliance to EU rules is the legitimacy that being part of the EU brings to the post-socialist countries of the EU-11. By complying with EU rules, leaders and their political elites in the EU-11 are able to influence and participate in global governance regimes (for example, global trade deals) in a way in which as independent, small economies they would not be able to. Being on the European and global stage, leaders from the EU-11 gain credibility and shared power. This is no better illustrated than an EU-11 country holding the rotating six-month presidency of the European Council. The holder of this presidency has numerous obligations related to managing and organizing the legislative activities of the Council of Ministers and, indirectly, the European Parliament. However, the presidency also allows the EU-11 member state to set the agenda for the six months, as well as setting legislative priorities for the EU.

Third, compliance with EU rules on free movement of goods, services, capital and people (the so-called 'Four Freedoms') has brought significant economic rewards in the form of inward foreign direct investment (FDI) boosting EU-11 capital formation and increasing the skills base of its labour force. Inward FDI has also become an important source of exports for EU-11 countries, contributing to these countries' current accounts.

After the expiration of limits on free movement of people, EU-11 countries' citizens now have full access to the EU labour market. While the impact of outward migration from the EU-11 towards the other EU countries has generated much political rhetoric about creating unemployment in migrant recipient countries, and about 'welfare tourism' of EU-11 citizens moving to West Europe to gain access to the more generous welfare benefits there, the overall balance of objective analysis has demonstrated that a combination of new employment opportunities for EU-11 workers and financial remittances back to the EU-11 has created overall positive impacts for EU-11 countries.

Contrast the rewards of compliance offered to EU-11 countries of the EECA with those countries that remain outside the EU. While they have fewer constraints on domestic policy, allowing them to more actively use discretionary industrial policy or selective protectionism through trade policy, the lack of effective conditionality has radically altered the incentives of local political elites. These elites face a typical case of the Prisoner's Dilemma: while effective and independent institutions may generally be beneficial for the country and its elites, an individual political party, when in power, may be interested in facing as few limitations on its rule as possible. This tendency to undermine independent institutions may be exacerbated by the objective reality of the periphery becoming the arena of an intense clash between two distinct political projects: one oriented toward the integration with the West, and one focused on the ties with the Russian Federation, which would imply renewing historical and cultural ties. The clash of radically conflicting geopolitical directions often produces abrupt, dramatic political changes, which are particularly damaging for the process of building durable and impartial institutions.

The ultimate effect of these trends is persistent, well-documented institutional gaps across the transitional periphery. They can be found in almost every area of governance. The very electoral process and accountability – the freedom to challenge those in power at the ballot box – is severely constrained in the non-EU EECA countries. The 2016 Democracy Score, a widely respected measure of the quality of democratic governance in the EECA region (Freedom House, 2016a) illustrates this point rather starkly. As part of its assessment, the Democracy Score directly evaluates electoral process. On a 1–7 scale, where 1 represents a fully democratic process and 7 a fully authoritarian one, the mean score for the electoral process of non-EU EECA countries was 5.18. The corresponding measure of the EU-11 countries was 3.16.

The quality of other political and economic institutions is even more divergent. In most non-EU EECA countries, the independent media is either weak or non-existent. The mean Democracy Score measure of media independence is 5.58 for our transitional periphery, with six countries accounting for nearly 80 per cent of the region's population (Azerbaijan, Belarus, Kazakhstan, Russia, Turkmenistan and Uzbekistan) scoring 6.5 or higher (which indicates nearly total governmental control of the media). As dire as freedom of the media looks across the transitional periphery, it still fares better than judicial independence. The mean Democracy Score measure here is 5.71 for the region under our consideration, compared to just 3.07 for the EU-11 countries. What that means in particular is that independent protections of owners of physical and intellectual property, and creditors, are much harder to find, and that court systems are unable to effectively protect them (Gelbudaa et al., 2008; Kühn, 2012). That problem with judicial independence extends to many other important governance institutions such as antitrust authorities, which are either non-existent or extraordinarily opaque in their practices.

In view of this weakness of institutional safeguards, it comes as no surprise that numerous measures of corruption and bribery suggest that EECA countries outside the EU-11 have systematically higher corruption. In the 2015 Transparency International Corruption Perceptions Index, a median position of a non-EU EECA country was 103rd in the world. Western Europe's corresponding median was 13th (Transparency International, 2016).

The differences between the non-EU EECA and EU-11 countries extend beyond formal legal institutions and also encompass the so-called 'soft' institutions. What we have particularly in mind is the levels of professionalization of the managerial cadre (Horwitch and Kisilowski, 2014). The difference here is partly the consequence of the lower level of foreign direct investment and a much less pronounced presence of multinational corporations in the transitional periphery (Akbar and McBride, 2004). Yet, what is also important is 'heritage' in management, to use the Bartlett and Ghoshal (1995) expression. 'Each company,' the authors observed, 'is influenced by the path by which it developed – its organizational history and the values, norms and practices of its management' (Bartlett and Ghoshal, 1995, p.472). Factors that influence such heritage include both internal, idiosyncratic management styles, and external factors such as national cultures, histories, and established practices and norms of management.

Thus while many of the institutions of communism such as central planning ministries and state-owned monopolies no longer exist because they have either collapsed, been privatized, or been reformed or transformed, residual values and practices of these institutions have been transferred to the managers and policy-makers who worked during communism. From the perspective of managers in these institutions, it is neither easy nor desirable to reform such practices based on several decades of experience. That process of changing norms and practices is naturally accelerated when a new, powerful source of cultural reproduction emerges. In the EU-11 countries, this model is represented by Western managerial practices brought by numerous foreign-owned companies and strengthened through the personal experience of millions of Central Europeans of studying and working in Western Europe. Such impact is simply missing in non-EU EECA countries. All in all, the post-socialist reform in the transitional periphery has been piecemeal, partial and subject to capture of vested interests (Arnold and Quelch, 1998; Palepu and Khanna, 2010). Some evidence exists that liberalization has outright failed (Wandel et al., 2011; Williams et al., 2011).

THE HILLMAN–HITT MODEL IN THE TRANSITIONAL PERIPHERY

The institutional characteristics of the transitional periphery significantly affect the palette of nonmarket strategies that managers have at their disposal in EECA countries. The research that we present below demonstrates that the three categories of strategies outlined in the Hillman–Hitt framework – financial, informational and constituency-based – altogether constitute only a small portion of how managers in EECA countries endeavour to seek advantage in the nonmarket realm. This conclusion can be quantified based on the results of our survey of 56 executives working in non-EU EECA countries. Table 10.1 summarizes these results, which we juxtapose with our earlier qualitative findings reported in Akbar and Kisilowski (2015).

Our survey asked respondents to indicate up to five strategic initiatives which they considered the most important in their interactions with the nonmarket environment. We coded the top five choices by giving 5 points for the initiative chosen as the most important, 4 for the second most important, 3 for the third most important, and so on. If a respondent selected fewer than five strategies, we 'divided' the missing points proportionally to the choices made. The resulting Strategic Importance Index (SII), reported in Table 10.1, is the sum of all the points generated by our respondents. As one can notice, the three Hillman–Hitt strategies altogether account for less than a quarter of the nonmarket strategic choices of companies operating in non-EU EECA countries.

To understand why this is the case, let us consider each strategy. Outreach to constituents of a politician is understandably not at the top of the list of a manager operating in the transitional periphery. After all, as highlighted

Table 10.1   *Relative importance of various nonmarket strategies across the transitional periphery*

Strategic initiatives	Strategic Importance Index	Relative importance in the nonmarket strategic palette (%)	
Gifts, bribes	18.2	2.2	Financial strategies
Lobbying	76.6	13.0	Informational
Seeking international assistance	20.5		strategies
Public exposure	12.2		
CSR and other community investments	60.8	7.2	Constituency-based strategies
		22.4	*Hillman–Hitt strategies (total)*
Local partner	59.6	29.6	Relational
Networking	83.3		strategies
Threats	17.0		
Collusion	88.5		
Litigation	25.1	48.0	Procedural
Theft	15.0		strategies
Tenders	72.0		
Compliance	236.8		
Avoiding regulations	54.6		

above, most of the countries that constitute that periphery are either con-solidated authoritarian regimes or, at best, democracies with mechanisms of political accountability so flawed that they are hardly comparable to what is standard in the West. If voters lack an effective way to reward and punish politicians at the ballot box, or otherwise hold them accountable, then it is entirely normal for a manager not to invest significant time and resources into recruiting constituents to support corporate interests and positions. Put another way, constituent-oriented nonmarket strategies are not particularly important in the transitional periphery, because constitu-ents are neither particularly relevant nor empowered political actors.

A similar argument can be made about informational strategies. Here too, the institutional features of the transitional periphery are at the root of the differences. After all, information that a business can provide to politicians, including industry expert knowledge and managerial know-how, is valuable only when technocratic, professional considerations are important determinants of policy outcomes. Politicians care about access to insights if the system requires them to find such insights to back their policy proposals. That expectation is rarely at the centre of policy-making in the countries under our consideration. In part, this is a consequence of the lack of effective electoral competition in those countries. Without effective opposition, a politician does not face the need to use data and analysis, as they simply do not have to convince anybody in the broader socio-economic realm. But there are also cultural factors at play. The notion of fact-based, data-driven policy-making is a relatively new concept to policy-makers in the transitional periphery. And while that approach to policy-making is actively promoted by international institutions such as the World Bank or European Bank for Reconstruction and Development, the impact of these efforts on the ground is still rather shallow (Chakrabarty, 2016).

Finally, information is an important currency of business–political exchange in developed democracies, in large part because of the role of an independent media. Journalists require a steady stream of facts and insights to produce their stories. Providing them with information is thus a natural way to generate content favourable to business. That way, information can create a powerful narrative that effectively constrains the viable policy choices of a politician. That mechanism crucially depends on the willingness of the media to provide an effective constraint on those in power. The Nations in Transit indexes (Freedom House, 2016b) make it clear, however, that such journalistic independence simply does not exist in the transitional periphery. With the nearly total governmental control over the media, there is simply no space for industry lobbies, much less an individual business, to effectively drive media narrative in the direction not already favoured by those in power. And without the ability to influence the discussion, feeding journalists with data, views and insights simply loses its rationale.

Finally, let us turn to the financial nonmarket strategies. Here our results may be viewed as perhaps the most surprising. After all, the non-EU EECA countries are known for generally high levels of perceived corruption. If corruption is so prevalent in the countries under our consideration, why would it play such a relatively minor role in the palette of strategically important initiatives undertaken by businesses? One potential response may focus on a possibility of social desirability bias skewing the results of our survey. That is unlikely, however. Our survey included questions about equally or even more legally questionable types of strategic initiatives than bribery, including violence and threats, or theft and collusion. As one can observe in Table 10.1, most of these other objectionable strategies still generated similar or even higher SII scores than bribery.

Rather than being a reporting quirk, the result may be telling us something significant about the region under our consideration. To understand this difference, one needs to keep in mind a major difference between our research and virtually all available studies and indices of corruption: while corruption researchers ask respondents to ascertain absolute prevalence of corruption, our study asked for the relative strategic significance of providing politicians with financial incentives as opposed to other types of nonmarket strategic initiatives. Accordingly, while corruption may be more prevalent in the transitional periphery than in the West, it may still be less commonplace than other types of nonmarket strategies practised in the periphery.

Even more important, however, is to point out that the prevalence of an activity may not have a simple linear relation with its strategic significance. If strategy is an art of seeking lasting advantage over competitors, a widely prevalent activity may actually play a relatively minor strategic role. If it is customary to pay an unofficial fee while seeking a permit or a licence – that is, petty corruption – a manager may not consider the act of paying particularly significant in strategic terms. In business strategy we do not regard, for instance, 'producing a product' or 'charging a price' as particularly significant strategic initiatives in themselves, precisely because every market participant engages in such activities.

It is also worth noting that some specific tactics included under the financial strategy umbrella by the Hillman–Hitt framework – contribution to politicians or party, honoraria for speaking or paid travel – are plainly of rather low relevance for the transitional periphery. These types of incentives assume the existence of both a viable electoral process, in which campaign contributions matter, and reasonably effective corruption laws, which force companies to find legal workarounds for financial exchange rather than relying on direct bribery.

THE NONMARKET STRATEGIC FOCUS IN THE TRANSITIONAL PERIPHERY

Our research suggests that the Hillman–Hitt triad of financial, informational and constituency-based nonmarket strategies cannot comprehensively cover all nonmarket strategy initiatives in the context of the transitional periphery. What our research instead finds essential are two other types of strategies: relational strategy and procedural strategy.

Let us begin with relational strategy.[2] This strategy relies on a mechanism of exchange quite similar to the one underlying the Hillman–Hitt strategies. Yet what is traded here is not money, information or votes, but a diffused set of goods (and bads) that centre on human relations. The most straightforward type of initiatives that fall under this strategic category concerns developing personal rapport with influential politicians. The qualitative part of our research suggests that this 'networking' goes very much along the traditional lines of family, clan, ethnic or geographic pedigree. The importance of these ties across the transitional periphery has been emphasized by other authors (Schatz, 2004; Bigo and Hale, 2013). But these relations – often referred to as cronyism or nepotism – are often conceptually fused with bribery in the research on the transitional periphery. This is rather misleading. Our respondents emphasize that a familial, clan-based or otherwise strong relationship is frequently a substitute for, rather than a complement to, bribery. In our sample, the correlation between including 'networking' and 'bribery' among the top five non-market strategic initiatives was, in our sample, only 0.36. Qualitatively, a number of our respondents explained that well-connected people actually do not need to pay bribes to receive favourable governmental treatment. Bribes and contacts are indeed substitutes.

Proponents of subsuming the discussion about relationships and kinships under the corruption umbrella have a point in emphasizing a tendency of anti-corruption laws promoted by Western institutions to broaden the definition of bribery. Rather than covering mere exchange of money or tangible goods as a *quid pro quo* for governmental actions, laws increasingly refer to 'illegal advantages' of any kind (Eicher et al., 2009). Yet, to follow this legal trend in the social science research is methodologically risky: if one follows the rational choice approach, modelling political interactions as business–government exchanges, virtually all corporate political activity becomes by construction a form of bribery. The above-mentioned Hillman–Hitt strategies, for instance, posit that businesses effectively trade information, votes or campaign contributions with at least an implicit intention of seeking competitive advantage through favourable governmental action. If those strategies do not constitute corruption, then one would wonder whether insisting on the corrupt designation of relations of kin or friendship in the EECA context is a conceptual oversight or error.

In general, in social science, putting too many eggs into one conceptual basket is rarely helpful. Our survey demonstrates, for instance, that many types of initiatives can be distinguished under the umbrella of relational strategies. Other than forging direct relations with politicians, managers can also rely on a well-connected partner or contractor. Indeed, the strategically valuable relations may not even involve politicians. Firms may collude with one another, fixing prices or quantities of product sold. Relations can also involve exchanging 'bads' rather than goods; our main example here is the use of pressure, blackmailing and threats of violence by some businesses, to get paid or to intimidate competition.

The examples of collusion and threats bring us to another important point: in peripheral environments marked by low levels of institutionaliza-tion, it is especially important to see the nonmarket environment of a business in terms that are not limited only to governmental institutions. As we have already mentioned, in the extant literature concerning Western countries, the terms 'nonmarket strategy' and 'corporate political strategy' are used almost interchangeably. That reflects the reality of formal political institutions being by far the most important wielders of nonmarket power. But in the transitional periphery, political institutions are frequently either ineffective or not sufficiently interested in listening to corporate interest groups. In such a setting, thinking about nonmarket strategy purely in terms of exchanges with politicians becomes seriously limiting. It is entirely rational for companies to search for alternative ways of seeking nonmarket advantage. If in a Western country an industry lobby would seek preferential treatment through favourable legislation, in a transitional periphery a collusion between the largest market players, with no involve-ment of government and absent functioning regulatory statutes, may be an alternative way to reach a similar strategic objective. Threats and the use of violence are likewise alternatives often pursued if the official system of enforcement of laws and contracts is ineffective.

The vital importance of seeing the nonmarket environment beyond the exchanges with politicians, however, becomes most visible in the results of our survey concerning what we call procedural strategies. These strategies not only are directed elsewhere than the political elite, but they actually are not based on the transactional logic that characterizes both the three Hillman–Hitt strategies and the relational strategy we have discussed above. As the name suggests, procedural strategies rely instead on the selective, strategic use of established processes regulating business conduct. Litigation, participating in (non-corrupt) grant and tender procedures, or simple compliance with the formal laws are examples of affirmative use of the process. Stealing resources, which includes producing harmful externalities such as pollution or toxic waste, as well as actively avoiding compliance with laws and regulations, are procedural strategic initiatives that subvert or ignore official rules of doing business in a given country.

As one can notice from Table 10.1, procedural strategies are the single most important category among those reported by our respondents, accounting for 48 per cent of the total SII score. At first glance, those figures might seem to be in contrast to the available data on the effective-ness of formal legal institutions. As we mentioned earlier, Freedom House (2016b) evaluated the judicial system as one of the weakest aspects of democratic governance of non-EU EECA countries. And yet, litigation has still been reported as a significantly more important nonmarket strategy than, for instance, bribery. In the 2015 World Bank Doing Business ranking, the non-EU EECA countries' median average was at the 57th country in the world, compared to the EU-11's median of 29th (World Bank, 2016). The difference here is not as stark as in the case of other governance and democracy indicators, but most non-EU EECA countries still have a rather cumbersome regulatory framework. And yet, compliance with these business-unfriendly regulations is the single most important nonmarket strategic initiative reported by our respondents, accounting alone for a full 30 per cent of the total importance score.

It is difficult to quantitatively ascertain the impact of the contextual specificities of the transitional periphery on the prevalence of procedural strategies. Hillman and Hitt (1999), and other similar researchers focusing on Western countries, do not study procedural strategies, perhaps because they do not fit the narrower definition of corporate political activity. It is thereby entirely likely that this definitional choice skews our picture of the nonmarket behaviour of Western businesses. Nevertheless, our qualitative research also suggests that the prominent importance of procedural strategies may, in somewhat surprising ways, be related to the contextual nature of the transitional periphery.

Our observations here are the flip-side of our arguments concerning bribery mentioned above: that bribery may not be considered strategically important for our respondents precisely because it is so prevalent. Conversely, the sheer cumbersomeness of most legal, procedural and regulatory frameworks in the transitional periphery makes the decisions about using or avoiding those frameworks quite significant indeed. A number of our interviewees emphasized, for instance, that in EECA realities, full compliance with the myriad of arbitrary and internally incoherent regulations is simply impossible. Each business must thereby make a strategically important decision about which laws to comply with and which to avoid. Unlike corruption, where there are often clear unwritten social rules about when a businessperson should pay a kickback or a facilitation fee, the approach to compliance may differ widely from company to company, becoming an important source of competitive advantage.

A similar case can be made for other types of procedural strategies. In the face of a persistently ineffective and slow court system, a decision about when to rely on it may actually carry significant strategic consequences, not least because of the sheer time and effort required to litigate in the countries under our consideration. And with the highly uneven levels of law enforcement, the decision on whether to engage in illegal appropriation of resources or collusion also becomes strategically significant.

CONCLUSIONS AND IMPLICATIONS

While much scholarly work on nonmarket strategy to date has either focused on developed-country contexts or the activities of MNEs (or both), our research on the transitional periphery has exposed a relatively limited conceptual breadth of current operationalization of nonmarket strategies. Although this chapter reports what in many ways is research work in progress, it appears that the extant literature misses a range of nonmarket strategies practised in EECA countries.

In particular, our chapter adds two new categories of nonmarket strategies to Hillman and Hitt's (1999) classifications: relational and procedural strategies. Relational strategies emphasize the importance of personal relationships between managers and politicians. As with other types of nonmarket strategy, a trade between manager and politician occurs, yet what is traded here is not money, information or votes, but a diffused set of goods (and bads) that centre around personal relationships between manager and politician. Procedural strategies rely on the selective, strategic use of established processes regulating business conduct. These strategies can cut both ways. On the one hand, simple compliance with the formal laws is an example of affirmative use of the process. On the other hand, stealing resources, as well as actively avoiding compliance with laws and regulations, are procedural strategic initiatives that do the opposite by subverting or ignoring the official rules of doing business in a given country.

To explain the divergence between our findings and the research on the nonmarket strategies in the Western context, we have focused primarily on institutional peculiarities of the transitional periphery. This is a natural direction, given the substantial differences between nonmarket environments that businesses face in the West and throughout the EECA. Yet our findings should motivate a broader reconsideration of methods and foundations adopted in our research of nonmarket strategy in non-Western contexts. Three such foundations deserve particular attention.

First, to the extent that the literature does look into nonmarket strategies beyond the West, it often models the nonmarket environment as dominated by a one-dimensional actor, 'the host government'. Businesses enter a game (frequently a zero-sum one) with that government, with the outcome predicted by a model (Dunning, 1998; Ramamurti, 2001). Our research suggests that this approach misses the point on many grounds. Governments are far from being homogeneous actors: they are collections of individuals with whom managers interact and 'trade' with various currencies (mostly non-financial ones). Even more importantly, as we have shown earlier, a significant part of nonmarket activity of businesses in the transitional periphery does not involve any strategic interaction with governments; it is instead focused on interaction with other market actors, or on strategically choosing areas of compliance and noncompliance with policies implemented by highly ineffective governmental apparatuses. Those apparently significant 'state-disengaged' strategies will obviously never enter the picture if firms–governments games are *a priori* taken as representative of the entire nonmarket picture.

Second, the literature focuses overwhelmingly on MNEs as the solely important business actors (Wright et al., 2005). What is missing are two important categories of local businesses: state-owned or state-influenced businesses, which typically tend to be larger; and genuinely independent enterprises, which in the transitional periphery invariably tend to be the smallest and weakest players. If one considers the institutional differences between the West, or even the EU-11 countries, on the one hand, and the transitional periphery on the other, the exclusive focus on MNEs appears to be seriously limiting. While a credible story might be offered as to why, in the West, local businesses approach their nonmarket environment in ways substantially similar to MNEs, this assumption is completely unwarranted in the transitional periphery. State-owned enterprises, for instance, will surely differ widely from MNEs as far as their interactions with the political elite are concerned. One obvious reason is that executives of those state-owned enterprises are often themselves prominent members of that political elite. Small local companies, by the same token, may approach compliance in very different ways from MNEs. On the one hand, being smaller and not bound by global rules and standards gives them significant flexibility and ability to exploit the system without detection. On the other hand, the significant power wielded by MNEs, combined with relatively weak links with local decision-makers, may make them more willing to disregard local rules that they consider unjust or unreasonable.

Third, the research on nonmarket strategies in peripheral environments has always been conducted in the shadow of enormously influential efforts to study corruption in these same environments. Corruption is a serious social problem affecting the EECA countries and other developing economies (Rose-Ackerman and Palifka, 2016). Recently, the Turkmenistan government ordered the construction of a new international airport at a cost of more than US$2.3 billion. While the autocratic leader of Turkmenistan, Gurbanguly Berdymukhamedov, proclaimed that the goal of the new airport was to strengthen his country's 'solid transit potential', in 2015 only 105000 tourists visited the country according to tourism ministry figures, and Turkmenistan is widely regarded as one of the most difficult countries to secure a visa to visit (BBC, 2016). As with many key decisions in Turkmenistan, President Berdymukhamedov is alleged to rely upon a close circle of influential business people. According to Jardine (2015), this group allegedly includes Yoseph Chalyk, the long-time Vice-Minister of Turkmenistan's Textile Industry and owner of the construction company Chalyk Holdings and the French construction company Bouygues. Furthermore, 'Carbonaro [Managing Director of Bouyges in Turkmenistan] also alleged that the company's CEO [chief executive officer], Martin Bouygues, was frequently treated like a head of state' (Jardine, 2015).

In nearby Azerbaijan, President Ilham Aliyev was named in the Panama Papers in 2016. The leaks from the Mossack Fonseca law firm based in Panama alleged that Aliyev had built a coterie of supporters who allegedly helped him and his family hide their assets overseas. In mid-2003, months before the October presidential election, Fazil Mammadov, Azerbaijan's tax minister, is alleged to have created AtaHolding, one of Azerbaijan's most important conglomerate firms. Mammadov then allegedly invited President Aliyev's family to join him in a business and political partnership at the company (Fitzgibbon et al., 2016).

Our research suggests that seeing nonmarket strategies solely through the prism of corruption distorts the picture. We cannot escape the conclusion that what produces such a distorted picture is at least partly a condescending attitude towards the peripheral countries under study. This is especially visible if corruption is defined in such a way that it covers practices similar, or functionally equivalent, to what rational choice models would suggest are also standard in the West. For example, it is questionable why we should regard relational strategies based on clan or family structures in the periphery as examples of corruption or cronyism, while we take instances of leveraging one's membership in an alumni community of US Ivy League colleges or French *Grandes Ecoles* as examples of socially accepted networking. While we ourselves emphasized earlier that Western institutions do tend to produce superior economic outcomes, and thus promoting Western practices may be desirable from a socio-economic standpoint, we should make sure to distinguish that prescriptive endeavour from our analytical accounts of how businesses actually interact with their nonmarket environment in the transitional periphery.

Shedding these three constraining assumptions will open up a number of interesting research avenues related to our understanding of the nature of nonmarket strategy, not just in the transitional periphery but more widely in other developing countries. Relational and procedural strategies seem, in particular, relevant not only to the transitional periphery but also to a broader set of developing countries in other parts of the world. Analysing those other non-Western regions with a more complete non-market strategic palette would be an especially fruitful avenue for future research. Another related area of empirical research with a strong practical relevance would be to consider 'best-practice' nonmarket strategy for managers and firms active in developing countries. Given the institutional weaknesses commonly encountered in developing countries, which kinds of nonmarket strategies (informational, financial, constituency, procedural or relational) discussed in this chapter are best suited to the specific context in which a firm finds itself? Is there a blend of these five categories that may be more effective than others in developing countries?

NOTES

1. These are: Albania, Armenia, Azerbaijan, Belarus, Bosnia and Herzegovina, Georgia, Kazakhstan, Kosovo, Kyrgyz Republic, Macedonia, Moldova, Mongolia, Montenegro, Russian Federation, Serbia, Tajikistan, Turkmenistan, Ukraine and Uzbekistan.
2. In a slightly confusing twist, Hillman and Hitt use the notion of 'relational approach' to nonmarket strategy, which they claim can be a feature of every nonmarket strategy. While it is beyond the scope of this chapter to discuss that point in detail, we use 'relational strategy' here in a different way: as a distinct group of nonmarket strategies.

REFERENCES

Akbar, Y. and Kisilowski, M. (2015). Managerial agency, risk, and strategic posture: nonmarket strategies in the transitional core and periphery. *International Business Review*, 24(6): 984–996.

Akbar, Y.H. and McBride, J.B. (2004). Multinational enterprise strategy, foreign direct investment and economic development: the case of the Hungarian banking industry. *Journal of World Business*, 39(1): 89–105.

Arnold, D.J. and Quelch, J.A. (1998). New strategies in emerging markets. *Sloan Management Review*, 40(1): 7–20.

Balcerowicz, L. (1993). Common fallacies in the debate on the economic transition in Central and Eastern Europe (No. 11). London: European Bank for Reconstruction and Development.

Bartlett, C.A. and Ghoshal, S. (1995). *Transnational Management: Text, Cases, and Readings in Cross-Border Management*, 2nd edn. Chicago, IL: Irwin.

Baysinger, B. and Richard W. Woodman (1982). Dimensions of the public affairs/government relations function in major American corporations. *Strategic Management Journal*, 3(1): 27–41.

BBC (2008). EU suspends funding for Bulgaria. Accessed at www.bbc.co.uk on 6 November 2016.

BBC (2016). Turkmenistan unveils bird-shaped airport in Ashgabat. Accessed at www.bbc.co.uk on 6 November 2016.

Bigo, P.O. and Hale, J. (2013). The EU and consolidating autocracies in Central Asia: a dialogue of the deaf?. Policy Brief, Civic Solidarity Forum.

Boddewyn, J.J. (2003). Understanding and advancing the concept of nonmarket. *Business and Society*, 42(3): 297–327.

Brewer, T.L. (1983). The instability of governments and the instability of controls on funds transfers by multinational enterprises: implications for political risk analysis. *Journal of International Business Studies*, 14(3): 147–157.

Casadesus-Masanell, R. and Ricart, J.E. (2010). From strategy to business models and onto tactics. *Long Range Planning*, 43(2/3): 95–215.

Chakrabarty, S. (2016). Shining a light on Central Asia. *EBRD News*, 17 February. Accessed at http://www.ebrd.com/news/2016/shining-a-light-on-central-asia.html on 6 November 2016.

Doh, J., Lawton, T. and Rajwani, T. (2012). Advancing nonmarket strategy research: institutional perspectives in a changing world. *Academy of Management Perspectives*, 26(3): 22–39.

Doh, J., McGuire, S. and Ozaki, T. (2015). Introduction to the special issue. *Journal of World Business*, Special Issue: Global Governance and International Nonmarket Strategies, 50(2), 256–261.

Dunning, J.H. (1998). An overview of relations with national governments. *New Political Economy*, 3(2): 280.

Eicher, T., García-Peñalosa, C. and Van Ypersele, T. (2009). Education, corruption, and the distribution of income. *Journal of Economic Growth*, 14(3): 205–231.

EU Commission (2016). Hungary. Accessed at https://europa.eu/european-union/about-eu/countries/member-countries/hungary_en on 6 November 2016.

Freedom House (2016a). *Freedom in the World*, 43rd edn. New York: Freedom House.

Freedom House (2016b). *Nations in Transit 2016*. Freedom House. Accessed at https://freedomhouse. org/sites/default/files/.

Fitzgibbon W., Patrucic, M. and Garcia Rey, M. (2016). Panama Papers: how family that runs Azerbaijan built an empire of hidden wealth. *Irish Times*, 4 April. Accessed at http://www.irishtimes.com/business/panama-papers-how-family-that-runs-azerbaijan-built-an-empire-of-hidden-wealth-1.2597762 on 6 November 2016.

Gelbudaa, M., Meyerb, K.M. and Deliosc, A. (2008). International business and institutional development in Central and Eastern Europe. *Journal of International Management*, 14(1): 1–11.

Healey, P (1991). Models of the development process: a review. *Journal of Property Research*, 8: 219–238.

Hillman, A. (2003). Determinants of political strategies in US multinationals. *Business and Society*, 42(4): 455–484.

Hillman, A.J. and Hitt, M.A. (1999). Corporate political strategy formulation: a model of approach, participation, and strategy decisions. *Academy of Management Review*, 24(4): 825–842.

Hillman, A.J. and Wan, W.P. (2005). The determinants of MNE subsidiaries' political strategies: evidence of institutional duality. *Journal of International Business Studies*, 36(3): 322–340.

Hillman, A.J., Keim, G.D. and Schuler, D. (2004). Corporate political activity: a review and research agenda. *Journal of Management*, 30(6): 837–857.

Horwitch, M. and Kisilowski, M. (2014). Joining the twenty-first century and the need for creative managerial professionalism. In M. Kisilowski (ed.), *Free Market in its Twenties: Modern Business Decision Making in Central and Eastern Europe*: 239–249 Budapest: CEU Press.

Jardine, B. (2015). Offshore Turkmenistan: 'Sultanism' in the construction industry.

Diplomat, 21 September. Accessed at http://thediplomat.com/2015/09/offshore-turkmenistan-sultanism-in-the-construction-industry/ on 6 November 2016.

Jimenez, A. (2010). Does political risk affect the scope of the expansion abroad? Evidence from Spanish MNEs. *International Business Review*, 19(6): 619–633.

Kostova, T., Roth, K. and Dacin, M.T. (2008). Institutional theory in the study of multinational corporations: a critique and new directions. *Academy of Management Review*, 33(4): 994–1006.

Kühn, Z. (2012). *Judicial Administration Reforms in Central-Eastern Europe: Lessons to be Learned*. Berlin: Springer.

Lux, S., Crook, T.R. and Woehr, D.J. (2011). Mixing business with politics: a meta-analysis of the antecedents and outcomes of corporate political activity. *Journal of Management*, 37(1): 223–247.

Mattingly, J.E. (2007). How to become your own worst adversary: examining the connection between managerial attributions and organizational relationships with public interest stakeholders. *Journal of Public Affairs*, 7(1): 7–21.

Mellahi, K., Frynas, G., Sun, P. and Siegel, D. (2016). A review of the non-market strategy literature: toward a multi-theoretical integration. *Journal of Management*, 42(1): 143–173.

Mintzberg, H. and Waters, J.A. (1985). Of strategies, deliberate and emergent. *Strategic Management Journal*, 6(3): 257–272.

Palepu, K.G. and Khanna, T. (2010). *Winning in Emerging Markets: A Road Map for Strategy and Execution*. Cambridge, MA: Harvard Business School Press.

Ramamurti, R. (2001). The obsolescing 'bargaining model'? MNC–host developing country relations revisited. *Journal of International Business Studies*, 32(1): 23–39.

Rose-Ackerman, S. and Palifka, B.J. (2016), *Corruption and Government: Causes, Consequences, and Reform*, 2nd edn. New York: Cambridge University Press.

Rybczynski, T. (1991). The sequencing of reform. *Oxford Review of Economic Policy*, 7(4): 26–34

Schatz, E. (2004), *Modern Clan Politics: The Power of 'Blood' in Kazakhstan and Beyond*. Seattle, WA: University of Washington Press.

Schimmelfennig, F. and Sedelmeier, U. (2004). Governance by conditionality: EU rule transfer to the candidate countries of Central and Eastern Europe. *Journal of European Public Policy*, 11(4): 661–679.

Shepsle, A.K. and Bonchek, M.S. (1997). *Analyzing Politics: Rationality, Behavior, and Institutions*. New York: Norton & Company.

Stigler, G.J. (1971). The theory of economic regulation. *Bell Journal of Economics and Management Science*, 2(1): 3–21.

Taminiau, Y. and Wilts, A. (2006). Corporate lobbying in Europe, managing knowledge and information strategies. *Journal of Public Affairs*, 6(2): 122–130.

Tenbücken, M. (2002). *Corporate Lobbying in the European Union: Strategies of Multinational Companies*. Frankfurt am Main: Peter Lang.

Transparency International (2016). Corruption Perception Survey. Accessed at www.transparency.org/research/cpi/overview on 6 November 2015.

Wandel, J., Pieniadz, A. and Glauben, T. (2011). What is success and what is failure of transition? A critical review of two decades of agricultural reform in the Europe and Central Asia region. *Post-Communist Economies*, 2(23): 139–162.

Williams, C., Nadin, S. and Rogers, p.(2011). Beyond a varieties of capitalism approach in Central and Eastern Europe: some lessons from Ukraine. *Employee Relations*, 33(4): 413–427.

World Bank (2016). *Doing Business: Measuring Business Regulations*. Washington, DC. Accessed at http://www.doingbusiness.org/ on 6 November 2016.

Wright, M., Filatotchev, I., Hoskisson, R.E. and Peng, M.W. (2005). Strategy research in emerging economies: challenging the conventional wisdom. *Journal of Management Studies*, 42(1): 1–33.

Index